The Second Common Reader

Virginia Woolf was born in London in 1882, the daughter of the editor and critic Sir Leslie Stephen, and a granddaughter of Thackeray. In 1912 she married Leonard Woolf, and together they founded the Hogarth Press. Her first novel, *The Voyage Out*, was published in 1915, and was followed by *Jacob's Room* (1922), *Mrs. Dalloway* (1925), *To the Lighthouse* (1927), *Orlando* (1928), *The Waves* (1931), *The Years* (1937), and *Between the Acts* (1941). Her books of essays include *The Common Reader* (1925), *The Second Common Reader* (1932), *The Death of the Moth* (1942), *The Moment and Other Essays* (1948), and *The Captain's Deathbed and Other Essays* (1950). She died in 1941. A portion of her journal was published in 1954 as *A Writer's Diary*.

Virginia Woolf

THE SECOND COMMON READER

I rejoice to concur with the common reader; for by the common sense of readers, uncorrupted by literary prejudices, after all the refinements of subtilty and the dogmatism of learning, must be generally decided all claim to poetical honours.

DR. JOHNSON, *Life of Gray*

A Harvest Book

HARCOURT, BRACE AND COMPANY
NEW YORK

PRINTED IN THE UNITED STATES OF AMERICA

AUTHOR'S NOTE

Most of the following papers have appeared in the *Times Literary Supplement*, *Life and Letters*, *The Nation*, *Vogue*, *The New York Herald*, *The Yale Review*, and *Figaro*. For permission to reprint two of them I have to thank the Oxford University Press and Mr. Jonathan Cape. Some are now published for the first time.

CONTENTS

The Second Common Reader

*

The Strange Elizabethans

*

There are few greater delights than to go back three or four hundred years and become in fancy at least an Elizabethan. That such fancies are only fancies, that this "becoming an Elizabethan," this reading sixteenth-century writing as currently and certainly as we read our own is an illusion, is no doubt true. Very likely the Elizabethans would find our pronunciation of their language unintelligible; our fancy picture of what it pleases us to call Elizabethan life would rouse their ribald merriment. Still, the instinct that drives us to them is so strong and the freshness and vigour that blow through their pages are so sweet that we willingly run the risk of being laughed at, of being ridiculous.

And if we ask why we go further astray in this particular region of English literature than in any other, the answer is no doubt that Elizabethan prose, for all its beauty and bounty, was a very imperfect medium. It was almost incapable of fulfilling one of the offices of prose which is to make people talk, simply and naturally, about ordinary things. In an age of utilitarian prose like our own, we know exactly how people spend the hours between breakfast and bed, how they behave when they are neither one thing nor the other, neither angry nor loving, neither happy nor miserable. Poetry ignores these slighter shades; the social student can pick up hardly any facts about daily life from Shakespeare's plays; and if prose refuses to enlighten us, then one avenue of approach to the men and women of another age is blocked. Elizabethan prose, still scarcely separated off from the body of its poetry, could speak magnificently, of course, about the great themes—how life is short, and death certain; how spring is lovely, and winter horrid—perhaps, indeed, the lavish and towering periods that it raises above these simple platitudes are due to the fact that it has not cheapened itself upon trifles. But the price it pays for this soaring splendour is to be found in its awkwardness when it comes to earth—when Lady Sidney, for example, finding herself cold at nights, has to solicit the Lord Chamberlain for a better bedroom at Court. Then any housemaid of her own age could put her case more simply and with greater force. Thus, if we go to the Elizabethan prose-writers to solidify the splendid world of Elizabethan poetry as we should go now to our biographers, novelists, and journalists to solidify the world of Pope, of Tennyson, of Conrad, we are perpetually baffled and driven from our quest. What, we ask, was the life of an ordinary man or woman in the time of Shakespeare? Even the familiar letters of the time give us little help. Sir Henry Wotton is pompous and ornate and keeps us stiffly at arm's length. Their histories resound with drums and trumpets. Their broadsheets reverberate with meditations upon death and reflections upon the immortality of the soul. Our best chance of finding them off their guard and so becoming at ease with them is to seek one of those unambitious men who haunt the outskirts of famous gatherings, listening, observing, sometimes taking a note in a book. But they are difficult to find. Gabriel Harvey perhaps, the friend of Spenser and of Sidney, might have fulfilled that function. Unfortunately the values of the time persuaded him that to write about rhetoric, to write about Thomas Smith, to write about Queen Elizabeth in Latin, was better worth doing than to record the table talk of Spenser and Sir Philip Sidney. But he possessed to some extent the modern instinct for preserving trifles, for keeping copies of letters, and for making notes of ideas that struck him in the margins of books. If we rummage among these fragments we shall, at any rate, leave the highroad and perhaps hear some roar of laughter from a tavern door, where poets are drinking; or meet humble people going about their milking and their love-making without a thought that this is the great Elizabethan age, or that Shakespeare is at this moment strolling down the Strand and might tell one, if one plucked him by the sleeve, to whom he wrote the sonnets, and what he meant by Hamlet.

The first person whom we meet is indeed a milkmaid—Gabriel Harvey's sister Mercy. In the winter of 1574 she was milking in the fields near Saffron Walden accompanied by an old woman, when a man approached her and offered her cakes and malmsey wine. When they had eaten and drunk in a wood and the old woman had wandered off to pick up sticks, the man proceeded to explain his business. He came from Lord Surrey, a youth of about Mercy's own age—seventeen or eighteen that is—and a married man. He had been bowling one day and had seen the milkmaid; her hat had blown off and "she had somewhat changed her colour." In short, Lord Surrey had fallen passionately in love with her; and sent her by the same man gloves, a silk girdle, and an enamel posy ring which he had torn from his own hat though his Aunt, Lady W——, had given it him for a very different purpose. Mercy at first stood her ground. She was a poor milkmaid, and he was a noble gentleman. But at last she agreed to meet him at her house in the village. Thus, one very misty, foggy night just before Christmas, Lord Surrey and his servant came to Saffron Walden. They peered in at the malthouse, but saw only her mother and sisters; they peeped in at the parlour, but only her brothers were there. Mercy herself was not to be seen; and "well mired and wearied for their labour," there was nothing for it but to ride back home again. Finally, after further parleys, Mercy agreed to meet Lord Surrey in a neighbour's house alone at midnight. She found him in the little parlour "in his doublet and hose, his points untrust, and his shirt lying round about him." He tried to force her on to the bed; but she cried out, and the good wife, as had been agreed between them, rapped on the door and said she was sent for. Thwarted, enraged, Lord Surrey cursed and swore, "God confound me, God confound me," and by way of lure emptied his pockets of all the money in them—thirteen shillings in shillings and testers it came to—and made her finger it. Still, however, Mercy made off, untouched, on condition that she would come again on Christmas Eve. But when Christmas Eve dawned she was up betimes and had put seven miles between her and Saffron Walden by six in the morning, though it snowed and rained so that the floods were out, and P., the servant, coming later to the place of assignation, had to pick his way through the water in pattens. So Christmas passed. And a week later, in the very nick of time to save her honour, the whole story very strangely was discovered and brought to an end. On New Year's Eve her brother Gabriel, the young fellow of Pembroke Hall, was riding back to Cambridge when he came up with a simple countryman whom he had met at his father's house. They rode on together, and after some country gossip, the man said that he had a letter for Gabriel in his pocket. Indeed, it was addressed "To my loving brother Mr. G. H.," but when Gabriel opened it there on the road, he found that the address was a lie. It was not from his sister Mercy, but to his sister Mercy. "Mine Own Sweet Mercy," it began; and it was signed "Thine more than ever his own Phil." Gabriel could hardly control himself—"could scarcely dissemble my sudden fancies and comprimitt my inward passions"—as he read. For it was not merely a love-letter; it was more; it talked about possessing Mercy according to promise. There was also a fair English noble wrapped up in the paper. So Gabriel, doing his best to control himself before the countryman, gave him back the letter and the coin and told him to deliver them both to his sister at Saffron Walden with this message: "To look ere she leap. She may pick out the English of it herself." He rode on to Cambridge; he wrote a long letter to the young lord, informing him with ambiguous courtesy that the game was up. The sister of Gabriel Harvey was not to be the mistress of a married nobleman. Rather she was to be a maid, "diligent, and trusty and tractable," in the house of Lady Smith at Audley End. Thus Mercy's romance breaks off; the clouds descend again; and we no longer see the milkmaid, the old woman, the treacherous serving man who came with malmsey and cakes and rings and ribbons to tempt a poor girl's honour while she milked her cows.

This is probably no uncommon story; there must have been many milkmaids whose hats blew off as they milked their cows, and many lords whose hearts leapt at the sight so that they plucked the jewels from their hats and sent their servants to make treaty for them. But it is rare for the girl's own letters to be preserved or to read her own account of the story as she was made to deliver it at her brother's inquisition. Yet when we try to use her words to light up the Elizabethan field, the Elizabethan house and living-room, we are met by the usual perplexities. It is easy enough, in spite of the rain and the fog and the floods, to make a fancy piece out of the milkmaid and the meadows and the old woman wandering off to pick up sticks. Elizabethan song-writers have taught us too well the habit of that particular trick. But if we resist the impulse to make museum pieces out of our reading, Mercy herself gives us little help. She was a milkmaid, scribbling love-letters by the light of a farthing dip in an attic. Nevertheless, the sway of the Elizabethan convention was so strong, the accent of their speech was so masterful, that she bears herself with a grace and expresses herself with a resonance that would have done credit to a woman of birth and literary training. When Lord Surrey pressed her to yield she replied:

> The thing you wot of, Milord, were a great trespass towards God, a great offence to the world, a great grief to my friends, a great shame to myself, and, as I think, a great dishonour to your lordship. I have heard my father say, Virginity is ye fairest flower in a maid's garden, and chastity ye richest dowry a poor wench can have. . . . Chastity, they say, is like unto time, which, being once lost, can no more be recovered.

Words chime and ring in her ears, as if she positively enjoyed the act of writing. When she wishes him to know that she is only a poor country girl and no fine lady like his wife, she exclaims, "Good Lord, that you should seek after so bare and country stuff abroad, that have so costly and courtly wares at home!" She even breaks into a jog-trot of jingling rhyme, far less sonorous than her prose, but proof that to write was an art, not merely a means of conveying facts. And if she wants to be direct and forcible, the proverbs she has heard in her father's house come to her pen, the Biblical imagery runs in her ears: "And then were I, poor wench, cast up for hawk's meat, to mine utter undoing, and my friends' exceeding grief." In short, Mercy the milkmaid writes a natural and noble style, which is incapable of vulgarity, and equally incapable of intimacy. Nothing, one feels, would have been easier for Mercy than to read her lover a fine discourse upon the vanity of grandeur, the loveliness of chastity, the vicissitudes of fortune. But of emotion as between one particular Mercy and one particular Phillip, there is no trace. And when it comes to dealing exactly in a few words with some mean object—when, for example, the wife of Sir Henry Sidney, the daughter of the Duke of Northumberland, has to state her claim to a better room to sleep in, she writes for all the world like an illiterate servant girl who can neither form her letters nor spell her words nor make one sentence follow smoothly after another. She haggles, she niggles, she wears our patience down with her repetitions and her prolixities. Hence it comes about that we know very little about Mercy Harvey, the milkmaid, who wrote so well, or Mary Sidney, daughter to the Duke of Northumberland, who wrote so badly. The background of Elizabethan life eludes us.

But let us follow Gabriel Harvey to Cambridge, in case we can there pick up something humble and colloquial that will make these strange Elizabethans more familiar to us. Gabriel, having discharged his duty as a brother, seems to have given himself up to the life of an intellectual young man with his way to make in the world. He worked so hard and he played so little that he made himself unpopular with his fellows. For it was obviously difficult to combine an intense interest in the future of English poetry and the capacity of the English language with card-playing, bear-baiting, and such diversions. Nor could he apparently accept everything that Aristotle said as gospel truth. But with congenial spirits he argued, it is clear, hour by hour, night after night, about poetry, and metre, and the raising of the despised English speech and the meagre English literature to a station among the great tongues and literatures of the world. We are sometimes made to think, as we listen, of such arguments as might now be going forward in the new Universities of America. The young English poets speak with a bold yet uneasy arrogance—"England, since it was England, never bred more honourable minds, more adventurous hearts, more valorous hands, or more excellent wits, than of late." Yet, to be English is accounted a kind of crime—"nothing is reputed so contemptible and so basely and vilely accounted of as whatsoever is taken for English." And if, in their hopes for the future and their sensitiveness to the opinion of older civilisations, the Elizabethans show much the same susceptibility that sometimes puzzles us among the younger countries today, the sense that broods over them of what is about to happen, of an undiscovered land on which they are about to set foot, is much like the excitement that science stirs in the minds of imaginative English writers of our own time. Yet however stimulating it is to think that we hear the stir and strife of tougues in Cambridge rooms about the year 1570, it has to be admitted that to read Harvey's pages methodically is almost beyond the limits of human patience. The words seem to run redhot, molten, hither and thither, until we cry out in anguish for the boon of some meaning to set its stamp on them. He takes the same idea and repeats it over and over again:

> In the sovereign workmanship of Nature herself, what garden of flowers without weeds? what orchard of trees without worms? what field of corn without cockle? what pond of fishes without frogs? what sky of light without darkness? what mirror of knowledge without ignorance? what man of earth without frailty? what commodity of the world without discommodity?

It is interminable. As we go round and round like a horse in a mill, we perceive that we are thus clogged with sound because we are reading what we should be hearing. The amplifications and the repetitions, the emphasis like that of a fist pounding the edge of a pulpit, are for the benefit of the slow and sensual ear which loves to dally over sense and luxuriate in sound—the ear which brings in, along with the spoken word, the look of the speaker and his gestures, which gives a dramatic value to what he says and adds to the crest of an extravagance some modulation which makes the word wing its way to the precise spot aimed at in the hearer's heart. Hence, when we lay Harvey's diatribes against Nash or his letters to Spenser upon poetry under the light of the eye alone, we can hardly make headway and lose our sense of any definite direction. We grasp any simple fact that floats to the surface as a drowning man grasps a plank—that the carrier was called Mrs. Kerke, that Perne kept a cub for his pleasure in his rooms at Peterhouse; that "Your last letter . . . was delivered me at mine hostesses by the fireside, being fast hedged in round about on every side with a company of honest, good fellows, and at that time reasonable, honest quaffers"; that Greene died begging Mistress Isam "for a penny pot of Malmsey," had borrowed her husband's shirt when his own was awashing, and was buried yesterday in the new churchyard near Bedlam at a cost of six shillings and fourpence. Light seems to dawn upon the darkness. But no; just as we think to lay hands on Shakespeare's coat-tails, to hear the very words rapped out as Spenser spoke them, up rise the fumes of Harvey's eloquence and we are floated off again into disputation and eloquence, windy, wordy, voluminous, and obsolete. How, we ask, as we slither over the pages, can we ever hope to come to grips with these Elizabethans? And then, turning, skipping and glancing, something fitfully and doubtfully emerges from the violent pages, the voluminous arguments—the figure of a man, the outlines of a face, somebody who is not "an Elizabethan" but an interesting, complex, and individual human being.

We know him, to begin with, from his dealings with his sister. We see him riding to Cambridge, a fellow of his college, when she was milking with poor old women in the fields. We observe with amusement his sense of the conduct that befits the sister of Gabriel Harvey, the Cambridge scholar. Education had put a great gulf between him and his family. He rode to Cambridge from a house in a village street where his father made ropes and his mother worked in the malthouse. Yet though his lowly birth and the consciousness that he had his way to make in the world made him severe with his sister, fawning to the great, uneasy and self-centred and ostentatious, it never made him ashamed of his family. The father who could send three sons to Cambridge and was so little ashamed of his craft that he had himself carved making ropes at his work and the carving let in above his fireplace, was no ordinary man. The brothers who followed Gabriel to Cambridge and were his best allies there, were brothers to be proud of. He could be proud of Mercy even, whose beauty could make a great nobleman pluck the jewel from his hat. He was undoubtedly proud of himself. It was the pride of a self-made man who must read when other people are playing cards, who owns no undue allegiance to authority and will contradict Aristotle himself, that made him unpopular at Cambridge and almost cost him his degree. But it was an unfortunate chance that led him thus early in life to defend his rights and insist upon his merits. Moreover, since it was true—since he was abler, quicker, and more learned than other people, handsome in person too, as even his enemies could not deny ("a smudge piece of a handsome fellow it hath been in his days" Nash admitted) he had reason to think that he deserved success and was denied it only by the jealousies and conspiracies of his colleagues. For a time, by dint of much caballing and much dwelling upon his own deserts, he triumphed over his enemies in the matter of the degree. He delivered lectures. He was asked to dispute before the Court when Queen Elizabeth came to Audley End. He even drew her favourable attention. "He lookt something like an Italian," she said when he was brought to her notice. But the seeds of his downfall were visible even in his moment of triumph. He had no self-respect, no self-control. He made himself ridiculous and his friends uneasy. When we read how he dressed himself up and "came ruffling it out huffty tuffty in his suit of velvet" how uneasy he was, at one moment cringing, at another "making no bones to take the wall of Sir Philip Sidney," now flirting with the ladies, now "putting bawdy riddles to them," how when the Queen praised him he was beside himself with joy and talked the English of Saffron Walden with an Italian accent, we can imagine how his enemies jeered and his friends blushed. And so, for all his merits, his decline began. He was not taken into Lord Leicester's service; he was not made Public Orator; he was not given the Mastership of Trinity Hall. But there was one society in which he succeeded. In the small, smoky rooms where Spenser and other young men discussed poetry and language and the future of English literature, Harvey was not laughed at. Harvey, on the contrary, was taken very seriously. To friends like these he seemed as capable of greatness as any of them. He too might be one of those destined to make English literature illustrious. His passion for poetry was disinterested. His learning was profound. When he held forth upon quantity and metre, upon what the Greeks had written and the Italians, and what the English might write, no doubt he created for Spenser that atmosphere of hope and ardent curiosity spiced with sound learning that serves to spur the imagination of a young writer and to make each fresh poem as it is written seem the common property of a little band of adventurers set upon the same quest. It was thus that Spenser saw him:

> Harvey, the happy above happiest men,
> I read: that, sitting like a looker-on
> Of this world's stage, doest note, with critic pen,
> The sharp dislikes of each condition.

Poets need such "lookers-on"; some one who discriminates from a watch-tower above the battle; who warns; who foresees. It must have been pleasant for Spenser to listen as Harvey talked; and then to cease to listen, to let the vehement, truculent voice run on, while he slipped from theory to practise and made up a few lines of his own poetry in his head. But the looker-on may sit too long and hold forth too curiously and domineeringly for his own health. He may make his theories fit too tight to accommodate the formlessness of life. Thus when Harvey ceased to theorise and tried to practise there issued nothing but a thin dribble of arid and unappetising verse or a copious flow of unctuous and servile eulogy. He failed to be a poet as he failed to be a statesman, as he failed to be a professor, as he failed to be a Master, as he failed, it might seem, in everything that he undertook, save that he had won the friendship of Spenser and Sir Philip Sidney.

But happily Harvey left behind him a commonplace book; he had the habit of making notes in the margins of books as he read. Looking from one to the other, from his public self to his private, we see his face lit from both sides, and the expression changes as it changes so seldom upon the face of the Elizabethans. We detect another Harvey lurking behind the superficial Harvey, shading him with doubt and effort and despondency. For, luckily, the commonplace book was small; the margins even of an Elizabethan folio narrow; Harvey was forced to be brief, and because he wrote only for his own eye at the command of some sharp memory or experience he seems to write as if he were talking to himself. That is true, he seems to say; or that reminds me, or again: If only I had done this— We thus become aware of a conflict between the Harvey who blundered among men and the Harvey who sat wisely at home among his books. The one who acts and suffers brings his case to the one who reads and thinks for advice and consolation.

Indeed, he had need of both. From the first his life was full of conflict and difficulty. Harvey the rope-maker's son might put a brave face on it, but still in the society of gentlemen the lowness of his birth galled him. Think, then, the sedentary Harvey counselled him, of all those unknown people who have nevertheless triumphed. Think of "Alexander, an Unexpert Youth"; think of David, "a forward stripling, but vanquished a huge Giant"; think of Judith and of Pope Joan and their exploits; think above all of that "gallant virago . . . Joan of Arc, a most worthy, valiant young wench . . . what may not an industrious and politic man do . . . when a lusty adventurous wench might thus prevail?" And then it seems as if the smart young men at Cambridge twitted the ropemaker's son for his lack of skill in the gentlemanly arts. "Leave writing," Gabriel counselled him, "which consumeth unreasonable much time. . . . You have already plagued yourself this way." Make yourself master of the arts of eloquence and persuasion. Go into the world. Learn swordsmanship, riding, and shooting. All three may be learnt in a week. And then the ambitious but uneasy youth began to find the other sex attractive and asked advice of his wise and sedentary brother in the conduct of his love affairs. Manners, the other Harvey was of opinion, are of the utmost importance in dealing with women; one must be discreet, self-controlled. A gentleman, this counsellor continued, is known by his "Good entertainment of Ladies and gentlewomen. No salutation, without much respect and ceremony"—a reflection inspired no doubt by the memory of some snub received at Audley End. Health and the care of the body are of the utmost importance. "We scholars make an Ass of our body and wit." One must "leap out of bed lustily, every morning in ye whole year." One must be sparing in one's diet, and active, and take regular exercise, like brother H., "who never failed to breathe his hound once a day at least." There must be no "buzzing or musing." A learned man must also be a man of the world. Make it your "daily charge" "to exercise, to laugh; to proceed boldly." And if your tormentors brawl and rail and scoff and mock at you, the best answer is "a witty and pleasant Ironie." In any case, do not complain, "It is gross folly, and a vile Sign of a wayward and forward disposition, to be eftsoons complaining of this, or that, to small purpose." And if as time goes on without preferment, one cannot pay one's bills, one is thrust into prison, one has to bear the taunts and insults of landladies, still remember "Glad poverty is no poverty"; and if, as time passes and the struggle increases, it seems as if "Life is warfare," if sometimes the beaten man has to own, "But for hope ye Hart would brust," still his sage counsellor in the study will not let him throw up the sponge. "He beareth his misery best, that hideth it most," he told himself.

So runs the dialogue that we invent between the two Harveys—Harvey the active and Harvey the passive, Harvey the foolish and Harvey the wise. And it seems on the surface that the two halves, for all their counselling together, made but a sorry business of the whole. For the young man who had ridden off to Cambridge full of conceit and hope and good advice to his sister returned empty-handed to his native village in the end. He dwindled out his last long years in complete obscurity at Saffron Walden. He occupied himself superficially by practising his skill as a doctor among the poor of the neighbourhood. He lived in the utmost poverty off buttered roots and sheep's trotters. But even so he had his consolations, he cherished his dreams. As he pottered about his garden in the old black velvet suit, purloined, Nash says, from a saddle for which he had not paid, his thoughts were all of power and glory; of Stukeley and Drake; of "the winners of gold and the wearers of gold." Memories he had in abundance—"The remembrance of best things will soon pass out of memory; if it be not often renewed and revived," he wrote. But there was some eager stir in him, some lust for action and glory and life and adventure that forbade him to dwell in the past. "The present tense only to be regarded" is one of his notes. Nor did he drug himself with the dust of scholarship. Books he loved as a true reader loves them, not as trophies to be hung up for display, but as living beings that "must be meditated, practised and incorporated into my body and soul." A singularly humane view of learning survived in the breast of the old and disappointed scholar. "The only brave way to learn all things with no study and much pleasure," he remarked. Dreams of the winners of gold and the wearers of gold, dreams of action and power, fantastic though they were in an old beggar who could not pay his reckoning, who pressed simples and lived off buttered roots in a cottage, kept life in him when his flesh had withered and his skin was "riddled and crumpled like a piece of burnt parchment." He had his triumph in the end. He survived both his friends and his enemies—Spenser and Sidney, Nash and Perne. He lived to a very great age for an Elizabethan, to eighty-one or eighty-two; and when we say that Harvey lived we mean that he quarrelled and was tiresome and ridiculous and struggled and failed and had a face like ours—a changing, a variable, a human face.

*

Donne After Three Centuries

*

When we think how many millions of words have been written and printed in England in the past three hundred years, and how the vast majority have died out without leaving any trace, it is tempting to wonder what quality the words of Donne possess that we should still hear them distinctly today. Far be it from us to suggest even in this year of celebration and pardonable adulation (1931) that the poems of Donne are popular reading or that the typist, if we look over her shoulder in the Tube, is to be discovered reading Donne as she returns from her office. But he is read; he is audible—to that fact new editions and frequent articles testify, and it is worth perhaps trying to analyse the meaning that his voice has for us as it strikes upon the ear after this long flight across the stormy seas that separate us from the age of Elizabeth.

But the first quality that attracts us is not his meaning, charged with meaning as his poetry is, but something much more unmixed and immediate; it is the explosion with which he bursts into speech. All preface, all parleying have been consumed; he leaps into poetry the shortest way. One phrase consumes all preparation:

> I long to talke with some old lover's ghost,

or

> He is starke mad, whoever sayes,
> That he hath beene in love an houre.

At once we are arrested. Stand still, he commands,

> Stand still, and I will read to thee
> A Lecture, Love, in love's philosophy.

And stand still we must. With the first words a shock passes through us; perceptions, previously numb and torpid, quiver into being; the nerves of sight and hearing are quickened; the "bracelet of bright hair" burns in our eyes. But, more remarkably, we do not merely become aware of beautiful remembered lines; we feel ourselves compelled to a particular attitude of mind. Elements that were dispersed in the usual stream of life become, under the stroke of Donne's passion, one and entire. The world, a moment before, cheerful, humdrum, bursting with character and variety, is consumed. We are in Donne's world now. All other views are sharply cut off.

In this power of suddenly surprising and subjugating the reader, Donne excels most poets. It is his characteristic quality; it is thus that he lays hold upon us, summing up his essence in a word or two. But it is an essence that, as it works in us, separates into strange contraries at odds with one another. Soon we begin to ask ourselves of what this essence is composed, what elements have met together to cut so deep and complex an impression. Some obvious clues lie strewn on the surface of the poems. When we read the *Satyres,* for example, we need no external proof to tell us that these are the work of a boy. He has all the ruthlessness and definiteness of youth, its hatred of the follies of middle age and of convention. Bores, liars, courtiers—detestable humbugs and hypocrites as they are, why not sum them up and sweep them off the face of the earth with a few strokes of the pen? And so these foolish figures are drubbed with an ardour that proves how much hope and faith and delight in life inspire the savagery of youthful scorn. But, as we read on, we begin to suspect that the boy with the complex and curious face of the early portrait—bold yet subtle, sensual yet nerve drawn—possessed qualities that made him singular among the young. It is not simply that the huddle and pressure of youth which outthinks its words had urged him on too fast for grace or clarity. It may be that there is in this clipping and curtailing, this abrupt heaping of thought on thought, some deeper dissatisfaction than that of youth with age, of honesty with corruption. He is in rebellion, not merely against his elders, but against something antipathetic to him in the temper of his time. His verse has the deliberate bareness of those who refuse to avail themselves of the current usage. It has the extravagance of those who do not feel the pressure of opinion, so that sometimes judgment fails them, and they heap up strangeness for strangeness' sake. He is one of those nonconformists, like Browning and Meredith, who cannot resist glorifying their nonconformity by a dash of wilful and gratuitous eccentricity. But to discover what Donne disliked in his own age, let us imagine some of the more obvious influences that must have told upon him when he wrote his early poems—let us ask what books he read. And by Donne's own testimony we find that his chosen books were the works of "grave Divines"; of philosophers; of "jolly Statesmen, which teach how to tie The sinewes of a cities mistique bodie"; and chroniclers. Clearly he liked facts and arguments. If there are also poets among his books, the epithets he applies to them, "Giddie fantastique," seem to disparage the art, or at least to show that Donne knew perfectly well what qualities were antipathetic to him in poetry. And yet he was living in the very spring of English poetry. Some of Spenser might have been on his shelves; and Sidney's *Arcadia;* and the *Paradise of Dainty Devices*, and Lyly's *Euphues*. He had the chance, and apparently took it—"I tell him of new playes"—of going to the theatre; of seeing the plays of Marlowe and Shakespeare acted. When he went abroad in London, he must have met all the writers of that time—Spenser and Sidney and Shakespeare and Jonson; he must have heard at this tavern or at that talk of new plays, of new fashions in verse, heated and learned discussion of the possibilities of the English language and the future of English poetry. And yet, if we turn to his biography, we find that he neither consorted with his contemporaries nor read what they wrote. He was one of those original beings who cannot draw profit, but are rather disturbed and distracted by what is being done round them at the moment. If we turn again to *Satyres*, it is easy to see why this should be so. Here is a bold and active mind that loves to deal with actual things, which struggles to express each shock exactly as it impinges upon his tight-stretched senses. A bore stops him in the street. He sees him exactly, vividly.

His cloths were strange, though coarse; and black, though bare;
Sleevelesse his jerkin was, and it had beene
Velvet, but t'was now (so much ground was seene)
Become Tufftaffatie;

Then he likes to give the actual words that people say:

He, like to a high stretcht lute string squeakt, O Sir,
'Tis sweet to talke of Kings. At Westminster,
Said I, The man that keepes the Abbey tombes,
And for his price doth with who ever comes,
Of all our Harries, and our Edwards talke,
From King to King and all their kin can walke:
Your eares shall heare nought, but Kings; your eyes meet
Kings only; The way to it, is Kingstreet.

His strength and his weakness are both to be found here. He selects one detail and stares at it until he has reduced it to the few words that express its oddity:

And like a bunch of ragged carrets stand
The short swolne fingers of thy gouty hand,

but he cannot see in the round, as a whole. He cannot stand apart and survey the large outline so that the description is always of some momentary intensity, seldom of the broader aspect of things. Naturally, then, he found it difficult to use the drama with its conflict of other characters; he must always speak from his own centre in soliloquy, in satire, in self-analysis. Spenser, Sidney, and Marlowe provided no helpful models for a man who looked out from this angle of vision. The typical Elizabethan with his love of eloquence, with his longing for brave new words, tended to enlarge and generalise. He loved wide landscapes, heroic virtues, and figures seen sublimely in outline or in heroic conflict. Even the prose-writers have the same habit of aggrandisement. When Dekker sets out to tell us how Queen Elizabeth died in the spring, he cannot describe her death in particular or that spring in particular; he must dilate upon all deaths and all springs:

> . . . the Cuckoo (like a single, sole Fiddler, that reels from Tavern to Tavern) plied it all the day long: Lambs frisked up and down in the vallies, kids and Goats leapt to and fro on the Mountains: Shepherds sat piping, country wenches singing: Lovers made Sonnets for their Lasses, whilst they made Garlands for their Lovers: And as the Country was frolic, so was the City merry . . . no Scritch-Owl frighted the silly Countryman at midnight, nor any Drum the Citizen at noon-day; but all was more calm than a still water, all husht, as if the Spheres had been playing in Consort: In conclusion, heaven lookt like a Pallace, and the great hall of the earth, like a Paradise. But O the short-liv'd Felicity of man! O world, of what slight and thin stuff is thy happiness!

—in short, Queen Elizabeth died, and it is no use asking Dekker what the old woman who swept his room for him said, or what Cheapside looked like that night if one happened to be caught in the thick of the throng. He must enlarge; he must generalise; he must beautify.

Donne's genius was precisely the opposite of this. He diminished; he particularised. Not only did he see each spot and wrinkle which defaced the fair outline; but he noted with the utmost curiosity his own reaction to such contrasts and was eager to lay side by side the two conflicting views and to let them make their own dissonance. It is this desire for nakedness in an age that was florid, this determination to record not the likenesses which go to compose a rounded and seemly whole, but the inconsistencies that break up semblances, the power to make us feel the different emotions of love and hate and laughter at the same time, that separate Donne from his contemporaries. And if the usual traffic of the day—to be buttonholed by a bore, to be snared by a lawyer, to be snubbed by a courtier—made so sharp an impression on Donne, the effect of falling in love was bound to be incomparably greater. Falling in love meant, to Donne, a thousand things; it meant being tormented and disgusted, disillusioned and enraptured; but it also meant speaking the truth. The love poems, the elegies, and the letters thus reveal a figure of a very different calibre from the typical figure of Elizabethan love poetry. That great ideal, built up by a score of eloquent pens, still burns bright in our eyes. Her body was of alabaster, her legs of ivory; her hair was golden wire and her teeth pearls from the Orient. Music was in her voice and stateliness in her walk. She could love and sport and be faithless and yielding and cruel and true; but her emotions were simple, as befitted her person. Donne's poems reveal a lady of a very different cast. She was brown but she was also fair; she was solitary but also sociable; she was rustic yet also fond of city life; she was sceptical yet devout, emotional but reserved—in short she was as various and complex as Donne himself. As for choosing one type of human perfection and restricting himself to love her and her only, how could Donne, or any man who allowed his senses full play and honestly recorded his own moods, so limit his nature and tell such lies to placate the conventional and the decorous? Was not "love's sweetest part, Variety"? "Of music, joy, life and eternity Change is the nursery," he sang. The timid fashion of the age might limit a lover to one woman. For his part he envied and admired the ancients, "who held plurality of loves no crime":

> But since this title honour hath been us'd,
> Our weak credulity hath been abus'd.

We have fallen from our high estate; the golden laws of nature are repealed.

So through the glass of Donne's poetry now darkly clouded, now brilliantly clear, we see pass in procession the many women whom he loved and hated—the common Julia whom he despised; the simpleton, to whom he taught the art of love; she who was married to an invalid husband, "cag'd in a basket chair"; she who could only be loved dangerously by strategy; she who dreamt of him and saw him murdered as he crossed the Alps; she whom he had to dissuade from the risk of loving him; and lastly, the autumnal, the aristocratic lady for whom he felt more of reverence than of love—so they pass, common and rare, simple and sophisticated, young and old, noble and plebeian, and each casts a different spell and brings out a different lover, although the man is the same man, and the women, perhaps, are also phases of womanhood rather than separate and distinct women. In later years the Dean of St. Paul's would willingly have edited some of these poems and suppressed one of these lovers—the poet presumably of "Going to Bed" and "Love's Warr." But the Dean would have been wrong. It is the union of so many different desires that gives Donne's love poetry not only its vitality but also a quality that is seldom found with such strength in the conventional and orthodox lover—its spirituality. If we do not love with the body, can we love with the mind? If we do not love variously, freely, admitting the lure first of this quality and then of that, can we at length choose out the one quality that is essential and adhere to it and so make peace among the warring elements and pass into a state of being which transcends the "Hee and Shee"? Even while he was at his most fickle and gave fullest scope to his youthful lusts, Donne could predict the season of maturity when he would love differently, with pain and difficulty, one and one only. Even while he scorned and railed and abused, he divined another relationship which transcended change and parting and might, even in the bodies' absence, lead to unity and communion:

> Rend us in sunder, thou canst not divide,
> Our bodies so, but that our souls are ty'd,
> And we can love by letters still and gifts,
> And thoughts and dreams;

Again,

> They who one another keepe alive
> N'er parted be.

And again,

> So to one neutrall thing both sexes fit,
> Wee dye and rise the same, and prove
> Mysterious by this love.

Such hints and premonitions of a further and finer state urge him on and condemn him to perpetual unrest and dissatisfaction with the present. He is tantalised by the sense that there is a miracle beyond any of these transient delights and disgusts. Lovers can, if only for a short space, reach a state of unity beyond time, beyond sex, beyond the body. And at last, for one moment, they reach it. In the "Extasie" they lie together on a bank,

> All day, the same our postures were,
> And wee said nothing, all the day. . . .
>
> This Extasie doth unperplex
> (We said) and tell us what we love,
> Wee see by this, it was not sexe,
> Wee see, we saw not what did move: . . .
>
> Wee then, who are this new soule, know,
> Of what we are compos'd, and made,
> For, th' Atomies of which we grow,
> Are soules, whom no change can invade.
>
> But O alas, so long, so farre
> Our bodies, why doe wee forbeare? . . .

But O alas, he breaks off, and the words remind us that however much we may wish to keep Donne in one posture—for it is in these Extasies that lines of pure poetry suddenly flow as if liquefied by a great heat—so to remain in one posture was against his nature. Perhaps it is against the nature of things also. Donne snatches the intensity because he is aware of the change that must alter, of the discord that must interrupt.

Circumstances, at any rate, put it beyond his power to maintain that ecstasy for long. He had married secretly; he was a father; he was, as we are soon reminded, a very poor yet a very ambitious man, living in a damp little house at Mitcham with a family of small children. The children were frequently ill. They cried, and their cries, cutting through the thin walls of the jerry-built house, disturbed him at his work. He sought sanctuary naturally enough elsewhere, and naturally had to pay rent for that relief. Great ladies—Lady Bedford, Lady Huntingdon, Mrs. Herbert—with well-spread tables and fair gardens, must be conciliated; rich men with the gift of rooms in their possession must be placated. Thus, after Donne the harsh satirist, and Donne the imperious lover, comes the servile and obsequious figure of Donne the devout servant of the great, the extravagant eulogist of little girls. And our relationship with him suddenly changes. In the satires and the love poems there was a quality—some psychological intensity and complexity—that brings him closer than his contemporaries, who often seem to be caught up in a different world from ours and to exist immune from our perplexities and swept by passions which we admire but cannot feel. Easy as it is to exaggerate affinities, still we may claim to be akin to Donne in our readiness to admit contrasts, in our desire for openness, in that psychological intricacy which the novelists have taught us with their slow, subtle, and analytic prose. But now, as we follow Donne in his progress, he leaves us in the lurch. He becomes more remote, inaccessible, and obsolete than any of the Elizabethans. It is as if the spirit of the age, which he had scorned and flouted, suddenly asserted itself and made this rebel its slave. And as we lose sight of the outspoken young man who hated society, and of the passionate lover, seeking some mysterious unity with his love and finding it miraculously, now here, now there, it is natural to abuse the system of patrons and patronage that thus seduced the most incorruptible of men. Yet it may be that we are too hasty. Every writer has an audience in view, and it may well be doubted if the Bedfords and the Drurys and the Herberts were worse influences than the libraries and the newspaper proprietors who fill the office of patron nowadays.

The comparison, it is true, presents great difficulties. The noble ladies who brought so strange an element into Donne's poetry, live only in the reflection, or in the distortion, that we find in the poems themselves. The age of memoirs and letter-writing was still to come. If they wrote themselves, and it is said that both Lady Pembroke and Lady Bedford were poets of merit, they did not dare to put their names to what they wrote, and it has vanished. But a diary here and there survives from which we may see the patroness more closely and less romantically. Lady Anne Clifford, for example, the daughter of a Clifford and a Russell, though active and practical and little educated—she was not allowed "to learn any language because her father would not permit it"—felt, we can gather from the bald statements of her diary, a duty towards literature and to the makers of it as her mother, the patroness of the poet Daniel, had done before her. A great heiress, infected with all the passion of her age for lands and houses, busied with all the cares of wealth and property, she still read good English books as naturally as she ate good beef and mutton. She read *The Faërie Queene* and Sidney's *Arcadia;* she acted in Ben Jonson's Masques at Court; and it is proof of the respect in which reading was held that a girl of fashion should be able to read an old corrupt poet like Chaucer without feeling that she was making herself a target for ridicule as a blue-stocking. The habit was part of a normal and well-bred life. It persisted even when she was mistress of one estate and claimant to even vaster possession of her own. She had Montaigne read aloud to her as she sat stitching at Knole; she sat absorbed in Chaucer while her husband worked. Later, when years of strife and loneliness had saddened her, she returned to her Chaucer with a deep sigh of content: ". . . if I had not excellent Chaucer's book here to comfort me," she wrote, "I were in a pitiable case having as many troubles as I have here, but, when I read in that, I scorn and make light of them all, and a little part of his beauteous spirit infuses itself in me." The woman who said that, though she never attempted to set up a salon or to found a library, felt it incumbent on her to respect the men of low birth and no fortune who could write *The Canterbury Tales* or *The Faërie Queene*. Donne preached before her at Knole. It was she who paid for the first monument to Spenser in Westminster Abbey, and if, when she raised a tomb to her old tutor, she dwelt largely upon her own virtues and titles, she still acknowledged that even so great a lady as herself owed gratitude to the makers of books. Words from great writers nailed to the walls of the room in which she sat, eternally transacting business surrounded her as she worked, as they surrounded Montaigne in his tower in Burgundy.

Thus we may infer that Donne's relation to the Countess of Bedford was very different from any that could exist between a poet and a countess at the present time. There was something distant and ceremonious about it. To him she was "as a vertuous Prince farre off." The greatness of her office inspired reverence apart from her personality, just as the rewards within her gift inspired humility. He was her Laureate, and his songs in her praise were rewarded by invitations to stay with her at Twickenham and by those friendly meetings with men in power which were so effective in furthering the career of an ambitious man—and Donne was highly ambitious, not indeed for the fame of a poet, but for the power of a statesman. Thus when we read that Lady Bedford was "God's Masterpiece," that she excelled all women in all ages, we realize that John Donne is not writing to Lucy Bedford; Poetry is saluting Rank. And this distance served to inspire reason rather than passion. Lady Bedford must have been a very clever woman, well versed in the finer shades of theology, to derive an instant or an intoxicating pleasure from the praises of her servant. Indeed, the extreme subtlety and erudition of Donne's poems to his patrons seem to show that one effect of writing for such an audience is to exaggerate the poet's ingenuity. What is not poetry but something tortured and difficult will prove to the patron that the poet is exerting his skill on her behalf. Then again, a learned poem can be handed round among statesmen and men of affairs to prove that the poet is no mere versifier, but capable of office and responsibility. But a change of inspiration that has killed many poets—witness Tennyson and the *Idylls of the King*—only stimulated another side of Donne's many-sided nature and many-faceted brain. As we read the long poems written ostensibly in praise of Lady Bedford, or in celebration of Elizabeth Drury (*An Anatomie of the World* and the *Progresse of the Soul*), we are made to reflect how much remains for a poet to write about when the season of love is over. When May and June are passed, most poets cease to write or sing the songs of their youth out of tune. But Donne survived the perils of middle age by virtue of the acuteness and ardour of his intellect. When "the satyrique fires which urg'd me to have writt in skorne of all" were quenched, when "My muse (for I had one), because I'm cold, Divorced herself," there still remained the power to turn upon the nature of things and dissect that. Even in the passionate days of youth Donne had been a thinking poet. He had dissected and analysed his own love. To turn from that to the anatomy of the world, from the personal to the impersonal, was the natural development of a complex nature. And the new angle to which his mind now pointed under the influence of middle age and traffic with the world, released powers that were held in check when they were directed against some particular courtier or some particular woman. Now his imagination, as if freed from impediment, goes rocketing up in flights of extravagant exaggeration. True, the rocket bursts; it scatters in a shower of minute, separate particles—curious speculations, wiredrawn comparisons, obsolete erudition; but, winged by the double pressure of mind and heart, of reason and imagination, it soars far and fast into a finer air. Working himself up by his own extravagant praise of the dead girl, he shoots on:

> We spur, we reine the starres, and in their race
> They're diversly content t'obey our pace.
> But keepes the earth her round proportion still?
> Doth not a Tenarif, or higher Hill
> Rise so high like a Rocke, that one might thinke
> The floating Moone would shipwracke there, and sinke?
> Seas are so deepe, that Whales being strooke today,
> Perchance tomorrow, scarce at middle way
> Of their wish'd journies end, the bottome, die.
> And men, to sound depths, so much line untie,
> As one might justly thinke, that there would rise
> At end thereof, one of th'Antipodies:

Or again, Elizabeth Drury is dead and her soul has escaped:

> she stayes not in the ayre,
> To looke what Meteors there themselves prepare;
> She carries no desire to know, nor sense,
> Whether th'ayres middle region be intense;
> For th'Element of fire, she doth not know,
> Whether she past by such a place or no;
> She baits not at the Moone, nor cares to trie
> Whether in that new world, men live, and die.
> *Venus* retards her not, to'enquire, how shee
> Can, (being one starre) *Hesper*, and *Vesper* bee;
> Hee that charm'd *Argus* eyes, sweet *Mercury*,
> Workes not on her, who now is growne all eye;

So we penetrate into distant regions, and reach rare and remote speculations a million miles removed from the simple girl whose death fired the explosion. But to break off fragments from poems whose virtue lies in their close-knit sinews and their long-breathed strength is to diminish them. They need to be read currently rather to grasp the energy and power of the whole than to admire those separate lines which Donne suddenly strikes to illumine the stages of our long climb.

Thus finally we reach the last section of the book, the Holy Sonnets and Divine Poems. Again the poetry changes with the change of circumstances and of years. The patron has gone with the need of patronage. Lady Bedford has been replaced by a Prince still more virtuous and still more remote. To Him the prosperous, the important, the famous Dean of St. Paul's now turns. But how different is the divine poetry of this great dignitary from the divine poetry of the Herberts and the Vaughans! The memory of his sins returns to him as he writes. He has been burnt with "lust and envy"; he has followed profane loves; he has been scornful and fickle and passionate and servile and ambitious. He has attained his end; but he is weaker and worse than the horse or the bull. Now too he is lonely. "Since she whom I lov'd" is dead "My good is dead." Now at last his mind is "wholly sett on heavenly things." And yet how could Donne—that "little world made cunningly of elements"—be wholly set on any one thing?

Oh, to vex me, contraryes meet in one:
Inconstancy unnaturally hath begott
A constant habit; that when I would not
I change in vowes, and in devotione.

It was impossible for the poet who had noted so curiously the flow and change of human life, and its contrast, who was at once so inquisitive of knowledge and so sceptical—

Doubt wisely; in strange way,
To stand inquiring right, is not to stray;
To sleep, or run wrong, is

—who had owned allegiance to so many great Princes, the body, the King, the Church of England, to reach that state of wholeness and certainty which poets of purer life were able to maintain. His devotions themselves were feverish and fitful. "My devout fitts come and goe away like a fantastique Ague." They are full of contraries and agonies. Just as his love poetry at its most sensual will suddenly reveal the desire for a transcendent unity "beyond the Hee and Shee," and his most reverential letters to great ladies will suddenly become love poems addressed by an amorous man to a woman of flesh and blood, so these last divine poems are poems of climbing and falling, of incongruous clamours and solemnities, as if the church door opened on the uproar of the street. That perhaps is why they still excite interest and disgust, contempt and admiration. For the Dean still retained the incorrigible curiosity of his youth. The temptation to speak the truth in defiance of the world even when he had taken all that the world had to give, still worked in him. An obstinate interest in the nature of his own sensations still troubled his age and broke its repose as it had troubled his youth and made him the most vigorous of satirists and the most passionate of lovers. There was no rest, no end, no solution even at the height of fame and on the edge of the grave for a nature plaited together of such diverse strands. The famous preparations that he made, lying in his shroud, being carved for his tomb, when he felt death approach are poles asunder from the falling asleep of the tired and content. He must still cut a figure and still stand erect—a warning perhaps, a portent certainly, but always consciously and conspicuously himself. That, finally, is one of the reasons why we still seek out Donne; why after three hundred years and more we still hear the sound of his voice speaking across the ages so distinctly. It may be true that when from curiosity we come to cut up and "survey each part," we are like the doctors and "know not why"—we cannot see how so many different qualities meet together in one man. But we have only to read him, to submit to the sound of that passionate and penetrating voice, and his figure rises again across the waste of the years more erect, more imperious, more inscrutable than any of his time. Even the elements seem to have respected that identity. When the fire of London destroyed almost every other monument in St. Paul's, it left Donne's figure untouched, as if the flames themselves found that knot too hard to undo, that riddle too difficult to read, and that figure too entirely itself to turn to common clay.

*

"The Countess of Pembroke's Arcadia"

*

If it is true that there are books written to escape from the present moment, and its meanness and its sordidity, it is certainly true that readers are familiar with a corresponding mood. To draw the blinds and shut the door, to muffle the noises of the street and shade the glare and flicker of its lights—that is our desire. There is then a charm even in the look of the great volumes that have sunk, like the "Countess of Pembroke's Arcadia," as if by their own weight down to the very bottom of the shelf. We like to feel that the present is not all; that other hands have been before us, smoothing the leather until the corners are rounded and blunt, turning the pages until they are yellow and dog-eared. We like to summon before us the ghosts of those old readers who have read their *Arcadia* from this very copy—Richard Porter, reading with the splendours of the Elizabethans in his eyes; Lucy Baxter, reading in the licentious days of the Restoration; Thos. Hake, still reading, though now the eighteenth century has dawned with a distinction that shows itself in the upright elegance of his signature. Each has read differently, with the insight and the blindness of his own generation. Our reading will be equally partial. In 1930 we shall miss a great deal that was obvious to 1655; we shall see some things that the eighteenth century ignored. But let us keep up the long succession of readers; let us in our turn bring the insight and the blindness of our own generation to bear upon the "Countess of Pembroke's Arcadia," and so pass it on to our successors.

If we choose the *Arcadia* because we wish to escape, certainly the first impression of the book is that Sidney wrote it with very much the same intention: ". . . it is done only for you, only to you," he tells his "dear lady and sister, the Countess of Pembroke." He is not looking at what is before him here at Wilton; he is not thinking of his own troubles or of the tempestuous mood of the great Queen in London. He is absenting himself from the present and its strife. He is writing merely to amuse his sister, not for "severer eyes." "Your dear self can best witness the manner, being done in loose sheets of Paper, most of it in your presence, the rest, by sheets sent unto you, as fast as they were done." So, sitting at Wilton under the downs with Lady Pembroke, he gazes far away into a beautiful land which he calls Arcadia. It is a land of fair valleys and fertile pastures, where the houses are "lodges of yellow stone built in the form of a star"; where the inhabitants are either great princes or humble shepherds; where the only business is to love and to adventure; where bears and lions surprise nymphs bathing in fields red with roses; where princesses are immured in the huts of shepherds; where disguise is perpetually necessary; where the shepherd is really a prince and the woman a man; where, in short, anything may be and happen except what actually is and happens here in England in the year 1580. It is easy to see why, as Sidney handed these dream pages to his sister, he smiled, entreating her indulgence. "Read it then at your idle times, and the follies your good judgment will find in it, blame not, but laugh at." Even for the Sidneys and the Pembrokes life was not quite like that. And yet the life that we invent, the stories we tell, as we sink back with half-shut eyes and pour forth our irresponsible dreams, have perhaps some wild beauty; some eager energy; we often reveal in them the distorted and decorated image of what we soberly and secretly desire. Thus the *Arcadia*, by wilfully flouting all contact with the fact, gains another reality. When Sidney hinted that his friends would like the book for its writer's sake, he meant perhaps that they would find there something that he could say in no other form, as the shepherds singing by the river's side will "deliver out, sometimes joys, sometimes lamentations, sometimes challengings one of the other, sometimes, under hidden forms, uttering such matters as otherwise they durst not deal with." There may be under the disguise of the *Arcadia* a real man trying to speak privately about something that is close to his heart. But in the first freshness of the early pages the disguise itself is enough to enchant us. We find ourselves with shepherds in spring on those sands which "lie against the Island of Cithera." Then, behold, something floats on the waters. It is the body of a man, and he grasps to his breast a small square coffer; and he is young and beautiful—"though he were naked, his nakedness was to him an apparel"; and his name is Musidorus; and he has lost his friend. So, warbling melodiously, the shepherds revive the youth, and row out in a bark from the haven in search of Pyrocles; and a stain appears on the sea, with sparks and smoke issuing from it. For the ship upon which the two princes Musidorus and Pyrocles were voyaging has caught fire; it floats blazing on the water with a great store of rich things round it, and many drowned bodies. "In sum, a defeat, where the conquered kept both field and spoil: a shipwrack without storm or ill footing: and a waste of fire in the midst of the water."

There in a little space we have some of the elements that are woven together to compose this vast tapestry. We have beauty of scene; a pictorial stillness; and something floating towards us, not violently but slowly and gently in time to the sweet warbling of the shepherds' voices. Now and again this crystallises into a phrase that lingers and haunts the ear—"and a waste of fire in the midst of the waters"; "having in their faces a certain waiting sorrow." Now the murmur broadens and expands into some more elaborate passage of description: "each pasture stored with sheep, feeding with sober security, while the pretty lambs with bleating oratory crav'd the dam's comfort: here a shepherd's boy piping, as though he should never be old: there a young shepherdess knitting, and withal singing, and it seemed that her voice comforted her hands to work, and her hands kept time to her voice-music"—a passage that reminds us of a famous description in Dorothy Osborne's *Letters*.

Beauty of scene; stateliness of movement; sweetness of sound—these are the graces that seem to reward the mind that seeks enjoyment purely for its own sake. We are drawn on down the winding paths of this impossible landscape because Sidney leads us without any end in view but sheer delight in wandering. The syllabling of the words even causes him the liveliest delight. Mere rhythm we feel as we sweep over the smooth backs of the undulating sentences intoxicates him. Words in themselves delight him. Look, he seems to cry, as he picks up the glittering handfuls, can it be true that there are such numbers of beautiful words lying about for the asking? Why not use them, lavishly and abundantly? And so he luxuriates. Lambs do not suck—"with bleating oratory [they] crav'd the dam's comfort"; girls do not undress—they "take away the eclipsing of their apparel"; a tree is not reflected in a river—"it seemed she looked into it and dressed her green locks by that running river." It is absurd; and yet there is a world of difference between writing like this with zest and wonder at the images that form upon one's pen and the writing of later ages when the dew was off the language—witness the little tremor that stirs and agitates a sentence that a more formal age would have made coldly symmetrical:

> And the boy fierce though beautiful; and beautiful, though dying, not able to keep his falling feet, fell down to the earth, which he bit for anger, repining at his fortune, and as long as he could, resisting death, which might seem unwilling too; so long he was in taking away his young struggling soul.

It is this inequality and elasticity that lend their freshness to Sidney's vast pages. Often as we rush through them, half laughing, half in protest, the desire comes upon us to shut the ear of reason completely and lie back and listen to this unformed babble of sound; this chorus of intoxicated voices singing madly like birds round the house before any one is up.

But it is easy to lay too much stress upon qualities that delight us because they are lost. Sidney doubtless wrote the *Arcadia* partly to wile away the time, partly to exercise his pen and experiment with the new instrument of the English language. But even so he remained young and a man; even in Arcadia the roads had ruts, and coaches were upset and ladies dislocated their shoulders; even the Princes Musidorus and Pyrocles have passions; Pamela and Philoclea, for all their sea-coloured satins and nets strung with pearls, are women and can love. Thus we stumble upon scenes that cannot be reeled off with a flowing pen; there are moments where Sidney stopped and thought, like any other novelist, what a real man or woman in this particular situation would say; where his own emotions come suddenly to the surface and light up the vague pastoral landscape with an incongruous glare. For a moment we get a surprising combination; crude daylight overpowers the silver lights of the tapers; shepherds and princesses suddenly stop their warbling and speak a few rapid words in their eager human voices.

> . . . many times have I, leaning to yonder Palm, admired the blessedness of it, that it could bear love without sense of pain; many times, when my Master's cattle came hither to chew their cud in this fresh place, I might see the young Bull testify his love; but how? with proud looks and joyfulness. O wretched mankind (said I then to myself) in whom wit (which should be the governor of his welfare) become's the traitor to his blessedness: these beasts like children to nature, inherit her blessings quietly; we like bastards are laid abroad, even as foundlings, to be trained up by grief and sorrow. Their minds grudge not at their bodies comfort, nor their senses are letted from enjoying their objects; we have the impediments of honour, and the torments of conscience.

The words ring strangely on the finicking, dandified lips of Musidorus. There is Sidney's own anger in them and his pain. And then the novelist Sidney suddenly opens his eyes. He watches Pamela as she takes the jewel in the figure of a crab-fish to signify "because it looks one way and goes another" that though he pretended to love Mopsa his heart was Pamela's. And she takes it, he notes, with a calm carelessness letting each thing slide (just as we do by their speeches who neither in matter nor person do any way belong unto us) which kind of cold temper, mixt with that lightning of her natural majesty, is of all others most terrible unto me. . . .

Had she despised him, had she hated him, it would have been better.

But this cruel quietness, neither retiring to mislike, nor proceeding to favour; gracious, but gracious still after one manner; all her courtesies having this engraven in them, that what is done, is for virtue's sake, not for the parties. . . . This (I say) heavenliness of hers . . . is so impossible to reach unto that I almost begin to submit myself unto the tyranny of despair, not knowing any way of persuasion. . . .

—surely an acute and subtle observation made by a man who had felt what he describes. For a moment the pale and legendary figures, Gynecia, Philoclea, and Zelmane, become alive; their featureless faces work with passion; Gynecia, realising that she loves her daughter's lover, foams into grandeur, "crying vehemently Zelmane help me, O Zelmane have pity on me"; and the old King, in whom the beautiful strange Amazon has awakened a senile amorosity, shows himself old and foolish, looking "very curiously upon himself, sometimes fetching a little skip, as if he had said his strength had not yet forsaken him."

But that moment of illumination, as it dies down and the princes once more resume their postures and the shepherds apply themselves to their lutes, throws a curious light upon the book as a whole. We realise more clearly the boundaries within which Sidney was working. For a moment he could note and observe and record as keenly and exactly as any modern novelist. And then, after this one glimpse in our direction, he turns aside, as if he heard other voices calling him and must obey their commands. In prose, he bethinks himself, one must not use the common words of daily speech. In a romance one must not make princes and princesses feel like ordinary men and women. Humour is the attribute of peasants. They can behave ridiculously; they can talk naturally; like Dametas they can come "whistling, and counting upon his fingers, how many load of hay seventeen fat oxen eat up on a year"; but the language of great people must always be long-winded and abstract and full of metaphors. Further, they must either be heroes of stainless virtue, or villains untouched by humanity. Of human oddities and littleness they must show no trace. Prose also must be careful to turn away from what is actually before it. Sometimes for a moment in looking at Nature one may fit the word to the sight; note the heron "wagling" as it rises from the marsh, or observe the water-spaniel hunting the duck "with a snuffling grace." But this realism is only to be applied to Nature and animals and peasants. Prose, it seems, is made for slow, noble, and generalised emotions; for the description of wide landscapes; for the conveyance of long, equable discourses uninterrupted for pages together by any other speaker. Verse, on the other hand, had quite a different office. It is curious to observe how, when Sidney wished to sum up, to strike hard, to register a single and definite impression, he turns to verse. Verse in the *Arcadia* performs something of the function of dialogue in the modern novel. It breaks up the monotony and strikes a high light. In those snatches of song that are scattered about the interminable adventures of Pyrocles and Musidorus our interest is once more fanned into flame. Often the realism and vigour of the verse comes with a shock after the drowsy languor of the prose:

> What needed so high spirits such mansions blind?
> Or wrapt in flesh what do they here obtain,
> But glorious name of wretched human kind?
> Balls to the stars, and thralls to fortune's reign;
> Turn'd from themselves, infected with their cage,
> Where death is fear'd, and life is held with pain.
> Like players plac't to fill a filthy stage. . . .

—one wonders what the indolent princes and princesses will make of that vehement speaking? Or of this:

> A shop of shame, a Book where blots be rife,
> This body is . . .
> This man, this talking beast, this walking tree

—thus the poet turns upon his languid company as if he loathed their self-complacent foppery; and yet must indulge them. For though it is clear that the poet Sidney had shrewd eyes—he talks of "hives of wisely painful bees," and knew like any other country-bred Englishman "how shepherds spend their days. At blow-point, hot-cockles or else at keels,"—still he must drone on about Plangus and Erona, and Queen Andromana and the intrigues of Amphialus and his mother Cecropia in deference to his audience. Incongruously enough, violent as they were in their lives, with their plots and their poisonings, nothing can be too sweet, too vague, too long-winded for those Elizabethan listeners. Only the fact that Zelmane had received a blow from a lion's paw that morning can shorten the story and suggest to Basilius that it might be better to reserve the complaint of Klaius till another day.

> Which she, perceiving the song had already worn out much time, and not knowing when Lamon would end, being even now stepping over to a new matter, though much delighted with what was spoken, willingly agreed unto. And so of all sides they went to recommend themselves to the elder brother of death.

And as the story winds on its way, or rather as the succession of stories fall on each other like soft snowflakes, one obliterating the other, we are much tempted to follow their example. Sleep weighs down our eyes. Half dreaming, half yawning, we prepare to seek the elder brother of death. What, then, has become of that first intoxicating sense of freedom? We who wished to escape have been caught and enmeshed. Yet how easy it seemed in the beginning to tell a story to amuse a sister—how inspiriting to escape from here and now and wander wildly in a world of lutes and roses! But alas, softness has weighed down our steps; brambles have caught at our clothing. We have come to long for some plain statement, and the decoration of the style, at first so enchanting, has dulled and decayed. It is not difficult to find the reason. High spirited, flown with words, Sidney seized his pen too carelessly. He had no notion when he set out where he was going. Telling stories, he thought, was enough—one could follow another interminably. But where there is no end in view there is no sense of direction to draw us on. Nor, since it is part of his scheme to keep his characters simply bad and simply good without distinction, can he gain variety from the complexity of character. To supply change and movement he must have recourse to mystification. These changes of dress, these disguises of princes as peasants, of men as women, serve instead of psychological subtlety to relieve the stagnancy of people collected together with nothing to talk about. But when the charm of that childish device falls flat, there is no breath left to fill his sails. Who is talking, and to whom, and about what we no longer feel sure. So slack indeed becomes Sidney's grasp upon these ambling phantoms that in the middle he has forgotten what his relation to them is—is it "I" the author who is speaking or is it "I" the character? No reader can be kept in bondage, whatever the grace and the charm, when the ties between him and the writer are so irresponsibly doffed and assumed. So by degrees the book floats away into the thin air of limbo. It becomes one of those half-forgotten and deserted places where the grasses grow over fallen statues and the rain drips and the marble steps are green with moss and vast weeds flourish in the flower-beds. And yet it is a beautiful garden to wander in now and then; one stumbles over lovely broken faces, and here and there a flower blooms and the nightingale sings in the lilac-tree.

Thus when we come to the last page that Sidney wrote before he gave up the hopeless attempt to finish the *Arcadia*, we pause for a moment before we return the folio to its place on the bottom shelf. In the *Arcadia*, as in some luminous globe, all the seeds of English fiction lie latent. We can trace infinite possibilities: it may take any one of many different directions. Will it fix its gaze upon Greece and prince and princesses, and seek as it might so nobly, the statuesque, the impersonal? Will it keep to simple lines and great masses and the vast landscapes of the epic? Or will it look closely and carefully at what is actually before it? Will it take for its heroes Dametas and Mopsa, ordinary people of low birth and rough natural speech, and deal with the normal course of daily human life? Or will it brush through those barriers and penetrate within to the anguish and complexity of some unhappy woman loving where she may not love; to the senile absurdity of some old man tortured by an incongruous passion? Will it make its dwelling in their psychology and the adventures of the soul? All these possibilities are present in the *Arcadia*—romance and realism, poetry and psychology. But as if Sidney knew that he had broached a task too large for his youth to execute, had bequeathed a legacy for others ages to inherit, he put down his pen, mid-way, and left unfinished in all its beauty and absurdity this attempt to wile away the long days at Wilton, telling a story to his sister.

❋

"*Robinson Crusoe*"

❋

There are many ways of approaching this classical volume; but which shall we choose? Shall we begin by saying that, since Sidney died at Zutphen leaving the *Arcadia* unfinished, great changes had come over English life, and the novel had chosen, or had been forced to choose, its direction? A middle class had come into existence, able to read and anxious to read not only about the loves of princes and princesses, but about themselves and the details of their humdrum lives. Stretched upon a thousand pens, prose had accommodated itself to the demand; it had fitted itself to express the facts of life rather than the poetry. That is certainly one way of approaching *Robinson Crusoe*—through the development of the novel; but another immediately suggests itself—through the life of the author. Here too, in the heavenly pastures of biography, we may spend many more hours than are needed to read the book itself from cover to cover. The date of Defoe's birth, to begin with, is doubtful—was it 1660 or 1661? Then again, did he spell his name in one word or in two? And who were his ancestors? He is said to have been a hosier; but what, after all, was a hosier in the seventeenth century? He became a pamphleteer, and enjoyed the confidence of William the Third; one of his pamphlets caused him to be stood in the pillory and imprisoned at Newgate; he was employed by Harley and later by Godolphin; he was the first of the hireling journalists; he wrote innumerable pamphlets and articles; also *Moll Flanders* and *Robinson Crusoe;* he had a wife and six children; was spare in figure, with a hooked nose, a sharp chin, grey eyes, and a large mole near his mouth. Nobody who has any slight acquaintance with English literature needs to be told how many hours can be spent and how many lives have been spent in tracing the development of the novel and in examining the chins of the novelists. Only now and then, as we turn from theory to biography and from biography to theory, a doubt insinuates itself—if we knew the very moment of Defoe's birth and whom he loved and why, if we had by heart the history of the origin, rise, growth, decline, and fall of the English novel from its conception (say) in Egypt to its decease in the wilds (perhaps) of Paraguay, should we suck an ounce of additional pleasure from *Robinson Crusoe* or read it one whit more intelligently?

For the book itself remains. However we may wind and wriggle, loiter and dally in our approach to books, a lonely battle waits us at the end. There is a piece of business to be transacted between writer and reader before any further dealings are possible, and to be reminded in the middle of this private interview that Defoe sold stockings, had brown hair, and was stood in the pillory is a distraction and a worry. Our first task, and it is often formidable enough, is to master his perspective. Until we know how the novelist orders his world, the ornaments of that world, which the critics press upon us, the adventures of the writer, to which biographers draw attention, are superfluous possessions of which we can make no use. All alone we must climb upon the novelist's shoulders and gaze through his eyes until we, too, understand in what order he ranges the large common objects upon which novelists are fated to gaze: man and men; behind them Nature; and above them that power which for convenience and brevity we may call God. And at once confusion, misjudgment, and difficulty begin. Simple as they appear to us, these objects can be made monstrous and indeed unrecognisable by the manner in which the novelist relates them to each other. It would seem to be true that people who live cheek by jowl and breathe the same air vary enormously in their sense of proportion; to one the human being is vast, the tree minute; to the other, trees are huge and human beings insignificant little objects in the background. So, in spite of the text-books, writers may live at the same time and yet see nothing the same size. Here is Scott, for example, with his mountains looming huge and his men therefore drawn to scale; Jane Austen picking out the roses on her tea-cups to match the wit of her dialogues; while Peacock bends over heaven and earth one fantastic distorting mirror in which a tea-cup may be Vesuvius or Vesuvius a tea-cup. Nevertheless Scott, Jane Austen, and Peacock lived through the same years; they saw the same world; they are covered in the text-books by the same stretch of literary history. It is in their perspective that they are different. If, then, it were granted us to grasp this firmly, for ourselves, the battle would end in victory; and we could turn, secure in our intimacy, to enjoy the various delights with which the critics and biographers so generously supply us.

But here many difficulties arise. For we have our own vision of the world; we have made it from our own experience and prejudices, and it is therefore bound up with our own vanities and loves. It is impossible not to feel injured and insulted if tricks are played and our private harmony is upset. Thus when *Jude the Obscure* appears or a new volume of Proust, the newspapers are flooded with protests. Major Gibbs of Cheltenham would put a bullet through his head tomorrow if life were as Hardy paints it; Miss Wiggs of Hampstead must protest that though Proust's art is wonderful, the real world, she thanks God, has nothing in common with the distortions of a perverted Frenchman. Both the gentleman and the lady are trying to control the novelist's perspective so that it shall resemble and reinforce their own. But the great writer—the Hardy or the Proust—goes on his way regardless of the rights of private property; by the sweat of his brow he brings order from chaos; he plants his tree there, and his man here; he makes the figure of his deity remote or present as he wills. In masterpieces—books, that is, where the vision is clear and order has been achieved—he inflicts his own perspective upon us so severely that as often as not we suffer agonies—our vanity is injured because our own order is upset; we are afraid because the old supports are being wrenched from us; and we are bored—for what pleasure or amusement can be plucked from a brand new idea? Yet from anger, fear, and boredom a rare and lasting delight is sometimes born.

Robinson Crusoe, it may be, is a case in point. It is a masterpiece, and it is a masterpiece largely because Defoe has throughout kept consistently to his own sense of perspective. For this reason he thwarts us and flouts us at every turn. Let us look at the theme largely and loosely, comparing it with our preconceptions. It is, we know, the story of a man who is thrown, after many perils and adventures, alone upon a desert island. The mere suggestion—peril and solitude and a desert island—is enough to rouse in us the expectation of some far land on the limits of the world; of the sun rising and the sun setting; of man, isolated from his kind, brooding alone upon the nature of society and the strange ways of men. Before we open the book we have perhaps vaguely sketched out the kind of pleasure we expect it to give us. We read; and we are rudely contradicted on every page. There are no sunsets and no sunrises; there is no solitude and no soul. There is, on the contrary, staring us full in the face nothing but a large earthenware pot. We are told, that is to say, that it was the 1st of September 1651; that the hero's name is Robinson Crusoe; and that his father has the gout. Obviously, then, we must alter our attitude. Reality, fact, substance is going to dominate all that follows. We must hastily alter our proportions throughout; Nature must furl her splendid purples; she is only the giver of drought and water; man must be reduced to a struggling, life-preserving animal; and God shrivel into a magistrate whose seat, substantial and somewhat hard, is only a little way above the horizon. Each sortie of ours in pursuit of information upon these cardinal points of perspective—God, man, Nature—is snubbed back with ruthless common-sense. Robinson Crusoe thinks of God: "Sometimes I would expostulate with myself, why providence should thus completely ruin its creatures. . . . But something always return'd swift upon me to check these thoughts." God does not exist. He thinks of Nature, the fields "adorn'd with flowers and grass, and full of very fine woods," but the important thing about a wood is that it harbours an abundance of parrots who may be tamed and taught to speak. Nature does not exist. He considers the dead, whom he has killed himself. It is of the utmost importance that they should be buried at once, for "they lay open to the sun and would presently be offensive." Death does not exist. Nothing exists except an earthenware pot. Finally, that is to say, we are forced to drop our own preconceptions and to accept what Defoe himself wishes to give us.

Let us then go back to the beginning and repeat again, "I was born in the year 1632 in the city of York of a good family." Nothing could be plainer, more matter of fact, than that beginning. We are drawn on soberly to consider all the blessings of orderly, industrious middle-class life. There is no greater good fortune we are assured than to be born of the British middle class. The great are to be pitied and so are the poor; both are exposed to distempers and uneasiness; the middle station between the mean and the great is the best; and its virtues—temperance, moderation, quietness, and health—are the most desirable. It was a sorry thing, then, when by some evil fate a middle-class youth was bitten with the foolish love of adventure. So he proses on, drawing, little by little, his own portrait, so that we never forget it—imprinting upon us indelibly, for he never forgets it either, his shrewdness, his caution, his love of order and comfort and respectability; until by whatever means, we find ourselves at sea, in a storm; and, peering out, everything is seen precisely as it appears to Robinson Crusoe. The waves, the seamen, the sky, the ship—all are seen through those shrewd, middle-class, unimaginative eyes. There is no escaping him. Everything appears as it would appear to that naturally cautious, apprehensive, conventional, and solidly matter-of-fact intelligence. He is incapable of enthusiasm. He has a natural slight distaste for the sublimities of Nature. He suspects even Providence of exaggeration. He is so busy and has such an eye to the main chance that he notices only a tenth part of what is going on round him. Everything is capable of a rational explanation, he is sure, if only he had time to attend to it. We are much more alarmed by the "vast great creatures" that swim out in the night and surround his boat than he is. He at once takes his gun and fires at them, and off they swim—whether they are lions or not he really cannot say. Thus before we know it we are opening our mouths wider and wider. We are swallowing monsters that we should have jibbed at if they had been offered us by an imaginative and flamboyant traveller. But anything that this sturdy middle-class man notices can be taken for a fact. He is for ever counting his barrels, and making sensible provisions for his water supply; nor do we ever find him tripping even in a matter of detail. Has he forgotten, we wonder, that he has a great lump of beeswax on board? Not at all. But as he had already made candles out of it, it is not nearly as great on page thirty-eight as it was on page twenty-three. When for a wonder he leaves some inconsistency hanging loose—why if the wild cats are so very tame are the goats so very shy?—we are not seriously perturbed, for we are sure that there was a reason, and a very good one, had he time to give it us. But the pressure of life when one is fending entirely for oneself alone on a desert island is really no laughing matter. It is no crying one either. A man must have an eye to everything; it is no time for raptures about Nature when the lightning may explode one's gunpowder—it is imperative to seek a safer lodging for it. And so by means of telling the truth undeviatingly as it appears to him—by being a great artist and forgoing this and daring that in order to give effect to his prime quality, a sense of reality—he comes in the end to make common actions dignified and common objects beautiful. To dig, to bake, to plant, to build—how serious these simple occupations are; hatchets, scissors, logs, axes,—how beautiful these simple objects become. Unimpeded by comment, the story marches on with magnificent downright simplicity. Yet how could comment have made it more impressive? It is true that he takes the opposite way from the psychologist's—he describes the effect of emotion on the body, not on the mind. But when he says how, in a moment of anguish, he clinched his hands so that any soft thing would have been crushed; how "my teeth in my head would strike together, and set against one another so strong, that for the time I could not part them again," the effect is as deep as pages of analysis could have made it. His own instinct in the matter is right. "Let the naturalists," he says, "explain these things, and the reason and manner of them; all I can say to them is, to describe the fact. . . ." If you are Defoe, certainly to describe the fact is enough; for the fact is the right fact. By means of this genius for fact Defoe achieves effects that are beyond any but the great masters of descriptive prose. He has only to say a word or two about "the grey of the morning" to paint vividly a windy dawn. A sense of desolation and of the deaths of many men is conveyed by remarking in the most prosaic way in the world, "I never saw them afterwards, or any sign of them except three of their hats, one cap, and two shoes that were not fellows." When at last he exclaims, "Then to see how like a king I din'd too all alone, attended by my servants"—his parrot and his dog and his two cats, we cannot help but feel that all humanity is on a desert island alone—though Defoe at once informs us, for he has a way of snubbing off our enthusiasms, that the cats were not the same cats that had come in the ship. Both of those were dead; these cats were new cats, and as a matter of fact cats became very troublesome before long from their fecundity, whereas dogs, oddly enough, did not breed at all.

Thus Defoe, by reiterating that nothing but a plain earthenware pot stands in the foreground, persuades us to see remote islands and the solitudes of the human soul. By believing fixedly in the solidity of the pot and its earthiness, he has subdued every other element to his design; he has roped the whole universe into harmony. And is there any reason, we ask as we shut the book, why the perspective that a plain earthenware pot exacts should not satisfy us as completely, once we grasp it, as man himself in all his sublimity standing against a background of broken mountains and tumbling oceans with stars flaming in the sky?

❋

Dorothy Osborne's "Letters"

❋

It must sometimes strike the casual reader of English literature that there is a bare season in it, sometimes like early spring in our countryside. The trees stand out; the hills are unmuffled in green; there is nothing to obscure the mass of the earth or the lines of the branches. But we miss the tremor and murmur of June, when the smallest wood seems full of movement, and one has only to stand still to hear the whispering and the pattering of nimble, inquisitive animals going about their affairs in the undergrowth. So in English literature we have to wait till the sixteenth century is over and the seventeenth well on its way before the bare landscape becomes full of stir and quiver and we can fill in the spaces between the great books with the voices of people talking.

Doubtless great changes in psychology were needed and great changes in material comfort—arm-chairs and carpets and good roads—before it was possible for human beings to watch each other curiously or to communicate their thoughts easily. And it may be that our early literatures owes something of its magnificence to the fact that writing was an uncommon art, practised, rather for fame than for money, by those whose gifts compelled them. Perhaps the dissipation of our genius in biography, and journalism, and letter- and memoir-writing has weakened its strength in any one direction. However this may be, there is a bareness about an age that has neither letter-writers nor biographers. Lives and characters appear in stark outline. Donne, says Sir Edmund Gosse, is inscrutable; and that is largely because, though we know what Donne thought of Lady Bedford, we have not the slightest inkling what Lady Bedford thought of Donne. She had no friend to whom she described the effect of that strange visitor; nor, had she a confidante, could she have explained for what reasons Donne seemed to her strange.

And the conditions that made it impossible for Boswell or Horace Walpole to be born in the sixteenth century were obviously likely to fall with far heavier force upon the other sex. Besides the material difficulty—Donne's small house at Mitcham with its thin walls and crying children typifies the discomfort in which the Elizabethans lived—the woman was impeded also by her belief that writing was an act unbefitting her sex. A great lady here and there whose rank secured her the toleration and it may be the adulation of a servile circle, might write and print her writings. But the act was offensive to a woman of lower rank. "Sure the poore woman is a little distracted, she could never bee soe ridiculous else as to venture writeing book's and in verse too," Dorothy Osborne exclaimed when the Duchess of Newcastle published one of her books. For her own part, she added, "If I could not sleep this fortnight I should not come to that." And the comment is the more illuminating in that it was made by a woman of great literary gift. Had she been born in 1827, Dorothy Osborne would have written novels; had she been born in 1527, she would never have written at all. But she was born in 1627, and at that date though writing books was ridiculous for a woman there was nothing unseemly in writing a letter. And so by degrees the silence is broken; we begin to hear rustlings in the undergrowth; for the first time in English literature we hear men and women talking together over the fire.

But the art of letter-writing in its infancy was not the art that has since filled so many delightful volumes. Men and women were ceremoniously Sir and Madam; the language was still too rich and stiff to turn and twist quickly and freely upon half a sheet of notepaper.

The art of letter-writing is often the art of essay-writing in disguise. But such as it was, it was an art that a woman could practise without unsexing herself. It was an art that could be carried on at odd moments, by a father's sick-bed, among a thousand interruptions, without exciting comment, anonymously as it were, and often with the pretence that it served some useful purpose. Yet into these innumerable letters, lost now for the most part, went powers of observation and of wit that were later to take rather a different shape in *Evelina* and in *Pride and Prejudice*. They were only letters, yet some pride went to their making. Dorothy, without admitting it, took pains with her own writing and had views as to the nature of it: ". . . great Schollers are not the best writer's (of Letters I mean, of books perhaps they are) . . . all letters mee thinks should be free and easy as one's discourse." She was in agreement with an old uncle of hers who threw his standish at his secretary's head for saying "put pen to paper" instead of simply "wrote." Yet there were limits, she reflected, to free-and-easiness: ". . . many pritty things shuffled together" do better spoken than in a letter. And so we come by a form of literature, if Dorothy Osborne will let us call it so, which is distinct from any other, and much to be regretted now that it has gone from us, as it seems, for ever.

For Dorothy Osborne, as she filled her great sheets by her father's bed or by the chimney-corner, gave a record of life, gravely yet playfully, formally yet with intimacy, to a public of one, but to a fastidious public, as the novelist can never give it, or the historian either. Since it is her business to keep her lover informed of what passes in her home, she must sketch the solemn Sir Justinian Isham—Sir Solomon Justinian, she calls him—the pompous widower with four daughters and a great gloomy house in Northamptonshire who wished to marry her. "Lord what would I give that I had a Lattin letter of his for you," she exclaimed, in which he describes her to an Oxford friend and specially commended her that she was "capable of being company and conversation for him"; she must sketch her valetudinarian Cousin Molle waking one morning in fear of the dropsy and hurrying to the doctor at Cambridge; she must draw her own picture wandering in the garden at night and smelling the "Jessomin," "and yet I was not pleased" because Temple was not with her. Any gossip that comes her way is sent on to amuse her lover. Lady Sunderland, for instance, has condescended to marry plain Mr. Smith, who treats her like a princess, which Sir Justinian thinks a bad precedent for wives. But Lady Sunderland tells everyone she married him out of pity, and that, Dorothy comments, "was the pitty-full'st sayeing that ever I heard." Soon we have picked up enough about all her friends to snatch eagerly at any further addition to the picture which is forming in our mind's eye.

Indeed, our glimpse of the society of Bedfordshire in the seventeenth century is the more intriguing for its intermittency. In they come and out they go—Sir Justinian and Lady Diana, Mr. Smith and his countess—and we never know when or whether we shall hear of them again. But with all this haphazardry, the *Letters*, like the letters of all born letter-writers, provide their own continuity. They make us feel that we have our seat in the depths of Dorothy's mind, at the heart of the pageant which unfolds itself page by page as we read. For she possesses indisputably the gift which counts for more in letter-writing than wit or brilliance or traffic with great people. By being herself without effort or emphasis, she envelops all these odds and ends in the flow of her own personality. It was a character that was both attractive and a little obscure. Phrase by phrase we come closer into touch with it. Of the womanly virtues that befitted her age she shows little trace. She says nothing of sewing or baking. She was a little indolent by temperament. She browsed casually on vast French romances. She roams the commons, loitering to hear the milkmaids sing; she walks in the garden by the side of a small river, "where I sitt downe and wish you were with mee." She was apt to fall silent in company and dream over the fire till some talk of flying, perhaps, roused her, and she made her brother laugh by asking what they were saying about flying, for the thought had struck her, if she could fly she could be with Temple. Gravity, melancholy were in her blood. She looked, her mother used to say, as if all her friends were dead. She is oppressed by a sense of fortune and its tyranny and the vanity of things and the uselessness of effort. Her mother and sister were grave women too, the sister famed for her letters, but fonder of books than of company, the mother "counted as wise a woman as most in England," but sardonic. "I have lived to see that 'tis almost impossible to think People worse than they are and soe will you"—Dorothy could remember her mother saying that. To assuage her spleen, Dorothy herself had to visit the wells at Epsom and to drink water that steel had stood in.

With such a temperament her humour naturally took the form of irony rather than of wit. She loved to mock her lover and to pour a fine raillery over the pomps and ceremonies of existence. Pride of birth she laughed at. Pompous old men were fine subjects for her satire. A dull sermon moved her to laughter. She saw through parties; she saw through ceremonies; she saw through worldliness and display. But with all this clear-sightedness there was something that she did not see through. She dreaded with a shrinking that was scarcely sane the ridicule of the world. The meddling of aunts and the tyranny of brothers exasperated her. "I would live in a hollow Tree," she said, "to avoyde them." A husband kissing his wife in public seemed to her as "ill a sight as one would wish to see." Though she cared no more whether people praised her beauty or her wit than whether "they think my name Eliz: or Dor:," a word of gossip about her own behaviour would set her in a quiver. Thus when it came to proving before the eyes of the world that she loved a poor man and was prepared to marry him, she could not do it. "I confess that I have an humor that will not suffer mee to Expose myself to People's Scorne," she wrote. She could be "sattisfyed within as narrow a compass as that of any person liveing of my rank," but ridicule was intolerable to her. She shrank from any extravagance that could draw the censure of the world upon her. It was a weakness for which Temple had sometimes to reprove her.

For Temple's character emerges more and more clearly as the letters go on—it is a proof of Dorothy's gift as a correspondent. A good letter-writer so takes the colour of the reader at the other end, that from reading the one we can imagine the other. As she argues, as she reasons, we hear Temple almost as clearly as we hear Dorothy herself. He was in many ways the opposite of her. He drew out her melancholy by rebutting it; he made her defend her dislike of marriage by opposing it. Of the two Temple was by far the more robust and positive. Yet there was perhaps something—a little hardness, a little conceit—that justified her brother's dislike of him. He called Temple the "proudest imperious insulting ill-natured man that ever was." But, in the eyes of Dorothy, Temple had qualities that none of her other suitors possessed. He was not a mere country gentleman, nor a pompous Justice of the Peace, nor a town gallant, making love to every woman he met, nor a travelled Monsieur; for had he been any one of these things, Dorothy, with her quick sense of the ridiculous, would have had none of him. To her he had some charm, some sympathy, that the others lacked; she could write to him whatever came into her head; she was at her best with him; she loved him; she respected him. Yet suddenly she declared that marry him she would not. She turned violently against marriage indeed, and cited failure after failure. If people knew each other before marriage, she thought, there would be an end of it. Passion was the most brutish and tyrannical of all our senses. Passion had made Lady Anne Blount the "talk of all the footmen and Boy's in the street." Passion had been the undoing of the lovely Lady Izabella—what use was her beauty now married to "that beast with all his estate"? Torn asunder by her brother's anger, by Temple's jealously, and by her own dread of ridicule, she wished for nothing but to be left to find "an early and a quiet grave." That

Temple overcame her scruples and overrode her brother's opposition is much to the credit of his character. Yet it is an act that we can hardly help deploring. Married to Temple, she wrote to him no longer. The letters almost immediately cease. The whole world that Dorothy had bought into existence is extinguished. It is then that we realize how round and populous and stirring that world has become. Under the warmth of her affection for Temple the stiffness had gone out of her pen. Writing half asleep by her father's side, snatching the back of an old letter to write upon, she had come to write easily though always with the dignity proper to that age, of the Lady Dianas, and the Ishams, of the aunts and the uncles—how they come, how they go; what they say; whether she finds them dull, laughable, charming, or much as usual. More than that, she has suggested, writing her mind out to Temple, the deeper relationships, the more private moods, that gave her life its conflict and its consolation—her brother's tyranny; her own moodiness and melancholy; the sweetness of walking in the garden at night; of sitting lost in thought by the river; of longing for a letter and finding one. All this is around us; we are deep in this world, seizing its hints and suggestions when, in the moment, the scene is blotted out. She married, and her husband was a rising diplomat. She had to follow his fortunes in Brussels, at The Hague, wherever they called him. Seven children were born and seven children died "almost all in their cradle." Innumerable duties and responsibilities fell to the lot of the girl who had made fun of pomp and ceremony, who loved privacy and had wished to live secluded out of the world and "grow old together in our little cottage." Now she was mistress of her husband's house at The Hague with its splendid buffet of plate. She was his confidante in the many troubles of his difficult career. She stayed behind in London to negotiate if possible the payment of his arrears of salary. When her yacht was fired on, she behaved, the King said, with greater courage than the captain himself. She was everything that the wife of an ambassador should be: she was everything, too, that the wife of a man retired from the public service should be. And troubles came upon them—a daughter died; a son, inheriting perhaps his mother's melancholy, filled his boots with stones and leapt into the Thames. So the years passed; very full, very active, very troubled. But Dorothy maintained her silence.

At last, however, a strange young man came to Moor Park as secretary to her husband. He was difficult, ill-mannered, and quick to take offence. But it is through Swift's eyes that we see Dorothy once more in the last years of her life. "Mild Dorothea, peaceful, wise, and great," Swift called her; but the light falls upon a ghost. We do not know that silent lady. We cannot connect her after all these years with the girl who poured her heart out to her lover. "Peaceful, wise, and great"—she was none of those things when we last met her, and much though we honour the admirable ambassadress who made her husband's career her own, there are moments when we would exchange all the benefits of the Triple Alliance and all the glories of the Treaty of Nimuegen for the letters that Dorothy did not write.

Swift's "Journal to Stella"

In any highly civilised society disguise plays so large a part, politeness is so essential, that to throw off the ceremonies and conventions and talk a "little language" for one or two to understand, is as much a necessity as a breath of air in a hot room. The reserved, the powerful, the admired have the most need of such a refuge. Swift himself found it so. The proudest of men coming home from the company of great men who praised him, of lovely women who flattered him, from intrigue and politics, put all that aside, settled himself comfortably in bed, pursed his severe lips into baby language and prattled to his "two monkies," his "dear Sirrah," his "naughty rogues" on the other side of the Irish Channel.

> Well, let me see you now again. My wax candle's almost out, but however I'll begin. Well then don't be so tedious, Mr. Presto; what can you say to MD's letter? Make haste, have done with your preambles—why, I say, I am glad you are so often abroad.

So long as Swift wrote to Stella in that strain, carelessly, illegibly, for "methinks when I write plain, I do not know how, but we are not alone, all the world can see us. A bad scrawl is so snug . . . ," Stella had no need to be jealous. It was true that she was wearing away the flower of her youth in Ireland with Rebecca Dingley, who wore hinged spectacles, consumed large quantities of Brazil tobacco, and stumbled over her petticoats as she walked. Further, the conditions in which the two ladies lived, for ever in Swift's company when he was at home, occupying his house when he was absent, gave rise to gossip; so that though Stella never saw him except in Mrs. Dingley's presence, she was one of those ambiguous women who live chiefly in the society of the other sex. But surely it was well worth while. The packets kept coming from England, each sheet written to the rim in Swift's crabbed little hand, which she imitated to perfection, full of nonsense words, and capital letters, and hints which no one but Stella could understand, and secrets which Stella was to keep, and little commissions which Stella was to execute. Tobacco came for Dingley, and chocolate and silk aprons for Stella. Whatever people might say, surely it was well worth while.

Of this Presto, who was so different from that formidable character "t'other I," the world knew nothing. The world knew only that Swift was over in England again, soliciting the new Tory government on behalf of the Irish Church for those First Fruits which he had begged the Whigs in vain to restore. The business was soon accomplished; nothing indeed could exceed the cordiality and affection with which Harley and St. John greeted him; and now the world saw what even in those days of small societies and individual pre-eminence must have been a sight to startle and amaze—the "mad parson," who had marched up and down the coffee-houses in silence and unknown a few years ago, admitted to the inmost councils of State, the penniless boy who was not allowed to sit down at table with Sir William Temple dining with the highest Ministers of the Crown, making dukes do his bidding and so run after for his good offices that his servant's chief duty was to know how to keep people out. Addison himself forced his way up only by pretending that he was a gentleman come to pay a bill. For the time being Swift was omnipotent. Nobody could buy his services; everybody feared his pen. He went to Court, and "am so proud I make all the lords come up to me." The Queen wished to hear him preach; Harley and St. John added their entreaties; but he refused. When Mr. Secretary one night dared show his temper, Swift called upon him and warned him never to appear cold to me, for I would not be treated like a schoolboy. . . . He took all right; said I had reason . . . would have had me dine with him at Mrs. Masham's brother, to make up matters; but I would not. I don't know, but I would not.

He scribbled all this down to Stella without exultation or vanity. That he should command and dictate, prove himself the peer of great men and make rank abase itself before him, called for no comment on his part or on hers. Had she not known him years ago at Moor Park and seen him lose his temper with Sir William Temple, and guessed his greatness and heard from his own lips what he planned and hoped? Did she not know better than anyone how strangely good and bad were blent in him and all his foibles and eccentricities of temper? He scandalised the lords with whom he dined by his stinginess, picked the coals off his fire, saved halfpence on coaches; and yet by the help of these very economies he practised, she knew, the most considerate and secret of charities—he gave poor Patty Rolt "a pistole to help her a little forward against she goes to board in the country"; he took twenty guineas to young Harrison, the sick poet, in his garret. She alone knew how he could be coarse in his speech and yet delicate in his behaviour; how he could be cynical superficially and yet cherish a depth of feeling which she had never met with in any other human being. They knew each other in and out; the good and the bad, the deep and the trivial; so that without effort or concealment he could use those precious moments late at night or the first thing on waking to pour out upon her the whole story of his day, with its charities and meannesses, its affections and ambitions and despairs, as though he were thinking aloud.

With such proof of his affection, admitted to intimacy with this Presto whom no one else in the world knew, Stella had no cause to be jealous. It was perhaps the opposite that happened. As she read the crowded pages, she could see him and hear him and imagine so exactly the impression that he must be making on all these fine people that she fell more deeply in love with him than ever. Not only was he courted and flattered by the great;

everybody seemed to call upon him when they were in trouble. There was "young Harrison"; he worried to find him ill and penniless; carried him off to Knightsbridge; took him a hundred pounds only to find that he was dead an hour before. "Think what grief this is to me! . . . I could not dine with Lord Treasurer, nor anywhere else; but got a bit of meat toward evening." She could imagine the strange scene, that November morning, when the Duke of Hamilton was killed in Hyde Park, and Swift went at once to the Duchess and sat with her for two hours and heard her rage and storm and rail; and took her affairs, too, on his shoulders as if it were his natural office, and none could dispute his place in the house of mourning. "She has moved my very soul," he said. When young Lady Ashburham died he burst out, "I hate life when I think it exposed to such accidents; and to see so many thousand wretches burdening the earth, while such as her die, makes me think God did never intend life for a blessing." And then, with that instinct to rend and tear his own emotions which made him angry in the midst of his pity, he would round upon the mourners, even the mother and sister of the dead woman, and part them as they cried together and complain how "people will pretend to grieve more than they really do, and that takes off from their true grief."

All this was poured forth freely to Stella; the gloom and the anger, the kindness and the coarseness and the genial love of little ordinary human things. To her he showed himself fatherly and brotherly; he laughed at her spelling; he scolded her about her health; he directed her business affairs. He gossiped and chatted with her. They had a fund of memories in common. They had spent many happy hours together. "Do not you remember I used to come into your chamber and turn Stella out of her chair, and rake up the fire in a cold morning and cry *uth, uth, uth!*" She was often in his mind; he wondered if she was out walking when he was; when Prior abused one of his puns he remembered Stella's puns and how vile they were; he compared his life in London with hers in Ireland and wondered when they would be together again. And if this was the influence of Stella upon Swift in town among all the wits, the influence of Swift upon Stella marooned in an Irish village alone with Dingley was far greater. He had taught her all the little learning she had when she was a child and he a young man years ago at Moor Park. His influence was everywhere—upon her mind, upon her affections, upon the books she read and the hand she wrote, upon the friends she made and the suitors she rejected. Indeed, he was half responsible for her being.

But the woman he had chosen was no insipid slave. She had a character of her own. She was capable of thinking for herself. She was aloof, a severe critic for all her grace and sympathy, a little formidable perhaps with her love of plain speaking and her fiery temper and her fearlessness in saying what she thought. But with all her gifts she was little known. Her slender means and feeble health and dubious social standing made her way of life very modest. The society which gathered round her came for the simple pleasure of talking to a woman who listened and understood and said very little herself, but in the most agreeable of voices and generally "the best thing that was said in the company." For the rest she was not learned. Her health had prevented her from serious study, and though she had run over a great variety of subjects and had a fine severe taste in letters, what she did read did not stick in her mind. She had been extravagant as a girl, and flung her money about until her good sense took control of her and now she lived with the utmost frugality. "Five nothings on five plates of delf" made her supper. Attractive, if not beautiful, with her fine dark eyes and her raven black hair she dressed very plainly, and thus contrived to lay by enough to help the poor and to bestow upon her friends (it was an extravagance that she could not resist) "the most agreeable presents in the world." Swift never knew her equal in that art, "although it be an affair of as delicate a nature as most in the course of life." She had in addition that sincerity which Swift called "honour," and in spite of the weakness of her body "the personal courage of a hero." Once when a robber came to her window, she had shot him through the body with her own hand. Such, then, was the influence which worked on Swift as he wrote; such the presence that mingled with the thought of his fruit trees and the willows and the trout stream at Laracor when he saw the trees budding in St. James's Park and heard the politicians wrangle at Westminster. Unknown to all of them, he had his retreat; and if the Ministers again played him false, and once more, after making his friend's fortunes, he went empty-handed away, then after all he could retire to Ireland and to Stella and have "no shuddering at all" at the thought.

But Stella was the last woman in the world to press her claims. None knew better than she that Swift loved power and the company of men: that though he had his moods of tenderness and his fierce spasms of disgust at society, still for the most part he infinitely preferred the dust and bustle of London to all the trout streams and cherry trees in the world. Above all, he hated interference. If anyone laid a finger upon his liberty or hinted the least threat to his independence, were they men or women, queens or kitchenmaids, he turned upon them with a ferocity which made a savage of him on the spot. Harley once dared to offer him a banknote; Miss Waring dared hint that the obstacles to their marriage were now removed. Both were chastised, the woman brutally. But Stella knew better than to invite such treatment. Stella had learnt patience; Stella had learnt discretion. Even in a matter like this of staying in London or coming back to Ireland she allowed him every latitude. She asked nothing for herself and therefore got more than she asked. Swift was half annoyed:

> . . . your generosity makes me mad; I know you repine inwardly at Presto's absence; you think he has broken his word, of coming in three months, and that this is always his trick: and now Stella says, she does not see possibly how I can come away in haste, and that MD is satisfied, etc. An't you a rogue to overpower me thus?

But it was thus that she kept him. Again and again he burst into language of intense affection:

> Farewell dear Sirrahs, dearest lives: there is peace and quiet with MD, and nowhere else. . . . Farewell again, dearest rogues: I am never happy, but when I write or think of MD. . . . You are as welcome as my blood to every farthing I have in the world: and all that grieves me is, I am not richer, for MD's sake.

One thing alone dashed the pleasure that such words gave her. It was always in the plural that he spoke of her; it was always "dearest Sirrahs, dearest lives"; MD stood for Stella and Mrs. Dingley together. Swift and Stella were never alone. Grant that this was for form's sake merely, grant that the presence of Mrs. Dingley, busy with her keys and her lap-dog and never listening to a word that was said to her, was a form too. But why should such forms be necessary? Why impose a strain that wasted her health and half spoilt her pleasure and kept "perfect friends" who were happy only in each other's company apart? Why indeed? There was a reason; a secret that Stella knew; a secret that Stella did not impart. Divided they had to be. Since, then, no bond bound them, since she was afraid to lay the least claim upon her friend, all the more jealously must she have searched into his words and analysed his conduct to ascertain the temper of his mood and acquaint herself instantly with the least change in it. So long as he told her frankly of his "favourites" and showed himself the bluff tyrant who required every woman to make advances to him, who lectured fine ladies and let them tease him, all was well. There was nothing in that to rouse her suspicions. Lady Berkeley might steal his hat; the Duchess of Hamilton might lay bare her agony; and Stella, who was kind to her sex, laughed with the one and grieved with the other.

But were there traces in the *Journal* of a different sort of influence—something far more dangerous because more equal and more intimate? Suppose that there were some woman of Swift's own station, a girl, like the girl that Stella herself had been when Swift first knew her, dissatisfied with the ordinary way of life, eager, as Stella put it, to know right from wrong, gifted, witty, and untaught—she indeed, if she existed, might be a rival to be feared.

But was there such a rival? If so, it was plain that there would be no mention of her in the *Journal.* Instead, there would be hesitations, excuses, an occasional uneasiness and embarrassment when, in the midst of writing freely and fully, Swift was brought to a stop by something that he could not say. Indeed, he had only been a month or two in England when some such silence roused Stella's suspicions. Who was it, she asked, that boarded near him, that he dined with now and then? "I know no such person," Swift replied; "I do not dine with boarders. What the pox! You know whom I have dined with every day since I left you, better than I do. What do you mean, Sirrah?" But he knew what she meant: she meant Mrs. Vanhomrigh, the widow who lived near him; she meant her daughter Esther. "The Vans" kept coming again and again after that in the *Journal.* Swift was too proud to conceal the fact that he saw them, but he sought nine times out of ten to excuse it. When he was in Suffolk Street the Vanhomrighs were in St. James's Street and thus saved him a walk. When he was in Chelsea they were in London, and it was convenient to keep his best gown and periwig there. Sometimes the heat kept him there and sometimes the rain; now they were playing cards, and young Lady Ashburnham reminded him so much of Stella that he stayed on to help her. Sometimes he stayed out of listlessness; again he stayed because he was very busy and they were simple people who did not stand on ceremony. At the same time Stella had only to hint that these Vanhomrighs were people of no consequence for him to retort, "Why, they keep as good female company as I do male. . . . I saw two lady Bettys there this afternoon." In short, to tell the whole truth, to write whatever came into his head in the old free way, was no longer easy.

Indeed, the whole situation was full of difficulty. No man detested falsehood more than Swift or loved truth more whole-heartedly. Yet here he was compelled to hedge, to hide, and to prevaricate. Again, it had become essential to him to have "sluttery" or private chamber where he could relax and unbend and be Presto and not "t'other I." Stella satisfied this need as no one else could. But then Stella was in Ireland; Vanessa was on the spot. She was younger and fresher; she too had her charms. She too could be taught and improved and scolded into maturity as Stella had been. Obviously Swift's influence upon her was all to the good. And so with Stella in Ireland and Vanessa in London, why should it not be possible to enjoy what each could give him, confer benefits on both and do no serious harm to either? It seemed possible; at any rate he allowed himself to make the experiment. Stella, after all, had contrived for many years to make shift with her portion; Stella had never complained of her lot.

But Vanessa was not Stella. She was younger, more vehement, less disciplined, less wise. She had no Mrs. Dingley to restrain her. She had no memories of the past to solace her. She had no journals coming day by day to comfort her. She loved Swift and she knew no reason why she should not say so. Had he not himself taught her "to act what was right, and not to mind what the world said"? Thus when some obstacle impeded her, when some mysterious secret came between them she had the unwisdom to question him. "Pray what can be wrong in seeing and advising an unhappy young woman? I can't imagine." "You have taught me to distinguish," she burst out, "and then you leave me miserable." Finally in her anguish and her bewilderment she had the temerity to force herself upon Stella. She wrote and demanded to be told the truth—what was Stella's connection with Swift? But it was Swift himself who enlightened her. And when the full force of those bright blue eyes blazed upon her, when he flung her letter on the table and glared at her and said nothing and rode off, her life was ended. It was no figure of speech when she said that "his killing, killing words" were worse than the rack to her; when she cried out that there was "something in your look so awful that it strikes me dumb." Within a few weeks of that interview she was dead; she had vanished, to become one of those uneasy ghosts who haunted the troubled background of Stella's life, peopling its solitude with fears.

Stella was left to enjoy her intimacy alone. She lived on to practise those sad arts by which she kept her friend at her side until, worn out with the strain and the concealment, with Mrs. Dingley and her lap-dogs, with the perpetual fears and frustrations, she too died. As they buried her, Swift sat in a back room away from the lights in the churchyard and wrote an account of the character of "the truest, most virtuous, and valuable friend, that I, or perhaps any other person, was blessed with." Years passed; insanity overcame him; he exploded in violent outbursts of mad rage. Then by degrees he fell silent. Once they caught him murmuring. "I am what I am," they heard him say.

*

The "Sentimental Journey"

*

Tristram Shandy, though it is Sterne's first novel, was written at a time when many have written their twentieth, that is, when he was forty-five years old. But it bears every sign of maturity. No young writer could have dared to take such liberties with grammar and syntax and sense and propriety and the long-standing tradition of how a novel should be written. It needed a strong dose of the assurance of middle age and its indifference to censure to run such risks of shocking the lettered by the unconventionality of one's style, and the respectable by the irregularity of one's morals. But the risk was run and the success was prodigious. All the great, all the fastidious were enchanted. Sterne became the idol of the town. Only in the roar of laughter and applause which greeted the book, the voice of the simple-minded public at large was to be heard protesting that it was a scandal coming from a clergyman and that the Archbishop of York ought to administer, to say the least of it, a scolding. The Archbishop, it seems, did nothing. But Sterne, however little he let it show on the surface, laid the criticism to heart. That heart too had been afflicted since the publication of *Tristram Shandy*. Eliza Draper, the object of his passion, had sailed to join her husband in Bombay. In his next book Sterne was determined to give effect to the change that had come over him, and to prove, not only the brilliance of his wit, but the depths of his sensibility. In his own words, "my design in it was to teach us to love the world and our fellow creatures better than we do." It was with such motives animating him that he sat down to write that narrative of a little tour in France which he called *A Sentimental Journey*.

But if it were possible for Sterne to correct his manners, it was impossible for him to correct his style. That had become as much a part of himself as his large nose or his brilliant eyes. With the first words—They order, said I, this matter better in France—we are in the world of *Tristram Shandy*. It is a world in which anything may happen. We hardly know what jest, what jibe, what flash of poetry is not going to glance suddenly through the gap which this astonishingly agile pen has cut in the thick-set hedge of English prose. Is Sterne himself responsible? Does he know what he is going to say next for all his resolve to be on his best behaviour this time? The jerky, disconnected sentences are as rapid and it would seem as little under control as the phrases that fall from the lips of a brilliant talker. The very punctuation is that of speech, not writing, and brings the sound and associations of the speaking voice in with it. The order of the ideas, their suddenness and irrelevancy, is more true to life than to literature. There is a privacy in this intercourse which allows things to slip out unreproved that would have been in doubtful taste had they been spoken in public. Under the influence of this extraordinary style the book becomes semi-transparent. The usual ceremonies and conventions which keep reader and writer at arm's length disappear. We are as close to life as we can be.

That Sterne achieved this illusion only by the use of extreme art and extraordinary pains is obvious without going to his manuscript to prove it. For though the writer is always haunted by the belief that somehow it must be possible to brush aside the ceremonies and conventions of writing and to speak to the reader as directly as by word of mouth, anyone who has tried the experiment has either been struck dumb by the difficulty, or waylaid into disorder and diffusity unutterable. Sterne somehow brought off the astonishing combination. No writing seems to flow more exactly into the very folds and creases of the individual mind, to express its changing moods, to answer its lightest whim and impulse, and yet the result is perfectly precise and composed. The utmost fluidity exists with the utmost permanence. It is as if the tide raced over the beach hither and thither and left every ripple and eddy cut on the sand in marble.

Nobody, of course, stood more in need of the liberty to be himself than Sterne. For while there are writers whose gift is impersonal, so that a Tolstoy, for example, can create a character and leave us alone with it, Sterne must always be there in person to help us in our intercourse. Little or nothing of *A Sentimental Journey* would be left if all that we call Sterne himself were extracted from it. He has no valuable information to give, no reasoned philosophy to impart. He left London, he tells us, "with so much precipitation that it never enter'd my mind that we were at war with France." He has nothing to say of pictures or churches or the misery or well-being of the countryside. He was travelling in France indeed, but the road was often through his own mind, and his chief adventures were not with brigands and precipices but with the emotions of his own heart.

This change in the angle of vision was in itself a daring innovation. Hitherto, the traveller had observed certain laws of proportion and perspective. The Cathedral had always been a vast building in any book of travels and the man a little figure, properly diminutive, by its side. But Sterne was quite capable of omitting the Cathedral altogether. A girl with a green satin purse might be much more important than Notre-Dame. For there is, he seems to hint, no universal scales of values. A girl may be more interesting than a cathedral; a dead donkey more instructive than a living philosopher. It is all a question of one's point of view. Sterne's eyes were so adjusted that small things often bulked larger in them than big. The talk of a barber about the buckle of his wig told him more about the character of the French than the grandiloquence of her statesmen.

I think I can see the precise and distinguishing marks of national characters more in these nonsensical *minutiae*, than in the most important matters of state; where great men of all nations talk and stalk so much alike, that I would not give nine-pence to chuse amongst them.

So too if one wishes to seize the essence of things as a sentimental traveller should, one should seek for it, not at broad noonday in large and open streets, but in an unobserved corner up a dark entry. One should cultivate a kind of shorthand which renders the several turns of looks and limbs into plain words. It was an art that Sterne had long trained himself to practise.

For my own part, by long habitude, I do it so mechanically that when I walk the streets of London, I go translating all the way; and have more than once stood behind in the circle, where not three words had been said, and have brought off twenty different dialogues with me, which I could have fairly wrote down and swore to.

It is thus that Sterne transfers our interest from the outer to the inner. It is no use going to the guide-book; we must consult our own minds; only they can tell us what is the comparative importance of a cathedral, of a donkey, and of a girl with a green satin purse. In this preference for the windings of his own mind to the guide-book and its hammered high road, Sterne is singularly of our own age. In this interest in silence rather than in speech Sterne is the forerunner of the moderns. And for these reasons he is on far more intimate terms with us today than his great contemporaries the Richardsons and the Fieldings.

Yet there is a difference. For all his interest in psychology Sterne was far more nimble and less profound than the masters of this somewhat sedentary school have since become. He is after all telling a story, pursuing a journey, however arbitrary and zigzag his methods. For all our divagations, we do make the distance between Calais and Modane within the space of a very few pages. Interested as he was in the way in which he saw things, the things themselves also interested him acutely. His choice is capricious and individual, but no realist could be more brilliantly successful in rendering the impression of the moment. *A Sentimental Journey* is a succession of portraits —the Monk, the lady, the Chevalier selling *pâtés*, the girl in the bookshop, La Fleur in his new breeches;—it is a succession of scenes. And though the flight of this erratic mind is as zigzag as a dragon-fly's, one cannot deny that this dragon-fly has some method in its flight, and chooses the flowers not at random but for some exquisite harmony or for some brilliant discord. We laugh, cry, sneer, sympathise by turns. We change from one emotion to its opposite in the twinkling of an eye. This light attachment to the accepted reality, this neglect of the orderly sequence of narrative, allows Sterne almost the licence of a poet. He can express ideas which ordinary novelists would have to ignore in language which, even if the ordinary novelist could command it, would look intolerably outlandish upon his page.

> I walked up gravely to the window in my dusty black coat, and looking through the glass saw all the world in yellow, blue, and green, running at the ring of pleasure.—The old with broken lances, and in helmets which had lost their vizards —the young in armour bright which shone like gold, beplumed with each gay feather of the east—all—all tilting at it like fascinated knights in tournaments of yore for fame and love.

There are many passages of such pure poetry in Sterne. One can cut them out and read them apart from the text, and yet—for Sterne was a master of the art of contrast—they lie harmoniously side by side on the printed page. His freshness, his buoyancy, his perpetual power to surprise and startle are the results of these contrasts. He leads us to the very brink of some deep precipice of the soul; we snatch one short glance into its depths; next moment, we are whisked round to look at the green pastures glowing on the other side.

If Sterne distresses us, it is for another reason. And here the blame rests partly at least upon the public—the public which had been shocked, which had cried out after the publication of *Tristram Shandy* that the writer was a cynic who deserved to be unfrocked. Sterne, unfortunately, thought it necessary to reply.

> The world has imagined [he told Lord Shelburne] because I wrote *Tristram Shandy*, that I was myself more Shandean than I really ever was. . . . If it (*A Sentimental Journey*) is not thought a chaste book, mercy on them that read it, for they must have warm imaginations, indeed!

Thus in *A Sentimental Journey* we are never allowed to forget that Sterne is above all things sensitive, sympathetic, humane; that above all things he prizes the decencies, the simplicities of the human heart. And directly a writer sets out to prove himself this or that our suspicions are aroused. For the little extra stress he lays on the quality he desires us to see in him, coarsens it and over-paints it, so that instead of humour, we get farce, and instead of sentiment, sentimentality. Here, instead of being convinced of the tenderness of Sterne's heart—which in *Tristram Shandy* was never in question—we begin to doubt it. For we feel that Sterne is thinking not of the thing itself but of its effect upon our opinion of him. The beggars gather round him and he gives the *pauvre honteux* more than he had meant to. But his mind is not solely and simply on the beggars; his mind is partly on us, to see that we appreciate his goodness. Thus his conclusion, "and I thought he thank'd me more than them all," placed, for more emphasis, at the end of the chapter, sickens us with its sweetness like the drop of pure sugar at the bottom of a cup. Indeed, the chief fault of *A Sentimental Journey* comes from Sterne's concern for our good opinion of his heart. It has a monotony about it, for all its brilliance, as if the author had reined in the natural variety and vivacity of his tastes, lest they should give offence. The mood is subdued to one that is too uniformly kind, tender, and compassionate to be quite natural. One misses the variety, the vigour, the ribaldry of *Tristram Shandy*. His concern for his sensibility has blunted his natural sharpness, and we are called upon to gaze rather too long at modesty, simplicity, and virtue standing rather too still to be looked at.

But it is significant of the change of taste that has come over us that it is Sterne's sentimentality that offends us and not his immorality. In the eyes of the nineteenth century all that Stern wrote was clouded by his conduct as husband and lover. Thackeray lashed him with his righteous indignation, and exclaimed that "There is not a page of Sterne's writing but has something that were better away, a latent corruption—a hint as of an impure presence." To us at the present time, the arrogance of the Victorian novelist seems at least as culpable as the infidelities of the eighteenth-century parson. Where the Victorians deplored his lies and his levities, the courage which turned all the rubs of life to laughter and the brilliance of the expression are far more apparent now.

Indeed *A Sentimental Journey*, for all its levity and wit, is based upon something fundamentally philosophic. It is true that it is a philosophy that was much out of fashion in the Victorian age—the philosophy of pleasure; the philosophy which holds that it is as necessary to behave well in small things as in big, which makes the enjoyment, even of other people, seem more desirable than their suffering. The shameless man had the hardihood to confess to "having been in love with one princess or another almost all my life," and to add, "and I hope I shall go on so till I die, being firmly persuaded that if ever I do a mean action, it must be in some interval betwixt one passion and another." The wretch had the audacity to cry through the mouth of one of his characters, "Mais vive la joie . . . Vive l'amour! et vive la bagatelle!" Clergyman though he was, he had the irreverence to reflect, when he watched the French peasants dancing, that he could distinguish an elevation of spirit, different from that which is the cause or the effect of simple jollity.—"In a word, I thought I beheld *Religion* mixing in the dance."

It was a daring thing for a clergyman to perceive a relationship between religion and pleasure. Yet it may, perhaps, excuse him that in his own case the religion of happiness had a great deal of difficulty to overcome. If you are no longer young, if you are deeply in debt, if your wife is disagreeable, if, as you racket about France in a post-chaise, you are dying of consumption all the time, then the pursuit of happiness is not so easy after all. Still, pursue it one must. One must pirouette about the world, peeping and peering, enjoying a flirtation here, bestowing a few coppers there, and sitting in whatever little patch of sunshine one can find. One must crack a joke, even if the joke is not altogether a decent one. Even in daily life one must not forget to cry "Hail ye, small, sweet courtesies of life, for smooth do ye make the road of it!" One must—but enough of must; it is not a word that Sterne was fond of using. It is only when one lays the book aside and recalls its symmetry, its fun, its whole-hearted joy in all the different aspects of life, and the brilliant ease and beauty with which they are conveyed to us, that one credits the writer with a backbone of conviction to support him. Was not Thackeray's coward —the man who trifled so immorally with so many women and wrote love-letters on gilt-edged paper when he should have been lying on a sick-bed or writing sermons—was he not a stoic in his own way and a moralist, and a teacher? Most great writers are, after all. And that Sterne was a very great writer we cannot doubt.

*

Lord Chesterfield's Letters to His Son

*

When Lord Mahon edited the letters of Lord Chesterfield he thought it necessary to warn the intending reader that they are "by no means fitted for early or indiscriminate perusal." Only "those people whose understandings are fixed and whose principles are matured" can, so his Lordship said, read them with impunity. But that was in 1845. And 1845 looks a little distant now. It seems to us now the age of enormous houses without any bathrooms. Men smoke in the kitchen after the cook has gone to bed. Albums lie upon drawing-room tables. The curtains are very thick and the women are very pure. But the eighteenth century also has undergone a change. To us in 1930 it looks less strange, less remote than those early Victorian years. Its civilisation seems more rational and more complete than the civilisation of Lord Mahon and his contemporaries. Then at any rate a small group of highly educated people lived up to their ideals. If the world was smaller it was also more compact; it knew its own mind; it had its own standards. Its poetry is affected by the same security. When we read the *Rape of the Lock* we seem to find ourselves in an age so settled and so circumscribed that masterpieces were possible. Then, we say to ourselves, a poet could address himself whole-heartedly to his task and keep his mind upon it, so that the little boxes on a lady's dressing-table are fixed among the solid possessions of our imaginations. A game at cards or a summer's boating party upon the Thames has power to suggest the same beauty and the same sense of things vanishing that we receive from poems aimed directly at our deepest emotions. And just as the poet could spend all his powers upon a pair of scissors and a lock of hair, so too, secure in his world and its values, the aristocrat could lay down precise laws for the education of his son. In that world also there was a certainty, a security that we are now without. What with one thing and another times have changed. We can now read Lord Chesterfield's letters without blushing, or, if we do blush, we blush in the twentieth century at passages that caused Lord Mahon no discomfort whatever.

When the letters begin, Philip Stanhope, Lord Chesterfield's natural son by a Dutch governess, was a little boy of seven. And if we are to make any complaint against the father's moral teaching, it is that the standard is too high for such tender years. "Let us return to oratory, or the art of speaking well; which should never be entirely out of our thoughts," he writes to the boy of seven. "A man can make no figure without it in Parliament, or the Church, or in the law," he continues, as if the little boy were already considering his career. It seems, indeed, that the father's fault, if fault it be, is one common to distinguished men who have not themselves succeeded as they should have done and are determined to give their children—and Philip was an only child—the chances that they have lacked. Indeed, as the letters go on one may suppose that Lord Chesterfield wrote as much to amuse himself by turning over the stories of his experience, his reading, his knowledge of the world, as to instruct his son. The letter show an eagerness, an animation which prove that to write to Philip was not a task, but a delight. Tired, perhaps, with the duties of office and disillusioned with its disappointments, he takes up his pen and, in the relief of free communication at last, forgets that his correspondent is, after all, only a schoolboy who cannot understand half the things that his father says to him. But, even so, there is nothing to repel us in Lord Chesterfield's preliminary sketch of the unknown world. He is all on the side of moderation, toleration, ratiocination. Never abuse whole bodies of people, he counsels; frequent all churches, laugh at none;

inform yourself about all things. Devote your mornings to study, your evenings to good society. Dress as the best people dress, behave as they behave, never be eccentric, egotistical, or absent-minded. Observe the laws of proportion, and live every moment to the full.

So, step by step, he builds up the figure of the perfect man—the man that Philip may become, he is persuaded, if he will only—and here Lord Chesterfield lets fall the words which are to colour his teaching through and through —cultivate the Graces. These ladies are, at first, kept discreetly in the background. It is well that the boy should be indulged in fine sentiments about women and poets to begin with. Lord Chesterfield adjures him to respect them both. "For my own part, I used to think myself in company as much above me when I was with Mr. Addison and Mr. Pope, as if I had been with all the Princes in Europe," he writes. But as time goes on the Virtues are more and more taken for granted. They can be left to take care of themselves. But the Graces assume tremendous proportions. The Graces dominate the life of man in this world. Their service cannot for an instant be neglected. And the service is certainly exacting. For consider what it implies, this art of pleasing. To begin with, one must know how to come into a room and then how to go out again. As human arms and legs are notoriously perverse, this by itself is a matter needing considerable dexterity. Then one must be dressed so that one's clothes seem perfectly fashionable without being new or striking; one's teeth must be perfect; one's wig beyond reproach; one's finger-nails cut in the segment of a circle; one must be able to carve, able to dance, and, what is almost as great an art, able to sit gracefully in a chair. These things are the alphabet of the art of pleasing. We now come to speech. It is necessary to speak at least three languages to perfection. But before we open our lips we must take a further precaution—we must be on our guard never to laugh. Lord Chesterfield himself never laughed. He always smiled. When at length the young man is pronounced capable of speech he must avoid all proverbs and vulgar expressions; he must enunciate clearly and use perfect grammar; he must not argue; he must not tell stories; he must not talk about himself. Then, at last, the young man may begin to practise the finest of the arts of pleasing—the art of flattery. For every man and every woman has some prevailing vanity. Watch, wait, pry, seek out their weakness "and you will then know what to bait your hook with to catch them." For that is the secret of success in the world.

It is at this point, such is the idiosyncrasy of our age, that we begin to feel uneasy. Lord Chesterfield's views upon success are far more questionable than his views upon love. For what is to be the prize of this endless effort and self-abnegation? What do we gain when we have learnt to come into rooms and to go out again; to pry into people's secrets; to hold our tongues and to flatter, to forsake the society of low-born people which corrupts and the society of clever people which perverts? What is the prize which is to reward us? It is simply that we shall rise in the world. Press for a further definition, and it amounts perhaps to this: one will be popular with the best people. But if we are so exacting as to demand who the best people are we become involved in a labyrinth from which there is no returning. Nothing exists in itself. What is good society? It is the society that the best people believe to be good. What is wit? It is what the best people think to be witty. All value depends upon somebody else's opinion. For it is the essence of this philosophy that things have no independent existence, but live only in the eyes of other people. It is a looking-glass world, this, to which we climb so slowly; and its prizes are all reflections. That may account for our baffled feeling as we shuffle, and shuffle vainly, among these urbane pages for something hard to lay our hands upon. Hardness is the last thing we shall find. But, granted the deficiency, how much that is ignored by sterner moralists is here seized upon, and who shall deny, at least while Lord Chesterfield's enchantment is upon him, that these imponderable qualities have their value and these shining Graces have their radiance? Consider for a moment what the Graces have done for their devoted servant, the Earl.

Here is a disillusioned politician, who is prematurely aged, who has lost his office, who is losing his teeth, who, worst fate of all, is growing deafer day by day. Yet he never allows a groan to escape him. He is never dull; he is never boring; he is never slovenly. His mind is as well groomed as his body. Never for a second does he "welter in an easy-chair." Private though these letters are, and apparently spontaneous, they play with such ease in and about the single subject which absorbs them that it never becomes tedious or, what is still more remarkable, never becomes ridiculous. It may be that the art of pleasing has some connection with the art of writing. To be polite, considerate, controlled, to sink one's egotism, to conceal rather than to obtrude one's personality may profit the writer even as they profit the man of fashion.

Certainly there is much to be said in favour of the training, however we define it, which helped Lord Chesterfield to write his Characters. The little papers have the precision and formality of some old-fashioned minuet. Yet the symmetry is so natural to the artist that he can break it where he likes; it never becomes pinched and formal, as it would in the hands of an imitator. He can be sly; he can be witty; he can be sententious, but never for an instant does he lose his sense of time, and when the tune is over he calls a halt. "Some succeeded, and others burst" he says of George the First's mistresses: the King liked them fat. Again, "He was fixed in the house of lords, that hospital of incurables." He smiles: he does not laugh. Here the eighteenth century, of course, came to his help. Lord Chesterfield, though he was polite to everything, even to the stars and Bishop Berkeley's philosophy, firmly refused, as became a son of his age, to dally with infinity or to suppose that things are not quite as solid as they seem. The world was good enough and the world was big enough as it was. This prosaic temper, while it keeps him within the bounds of impeccable common sense, limits his outlook. No single phrase of his reverberates or penetrates as so many of La Bruyère's do. But he would have been the first to deprecate any comparison with that great writer; besides, to write as La Bruyère wrote, one must perhaps believe in something, and then how difficult to observe the Graces! One might perhaps laugh; one might perhaps cry. Both are equally deplorable.

But while we amuse ourselves with this brilliant nobleman and his views on life we are aware, and the letters owe much of their fascination to this consciousness, of a dumb yet substantial figure on the farther side of the page. Philip Stanhope is always there. It is true that he says nothing, but we feel his presence in Dresden, in Berlin, in Paris, opening the letters and poring over them and looking dolefully at the thick packets which have been accumulating year after year since he was a child of seven. He had grown into a rather serious, rather stout, rather short young man. He had a taste for foreign politics. A little serious reading was rather to his liking. And by every post the letters came—urbane, polished, brilliant, imploring and commanding him to learn to dance, to learn to carve, to consider the management of his legs, and to seduce a lady of fashion. He did his best. He worked very hard in the school of the Graces, but their service was too exacting. He sat down half-way up the steep stairs which lead to the glittering hall with all the mirrors. He could not do it. He failed in the House of Commons; he subsided into some small post in Ratisbon; he died untimely. He left it to his widow to break the news which he had lacked the heart or the courage to tell his father—that he had been married all these years to a lady of low birth, who had borne him children.

The Earl took the blow like a gentleman. His letter to his daughter-in-law is a model of urbanity. He began the education of his grandsons. But he seems to have become a little indifferent to what happened to himself after that. He did not care greatly if he lived or died. But still to the very end he cared for the Graces. His last words were a tribute of respect to those goddesses. Some one came into the room when he was dying; he roused himself: "Give Dayrolles a chair," he said, and said no more.

*

Two Parsons

*

I
JAMES WOODFORDE

One could wish that the psychoanalysts would go into the question of diary-keeping. For often it is the one mysterious fact in a life otherwise as clear as the sky and as candid as the dawn. Parson Woodforde is a case in point—his diary is the only mystery about him. For forty-three years he sat down almost daily to record what he did on Monday and what he had for dinner on Tuesday; but for whom he wrote or why he wrote it is impossible to say. He does not unburden his soul in his diary; yet it is no mere record of engagements and expenses. As for literary fame, there is no sign that he ever thought of it, and finally, though the man himself is peaceable above all things, there are little indiscretions and criticisms which would have got him into trouble and hurt the feelings of his friends had they read them. What purpose, then, did the sixty-eight little books fulfil? Perhaps it was the desire for intimacy. When James Woodforde opened one of his neat manuscript books he entered into conversation with a second James Woodforde, who was not quite the same as the reverend gentleman who visited the poor and preached in the church. These two friends said much that all the world might hear; but they had a few secrets which they shared with each other only. It was a great comfort, for example, that Christmas when Nancy, Betsy, and Mr. Walker seemed to be in conspiracy against him, to exclaim in the diary, "The treatment I meet with for my Civility this Christmas is to me abominable." The second James Woodforde sympathised and agreed. Again, when a stranger abused his hospitality it was a relief to inform the other self who lived in the little book that he had put him to sleep in the attic story, "and I treated him as one that would be too free if treated kindly." It is easy to understand why, in the quiet life of a country parish, these two bachelor friends became in time inseparable. An essential part of him would have died had he been forbidden to keep his diary. When indeed he thought himself in the grip of death he still wrote on and on. And as we read—if reading is the word for it—we seem to be listening to someone who is murmuring over the events of the day to himself in the quiet space which precedes sleep. It is not writing, and, to speak of the truth, it is not reading. It is slipping through half a dozen pages and strolling to the window and looking out. It is going on thinking about the Woodfordes while we watch the people in the street below. It is taking a walk and making up the life and character of James Woodforde as we go. It is not reading any more than it is writing—what to call it we scarcely know.

James Woodforde, then, was one of those smooth-cheeked, steady-eyed men, demure to look at, whom we can never imagine except in the prime of life. He was of an equable temper, with only such acerbities and touchinesses as are generally to be found in those who have had a love affair in their youth and remained, as they fancy, unwed because of it. The Parson's love affair, however, was nothing very tremendous. Once when he was a young man in Somerset he liked to walk over to Shepton and to visit a certain "sweet tempered" Betsy White who lived there. He had a great mind "to make a bold stroke" and ask her to marry him. He went so far, indeed, as to propose marriage "when opportunity served," and Betsy was willing. But he delayed; time passed; four years passed indeed, and Betsy went to Devonshire, met a Mr. Webster, who had five hundred pounds a year, and married him. When James Woodforde met them in the turnpike road he could say little, "being shy," but to his diary he remarked—and this no doubt was his private version of the affair ever after—"she has proved herself to me a mere jilt."

But he was a young man then, and as time went on we cannot help suspecting that he was glad to consider the question of marriage shelved once and for all so that he might settle down with his niece Nancy at Weston Longueville, and give himself simply and solely, every day and all day, to the great business of living. Again, what else to call it we do not know.

For James Woodforde was nothing in particular. Life had it all her own way with him. He had no special gift; he had no oddity or infirmity. It is idle to pretend that he was a zealous priest. God in Heaven was much the same to him as King George upon the throne—a kindly Monarch, that is to say, whose festivals one kept by preaching a sermon on Sunday much as one kept the Royal birthday by firing a blunderbuss and drinking a toast at dinner. Should anything untoward happen, like the death of a boy who was dragged and killed by a horse, he would instantly, but rather perfunctorily exclaim, "I hope to God the Poor Boy is happy," and add, "We all came home singing"; just as when Justice Creed's peacock spread its tail—"and most noble it is"—he would exclaim, "How wonderful are Thy Works O God in every Being." But there was no fanaticism, no enthusiasm, no lyric impulse about James Woodforde. In all these pages, indeed, each so neatly divided into compartments, and each of those again filled, as the days themselves were filled, quietly and fully in a hand steady as the pacing of a well-tempered nag, one can only call to mind a single poetic phrase about the transit of Venus. "It appeared as a black patch upon a fair Lady's face," he says. The words themselves are mild enough, but they hang over the undulating expanse of the Parson's prose with the resplendence of the star itself. So in the Fen country a barn or a tree appears twice its natural size against the surrounding flats. But what led him to this palpable excess that summer's night we cannot tell. It cannot have been that he was drunk. He spoke out too roundly against such failings in his brother Jack to be guilty himself. Temperamentally he was among the eaters of meat and not among the drinkers of wine. When we think of the Woodfordes, uncle and niece, we think of them as often as not waiting with some impatience for their dinner. Gravely they watch the joint as it is set upon the table; swiftly they get their knives to work upon the succulent leg or loin; without much comment, unless a word is passed about the gravy or the stuffing, they go on eating. So they munch, day after day, year in year out, until between them they must have devoured herds of sheep and oxen, flocks of poultry, an odd dozen or so of swans and cygnets, bushels of apples and plums, while the pastries and the jellies crumble and squash beneath their spoons in mountains, in pyramids, in pagodas. Never was there a book so stuffed with food as this one is. To read the bill of fare respectfully and punctually set forth gives one a sense of repletion. Trout and chicken, mutton and peas, pork and apple sauce—so the joints succeed each other at dinner, and there is supper with more joints still to come, all, no doubt, home grown, and of the juiciest and sweetest; all cooked, often by the mistress herself, in the plainest English way, save when the dinner was at Weston Hall and Mrs. Custance surprised them with a London dainty—a pyramid of jelly, that is to say, with a "landscape appearing through it." After dinner sometimes, Mrs. Custance, for whom James Woodforde had a chivalrous devotion, would play the "Sticcardo Pastorale," and make "very soft music indeed"; or would get out her work-box and show them how neatly contrived it was, unless indeed she were giving birth to another child upstairs. These infants the Parson would baptize and very frequently he would bury them. They died almost as frequently as they were born. The Parson had a deep respect for the Custances. They were all that country gentry should be—a little given to the habit of keeping mistresses, perhaps, but that peccadillo could be forgiven them in view of their generosity to the poor, the kindness they showed to Nancy, and their condescension in asking the Parson to dinner when they had great people staying with them. Yet great people were not much to James's liking. Deeply though he respected the nobility, "one must confess," he said, "that being with our equals is much more agreeable."

Not only did Parson Woodforde know what was agreeable; that rare gift was by the bounty of Nature supplemented by another equally rare—he could have what he wanted. The age was propitious. Monday, Tuesday, Wednesday—they follow each other and each little compartment seems filled with content. The days were not crowded, but they were enviably varied. Fellow of New College though he was, he did things with his own hands, not merely with his own head. He lived in every room of the house—in the study he wrote sermons, in the dining-room he ate copiously; he cooked in the kitchen, he played cards in the parlour. And then he took his coat and stick and went coursing his greyhounds in the fields. Year in, year out, the provisioning of the house and its defence against the cold of winter and the drought of summer fell upon him. Like a general he surveyed the seasons and took steps to make his own little camp safe with coal and wood and beef and beer against the enemy. His day thus had to accommodate a jumble of incongruous occupations. There is religion to be served, and the pig to be killed; the sick to be visited and dinner to be eaten; the dead to be buried and beer to be brewed; Convocation to be attended and the cow to be bolused. Life and death, mortality and immortality, jostle in his pages and make a good mixed marriage of it: ". . . found the old gentleman almost at his last gasp. Totally senseless with rattlings in his Throat. Dinner today boiled beef and Rabbit rosted." All is as it should be; life is like that.

Surely, surely, then, here is one of the breathing-spaces in human affairs—here in Norfolk at the end of the eighteenth century at the Parsonage. For once man is content with his lot; harmony is achieved; his house fits him; a tree is a tree; a chair is a chair; each knows its office and fulfils it. Looking through the eyes of Parson Woodforde, the different lives of men seem orderly and settled. Far away guns roar; a King falls; but the sound is not loud enough to scare the rooks here in Norfolk. The proportions of things are different. The Continent is so distant that it looks a mere blur; America scarcely exists; Australia is unknown. But a magnifying glass is laid upon the fields of Norfolk. Every blade of grass is visible there. We see every lane and every field; the ruts on the roads and the peasant's faces. Each house stands in its own breadth of meadow isolated and independent. No wires link village to village. No voices thread the air. The body also is more present and more real. It suffers more acutely. No anaesthetic deadens physical pain. The surgeon's knife hovers real and sharp above the limb. Cold strikes unmitigated upon the house. The milk freezes in the pans; the water is thick with ice in the basins. One can scarcely walk from one room to another in the parsonage in winter. Poor men and women are frozen to death upon the roads. Often no letters come and there are no visitors and no newspapers. The Parsonage stands alone in the midst of the frost-bound fields. At last, Heaven be praised, life circulates again; a man comes to the door with a Madagascar monkey; another brings a box containing a child with two distinct perfect heads; there is a rumour that a balloon is going to rise at Norwich. Every little incident stands out sharp and clear. The drive to Norwich even is something of an adventure. One must trundle every step of the way behind a horse. But look how distinct the trees stand in the hedges; how slowly the cattle move their heads as the carriage trots by; how gradually the spires of Norwich raise themselves above the hill. And then how clear-cut and familiar are the face of the few people who are our friends—the Custances, Mr. du Quesne. Friendship has time to solidify, to become a lasting, a valuable possession.

True, Nancy of the younger generation is visited now and then by a flighty notion that she is missing something, that she wants something. One day she complained to her uncle that life was very dull: she complained "of the dismal situation of my house, nothing to be seen, and little or no visiting or being visited, &c.," and made him very uneasy. We could read Nancy a little lecture upon the folly of wanting that "et cetera." Look what your "et cetera" has brought to pass, we might say; half the countries of Europe are bankrupt; there is a red line of villas on every green hillside; your Norfolk roads are black as tar; there is no end to "visiting or being visited." But Nancy has an answer to make us, to the effect that our past is her present. You, she says, think it a great privilege to be born in the eighteenth century, because one called cowslips pagles and rode in a curricle instead of driving in a car. But you are utterly wrong, you fanatical lovers of memoirs, she goes on. I can assure you, my life was often intolerably dull. I did not laugh at the things that make you laugh. It did not amuse me when my uncle dreamt of a hat or saw bubbles in the beer, and said that meant a death in the family; I thought so too. Betsy Davy mourned young Walker with all her heart in spite of dressing in sprigged paduasoy. There is a great deal of humbug talked of the eighteenth century. Your delight in old times and old diaries is half impure. You make up something that never had any existence. Our sober reality is only a dream to you—so Nancy grieves and complains, living through the eighteenth century day by day, hour by hour.

Still, if it is a dream, let us indulge it a moment longer. Let us believe that some things last, and some places and some people are not touched by change. On a fine May morning, with the rooks rising and the hares scampering and the plover calling among the long grass, there is much to encourage the illusion. It is we who change and perish. Parson Woodforde lives on. It is the kings and queens who lie in prison. It is the great towns that are ravaged with anarchy and confusion. But the river Wensum still flows; Mrs. Custance is brought to bed of yet another baby; there is the first swallow of the year. The spring comes, and summer with its hay and strawberries; then autumn, when the walnuts are exceptionally fine though the pears are poor; so we lapse into winter, which is indeed boisterous, but the house, thank God, withstands the storm; and then again there is the first swallow, and Parson Woodforde takes his greyhounds out a-coursing.

II

THE REV. JOHN SKINNER

A whole world separates Woodforde, who was born in 1740 and died in 1803, from Skinner, who was born in 1772 and died in 1839.

For the few years that separated the two parsons are those momentous years that separate the eighteenth century from the nineteenth. Camerton, it is true, lying in the heart of Somersetshire, was a village of the greatest antiquity; nevertheless, before five pages of the diary are turned we read of coal-works, and how there was a great shouting at the coal-works because a fresh vein of coal had been discovered, and the proprietors had given money to the workmen to celebrate an event which promised such prosperity to the village. Then, though the country gentlemen seemed set as firmly in their seats as ever, it happened that the manor house at Camerton, with all the rights and duties pertaining to it, was in the hands of the Jarretts, whose fortune was derived from the Jamaica trade. This novelty, this incursion of an element quite unknown to Woodforde in his day, had its disturbing influence no doubt upon the character of Skinner himself. Irritable, nervous, apprehensive, he seems to embody, even before the age itself had come into existence, all the strife and unrest of our distracted times. He stands, dressed in the prosaic and unbecoming stocks and pantaloons of the early nineteenth century, at the parting of the ways. Behind him lay order and discipline and all the virtues of the heroic past, but directly he left his study he was faced with drunkenness and immorality; with indiscipline and irreligion; with Methodism and Roman Catholicism; with the Reform Bill and the Catholic Emancipation Act, with a mob clamouring for freedom, with the overthrow of all that was decent and established and right. Tormented and querulous, at the same time conscientious and able, he stands at the parting of the ways, unwilling to yield an inch, unable to concede a point, harsh, peremptory, apprehensive, and without hope.

Private sorrow had increased the natural acerbity of his temper. His wife had died young, leaving him with four small children, and of these the best-loved, Laura, a child who shared his tastes and would have sweetened his life, for she already kept a diary and had arranged a cabinet of shells with the utmost neatness, died too. But these losses, though they served nominally to make him love God the better, in practice led him to hate men more. By the time the diary opens in 1822 he was fixed in his opinion that the mass of men are unjust and malicious, and that the people of Camerton are more corrupt even than the mass of men. But by that date he was also fixed in his profession. Fate had taken him from the lawyer's office, where he would have been in his element, dealing out justice, filling up forms, keeping strictly to the letter of the law, and had planted him at Camerton among church-wardens and farmers, the Gullicks and the Padfields, the old woman who had dropsy, the idiot boy, and the dwarf. Nevertheless, however sordid his tasks and disgusting his parishioners, he had his duty to them; and with them he would remain. Whatever insults he suffered, he would live up to his principles, uphold the right, protect the poor, and punish the wrongdoer. By the time the diary opens, this strenuous and unhappy career is in full swing.

Perhaps the village of Camerton in the year 1822, with its coal-miners and the disturbance they brought, was no fair sample of English village life. Certainly it is difficult, as one follows the Rector on his daily rounds, to indulge in pleasant dreams about the quaintness and amenity of old English rural life. Here, for instance, he was called to see Mrs. Gooch—a woman of weak mind, who had been locked up alone in her cottage and fallen into the fire and was in agony. "Why do you not help me, I say? Why do you not help me?" she cried. And the Rector, as he heard her screams, knew that she had come to this through no fault of her own. Her efforts to keep a home together had led to drink, and so she had lost her reason, and what with the squabbles between the Poor Law officials and the family as to who should support her, what with her husband's extravagance and drunkenness, she had been left alone, had fallen into the fire, and so died. Who was to blame? Mr. Purnell, the miserly magistrate, who was all for cutting down the allowance paid to the poor, or Hicks the Overseer, who was notoriously harsh, or the ale-houses, or the Methodists, or what? At any rate the Rector had done his duty. However he might be hated for it, he always stood up for the rights of the down-trodden; he always told people of their faults, and convicted them of evil. Then there was Mrs. Somer, who kept a house of ill fame and was bringing up her daughters to the same profession. Then there was Farmer Lippeatt, who, turned out of the Red Post at midnight, dead drunk, missed his way, fell into a quarry, and died of a broken breastbone. Wherever one turned there was suffering, wherever one looked one found cruelty behind that suffering. Mr. and Mrs. Hicks, for example, the Overseers, let an infirm pauper lie for ten days in the Poor House without care, "so that maggots had bred in his flesh and eaten great holes in his body." His only attendant was an old woman, who was so failing that she was unable to lift him. Happily the pauper died. Happily poor Garratt, the miner, died too. For to add to the evils of drink and poverty and the cholera there was constant peril from the mine itself. Accidents were common and the means of treating them elementary. A fall of coal had broken Garratt's back, but he lingered on, though exposed to the crude methods of country surgeons, from January to November, when at last death released him. Both the stern Rector and the flippant Lady of the Manor, to do them justice, were ready with their half-crowns, with their soups and their medicines, and visited sick-beds without fail. But even allowing for the natural asperity of Mr. Skinner's temper, it would need a very rosy pen and a very kindly eye to make a smiling picture of life in the village of Camerton a century ago. Half-crowns and soup went a very little way to remedy matters; sermons and denunciations made them perhaps even worse.

The Rector found refuge from Camerton neither in dissipation like some of his neighbours, nor in sport like others. Occasionally he drove over to dine with a brother cleric, but he noted acrimoniously that the entertainment was "better suited to Grosvenor Square than a clergyman's home—French dishes and French wines in profusion," and records with a note of exclamation that it was eleven o'clock before he drove home. When his children were young he sometimes walked with them in the fields, or amused himself by making them a boat, or rubbed up his Latin in an epitaph for the tomb of some pet dog or tame pigeon. And sometimes he leant back peacefully and listened to Mrs. Fenwick as she sang the songs of Moore to her husband's accompaniment on the flute. But even such harmless pleasures were poisoned with suspicion. A farmer stared insolently as he passed; some one threw a stone from a window; Mrs. Jarrett clearly concealed some evil purpose behind her cordiality. No, the only refuge from Camerton lay in Camalodunum. The more he thought of it the more certain he became that he had the singular good fortune to live on the identical spot where lived the father of Caractacus, where Ostorius established his colony, where Arthur had fought the traitor Modred, where Alfred very nearly came in his misfortunes. Camerton was undoubtedly the Camalodunum of Tacitus. Shut up in his study alone with his documents, copying, comparing, proving indefatigably, he was safe, at rest, even happy. He was also, he became convinced, on the track of an important etymological discovery, by which it could be proved that there was a secret significance "in every letter that entered into the composition of Celtic names." No archbishop was as content in his palace as Skinner the antiquary was content in his cell. To these pursuits he owed, too, those rare and delightful visits to Stourhead, the seat of Sir Richard Hoare, when at last he mixed with men of his own calibre, and met the gentlemen who were engaged in examining the antiquities of Wiltshire. However hard it froze, however high the snow lay heaped on the roads, Skinner rode over to Stourhead; and sat in the library, with a violent cold, but in perfect content, making extracts from Seneca, and extracts from Diodorum Siculus, and extracts from Ptolemy's *Geography*, or scornfully disposed of some rash and ill-informed fellow-antiquary who had the temerity to assert that Camalodunum was really situated at Colchester. On he went with his extracts, with his theories, with his proofs, in spite of the malicious present of a rusty nail wrapped in paper from his parishioners, in spite of the laughing warning of his host: "Oh, Skinner, you will bring everything at last to Camalodunum; be content with what you have already discovered, if you fancy too much you will weaken the authority of real facts." Skinner replied with a sixth letter thirty-four pages long; for Sir Richard did not know how necessary Camalodunum had become to an embittered man who had daily to encounter Hicks the Overseer and Purnell the magistrate, the brothels, the ale-houses, the Methodists, the dropsies and bad legs of Camerton. Even the floods were mitigated if one could reflect that thus Camalodunum must have looked in the time of the Britons.

So he filled three iron chests with ninety-eight volumes of manuscript. But by degrees the manuscripts ceased to be entirely concerned with Camalodunum; they began to be largely concerned with John Skinner. It was true that it was important to establish the truth about Camalodunum, but it was also important to establish the truth about John Skinner. In fifty years after his death, when the diaries were published, people would know not only that John Skinner was a great antiquary, but that he was a much wronged, much suffering man. His diary became his confidant, as it was to become his champion. For example, was he not the most affectionate of fathers, he asked the diary? He had spent endless time and trouble on his sons; he had sent them to Winchester and Cambridge, and yet now when the farmers were so insolent about paying him his tithes, and gave him a broken-backed lamb for his share, or fobbed him off with less than his due of cocks, his son Joseph refused to help him. His son said that the people of Camerton laughed at him; that he treated his children like servants; that he suspected evil where none was meant. And then he opened a letter by chance and found a bill for a broken gig; and then his sons lounged about smoking cigars when they might have helped him to mount his drawings. In short, he could not stand their presence in his house. He dismissed them in a fury to Bath. When they had gone he could not help admitting that perhaps he had been at fault. It was his querulous temper again—but then he had so much to make him querulous. Mrs. Jarrett's peacock screamed under his window all night. They jangled the church bells on purpose to annoy him. Still, he would try; he would let them come back. So Joseph and Owen came back. And then the old irritation overcame him again. He "could not help saying" something about being idle, or drinking too much cider, upon which there was a terrible scene and Joseph broke one of the parlour chairs. Owen took Joseph's part. So did Anna. None of his children cared for him. Owen went further. Owen said "I was a madman and ought to have a commission of lunacy to investigate my conduct." And, further, Owen cut him to the quick by pouring scorn on his verses, on his diaries and archaeological theories. He said: "No one would read the nonsense I had written. When I mentioned having gained a prize at Trinity College . . . his reply was that none but the most stupid fellows ever thought of writing for the college prize." Again there was a terrible scene; again they were dismissed to Bath, followed by their father's curses. And then Joseph fell ill with the family consumption. At once his father was all tenderness and remorse. He sent for doctors, he offered to take him for a sea trip to Ireland, he took him indeed to Weston and went sailing with him on the sea. Once more the family came together. And once more the querulous, exacting father could not help, for all his concern, exasperating the children whom, in his own crabbed way, he yet genuinely loved. The question of religion cropped up. Owen said his father was no better than a Deist or a Socinian. And Joseph, lying ill upstairs, said he was too tired for argument; he did not want his father to bring drawings to show him; he did not want his father to read prayers to him, "he would rather have some other person to converse with than me." So in the crisis of their lives, when a father should have been closest to them, even his children turned away from him. There was nothing left to live for. Yet what had he done to make everyone hate him? Why did the farmers call him mad? Why did Joseph say that no one would read what he wrote? Why did the villagers tie tin cans to the tail of his dog? Why did the peacocks shriek and the bells ring? Why was there no mercy shown to him and no respect and no love? With agonising repetition the diary asks these questions; but there was no answer. At last, one morning in December 1839, the Rector took his gun, walked into the beech wood near his home, and shot himself dead.

*

Dr. Burney's Evening Party

*

The party was given either in 1777 or in 1778; on which day or month of the year is not known, but the night was cold. Fanny Burney, from whom we get much of our information, was accordingly either twenty-five or twenty-six, as we choose. But in order to enjoy the party to the full it is necessary to go back some years and to scrape acquaintance with the guests.

Fanny, from the earliest days, had always been fond of writing. There was a cabin at the end of her stepmother's garden at King's Lynn, where she used to sit and write of an afternoon till the oaths of the seamen sailing up and down the river drove her in. But it was only in the afternoon and in remote places that her half-suppressed, uneasy passion for writing had its way. Writing was held to be slightly ridiculous in a girl; rather unseemly in a woman. Besides, one never knew, if a girl kept a diary, whether she might not say something indiscreet—so Miss Dolly Young warned her; and Miss Dolly Young, though exceedingly plain, was esteemed a woman of the highest character in King's Lynn. Fanny's stepmother also disapproved of writing. Yet so keen was the joy—"I cannot express the pleasure I have in writing down my thoughts at the very moment, and my opinion of people when I first see them"—that scribble she must. Loose sheets of paper fell from her pocket and were picked up and read by her father to her agony and shame; once she was forced to make a bonfire of all her papers in the back garden. At last some kind of compromise seems to have been arrived at. The morning was sacred to serious tasks like sewing; it was only in the afternoon that she allowed herself to scribble—

letters, diaries, stories, verses in the look-out place which overhung the river, till the oaths of the sailors drove her in.

There was something strange in that, perhaps, for the eighteenth century was the age of oaths. Fanny's early diary is larded with them. "God help me," "Split me," "Stap my vitals," together with damneds and devilishes dropped daily and hourly from the lips of her adored father and her venerated Daddy Crisp. Perhaps Fanny's attitude to language was altogether a little abnormal. She was immensely susceptible to the power of words, but not nervously or acutely as Jane Austen was. She adored fluency and the sound of language pouring warmly and copiously over the printed page. Directly she read *Rasselas*, enlarged and swollen sentences formed on the tip of her childish pen in the manner of Dr. Johnson. Quite early in life she would go out of her way to avoid the plain name of Tomkins. Thus, whatever she heard from her cabin at the end of the garden was sure to affect her more than most girls, and it is also clear that while her ears were sensitive to sound, her soul was sensitive to meaning. There was something a little prudish in her nature. Just as she avoided the name of Tomkins, so she avoided the roughnesses, the asperities, the plainnesses of daily life. The chief fault that mars the extreme vivacity and vividness of the early diary is that the profusion of words tends to soften the edges of the sentences, and the sweetness of the sentiment to smooth out the outlines of the thought. Thus, when she heard the sailors swearing, though Maria Allen, her half-sister, would, one believes, have liked to stay and toss a kiss over the water—her future history allows us to take the liberty of thinking so—Fanny went indoors.

Fanny went indoors, but not to solitary meditation. The house, whether it was in Lynn or in London—and by far the greater part of the year was spent in Poland Street—hummed with activity. There was the sound of the harpsichord; the sound of singing; there was the sound—for such concentration seems to pervade a whole house with its murmur—of Dr. Burney writing furiously, surrounded by notebooks, in his study; and there were great bursts of chatter and laughter when, returning from their various occupations, the Burney children met together. Nobody enjoyed family life more than Fanny did. For there her shyness only served to fasten the nickname of Old Lady upon her; there she had a familiar audience for her humour; there she need not bother about her clothes; there—perhaps the fact that their mother had died when they were all young was partly the cause of it—was that intimacy which expresses itself in jokes and legends and a private language ("The wig is wet," they would say, winking at each other); there were endless confabulations, and confidences between sisters and brothers and brothers and sisters. Nor could there be any doubt that the Burneys—Susan and James and Charles and Fanny and Hetty and Charlotte—were a gifted race. Charles was a scholar; James was a humorist; Fanny was a writer; Susan was musical—each had some special gift or characteristic to add to the common stock. And besides their natural gifts they were happy in the fact that their father was a very popular man; a man, too, so admirably situated by his talents, which were social, and his birth, which was gentle, that they could mix without difficulty either with lords or with bookbinders, and had, in fact, as free a run of life as could be wished.

As for Dr. Burney himself, there are some points about which, at this distance of time, one may feel dubious. It is difficult to be sure what, had one met him now, one would have felt for him. One thing is certain—one would have met him everywhere. Hostesses would be competing to catch him. Notes would wait for him. Telephone bells would interrupt him. For he was the most sought-after, the most occupied of men. He was always dashing in and dashing out. Sometimes he dined off a box of sandwiches in his carriage. Sometimes he went out at seven in the morning, and was not back from his round of music lessons till eleven at night. The "habitual softness of his manners," his great social charm, endeared him to everybody. His haphazard untidy ways—everything, notes, money, manuscripts, was tossed into a drawer, and he was robbed of all his savings once, but his friends were delighted to make it up for him; his odd adventures—did he not fall asleep after a bad crossing at Dover, and so return to France and so have to cross the Channel again? —gave him a claim upon people's kindness and sympathy. It is, perhaps, his diffuseness that makes him a trifle nebulous. He seems to be for ever writing and then re-writing, and requiring his daughters to write for him, endless books and articles, while over him, unchecked, unfiled, unread perhaps, pour down notes, letters, invitations to dinner which he cannot destroy and means some day to annotate and collect, until he seems to melt away at last in a cloud of words. When he died at the age of eighty-eight, there was nothing to be done by the most devoted of daughters but to burn the whole accumulation entire. Even Fanny's love of language was suffocated. But if we fumble a little as to our feeling for Dr. Burney, Fanny certainly did not. She adored her father. She never minded how many times she had to lay aside her own writing in order to copy out his. And he returned her affection. Though his ambition for her success at Court was foolish, perhaps, and almost cost her her life, she had only to cry when a distasteful suitor was pressed on her, "Oh, Sir, I wish for nothing! Only let me live with you!" for the emotional doctor to reply, "My Life! Thou shalt live with me for ever if thou wilt. Thou canst not think I meant to get rid of thee?" And not only were his eyes full of tears, but, what was more remarkable, he never mentioned Mr. Barlow again. Indeed, the Burneys were a happy family; a mixed composite, oddly assorted family; for there were the Allens, too, and little half-brothers and half-sisters were being born and growing up.

So time passed, and the passage of the years made it impossible for the family to continue in Poland Street any longer. First they moved to Queen Square, and then, in 1774, to the house where Newton had lived, in St. Martin's Street, Leicester Fields; where his Observatory still stood, and his room with the painted panels was still to be seen. Here in a mean street, but in the centre of the town, the Burneys set up their establishment. Here Fanny went on scribbling, stealing to the Observatory as she had stolen to the cabin at Lynn, for she exclaimed, "I cannot any longer resist what I find to be irresistible, the pleasure of popping down my thoughts from time to time upon paper." Here came so many famous people either to be closeted with the doctor, or, like Garrick, to sit with him while his fine head of natural hair was brushed, or to join the lively family dinner, or, more formally to gather together in a musical party, where all the Burney children played and their father "dashed away" on the harpsichord, and perhaps some foreign musician of distinction performed a solo—so many people came for one reason or another to the house in St. Martin's Street that it is only the eccentrics, the grotesques, that catch the eye. One remembers, for instance, the Ajujari, the astonishing soprano, because she had been "mauled as an infant by a pig, in consequence of which she is reported to have a silver side." One remembers Bruce, the traveller, because he had a

> most extraordinary complaint. When he attempted to speak, his whole stomach suddenly seemed to heave like an organ bellows. He did not wish to make any secret about it, but spoke of it as having originated in Abyssinia. However, one evening, when he appeared rather agitated, it lasted much longer than usual, and was so violent that it alarmed the company.

One seems to remember, for she paints herself while she paints the others, Fanny herself slipping eagerly and lightly in and out of all this company, with her rather prominent gnat-like eyes, and her shy, awkward manners. But the gnat-like eyes, the awkward manners, concealed the quickest observation, the most retentive memory. As soon as the company had gone, she stole to the Observatory and wrote down every word, every scene, in letters twelve pages long, for her beloved Daddy Crisp at Chessington. That old hermit—he had retired to a house in a field in dudgeon with society—though professing to be better pleased with a bottle of wine in his cellar and a horse in his stable, and a game of backgammon at night, than with all the fine company in the world, was always agog for news. He scolded his Fannikin if she did not tell him all about her fine goings-on. And he scolded her again if she did not write at full tilt exactly as the words came into her head.

Mr. Crisp wanted to know in particular "about Mr. Greville and his notions." For, indeed, Mr. Greville was a perpetual source of curiosity. It is a thousand pities that time with her poppy dust has covered Mr. Greville so that only his most prominent features, his birth, his person, and his nose emerge. Fulke Greville was the descendant—he must, one fancies, have emphasised the fact from the way in which it is repeated—of the friend of Sir Philip Sidney. A coronet, indeed, "hung almost suspended over his head." In person he was tall and well proportioned. "His face, features, and complexion were striking for masculine beauty." "His air and carriage were noble with conscious dignity"; his bearing was "lofty, yet graceful." But all these gifts and qualities, to which one must add that he rode and fenced and danced and played tennis to admiration, were marred by prodigious faults. He was supercilious in the extreme; he was selfish; he was fickle. He was a man of violent temper. His introduction to Dr. Burney in the first place was due to his doubt whether a musician could be fit company for a gentleman. When he found that young Burney not only played the harpsichord to perfection, but curved his finger and rounded his hand as he played; that he answered plain "Yes, Sir," or "No, Sir," being more interested in the music than in his patron; that it was only indeed when Greville himself thrummed pertinaciously from memory that he could stand it no longer, and broke into vivacious conversation—it was only when he found that young Burney was both gifted and well bred that, being himself a very clever man, he no longer stood upon his dignity. Burney became his friend and his equal. Burney, indeed, almost became his victim. For if there was one thing that the descendant of the friend of Sir Philip Sidney detested it was what he called "fogrum." By that expressive word he seems to have meant the middle-class virtues of discretion and respectability, as opposed to the aristocratic virtues of what he called "*ton*." Life must be lived dashingly, daringly, with perpetual display, even if the display was extremely expensive, and, as seemed possible to those who trailed dismally round his grounds praising the improvements, as boring to the man who made it as to the unfortunate guests whose admiration he insisted upon extorting. But Greville could not endure fogrum in himself or in his friends. He threw the obscure young musician into the fast life of White's and Newmarket, and watched with amusement to see if he sank or swam. Burney, most adroit of men, swam as if born to the water, and the descendant of the friend of Sir Philip Sidney was pleased. From being his protégé, Burney became his confidant. Indeed, the splendid gentleman, for all his high carriage, was in need of one. For Greville, could one wipe away the poppy dust that covers him, was one of those tortured and unhappy souls who find themselves torn asunder by opposite desires. On the one hand he was consumed with the wish to be in the first flight of fashion and to do "the thing," however costly or dreary "the thing" might be. On the other, he was secretly persuaded that "the proper bent of his mind and understanding was for metaphysics." Burney, perhaps, was a link between the world of *ton* and the world of fogrum. He was a man of breeding who could dice and bet with the bloods; he was also a musician who could talk of intellectual things and ask clever people to his house.

Thus Greville treated the Burneys as his equals, and came to their house, though his visits were often interrupted by the violent quarrels which he managed to pick even with the amiable Dr. Burney himself. Indeed, as time went on there was nobody with whom Greville did not quarrel. He had lost heavily at the gambling-tables. His prestige in society was sunk. His habits were driving his family from him. Even his wife, by nature gentle and conciliatory, though excessive thinness made her seem fitted to sit for a portrait "of a penetrating, puissant and sarcastic fairy queen," was wearied by his infidelities. Inspired by them she had suddenly produced that famous Ode to Indifference, "which had passed into every collection of fugitive pieces in the English language" and (it is Madam D'Arblay who speaks) "twined around her brow a garland of wide-spreading and unfading fragrance." Her fame, it may be, was another thorn in her husband's side; for he, too, was an author. He himself had produced a volume of Maxims and Characters; and having "waited for fame with dignity rather than anxiety, because with expectation unclogged with doubt," was beginning perhaps to become a little impatient when fame delayed. Meanwhile he was fond of the society of clever people, and it was largely at his desire that the famous party in St. Martin's Street met together that very cold night.

II

In those days, when London was so small, it was easier than now for people to stand on an eminence which they scarcely struggled to keep, but enjoyed by unanimous consent. Everybody knew and remembered when they saw her that Mrs. Greville had written an Ode to Indifference; everybody knew that Mr. Bruce had travelled in Abyssinia; so, too, everybody knew that there was a house at Streatham presided over by a lady called Mrs. Thrale. Without troubling to write an Ode, without hazarding her life among savages, without possessing either high rank or vast wealth, Mrs. Thrale was a celebrity. By the exercise of powers difficult to define—for to feel them one must have sat at table and noticed a thousand audacities and deftnesses and skilful combinations which die with the moment—Mrs. Thrale had the reputation of a great hostess. Her fame spread far beyond her house. People who had never seen her discussed her. People wanted to know what she was like; whether she was really so witty and so well read; whether it was a pose; whether she had a heart; whether she loved her husband the brewer, who seemed a dull dog; why she had married him; whether Dr. Johnson was in love with her—what, in short, was the truth of her story, the secret of her power. For power she had—that was indisputable.

Even then perhaps, it would have been difficult to say in what it consisted. For she possessed the one quality which can never be named; she enjoyed the one gift which never ceases to excite discussion. Somehow or other she was a personality. The young Burneys, for instance, had never seen Mrs. Thrale or been to Streatham, but the stir which she set going round her had reached them in St. Martin's Street. When their father came back from giving his first music lesson to Miss Thrale at Streatham they flocked about him to hear his account of her mother. Was she as brilliant as people made out? Was she kind? Was she cruel? Had he liked her? Dr. Burney was in high good temper—in itself a proof of his hostess's power—and he replied, not, we may be sure, as Fanny rendered it, that she was a "star of the first constellation of female wits: surpassing, rather than equalising the reputation which her extraordinary endowments, and the splendid fortune which made them conspicuous, had blazoned abroad"—that was written when Fanny's style was old and tarnished, and its leaves were fluttering and falling profusely to the ground; the doctor, we may suppose, answered briskly that he had enjoyed himself hugely; that the lady was a very clever lady; that she had interrupted the lesson all the time; that she had a very sharp tongue—there was no doubt of that; but he would go to the stake for it that she was a good-hearted woman at bottom. Then they must have pressed to know what she looked like. She looked younger than her age—which was about forty. She was rather plump, very small, fair with very blue eyes, and had a scar or cut on her lip. She painted her cheeks, which was unnecessary, because her complexion was rosy by nature. The whole impression she made was one of bustle and gaiety and good temper. She was, he said, a woman "full of sport," whom nobody could have taken for a creature that the doctor could not bear, a learned lady. Less obviously, she was very observant, as her anecdotes were to prove; capable of passion, though that was not yet visible at Streatham; and, while curiously careless and good-tempered about her dues as a wit or a blue-stocking, had an amusing pride in being descended from a long line of Welsh gentry (whereas the Thrales were obscure), and drew satisfaction now and then from the reflection that in her veins ran the blood, as the College of Heralds acknowledged, of Adam of Salzburg.

Many women might have possessed these qualities without being remembered for them. Mrs. Thrale possessed besides one that has given her immortality: the power of being the friend of Dr. Johnson. Without that addition, her life might have fizzled and flamed to extinction, leaving nothing behind it. But the combination of Dr. Johnson and Mrs. Thrale created something as solid, as lasting, as remarkable in its way as a work of art. And this was an achievement that called for much rarer powers on the part of Mrs. Thrale than the qualities of a good hostess. When the Thrales first met Johnson he was in a state of profound gloom, crying out such lost and terrible words that Mr. Thrale put his hand before his mouth to silence him. Physically, too, he was afflicted with asthma and dropsy; his manners were rough; his habits were gross; his clothes were dirty; his wig was singed; his linen was soiled; and he was the rudest of men. Yet Mrs. Thrale carried this monster off with her to Brighton and then domesticated him in her house at Streatham, where he was given a room to himself, and where he spent habitually some days in the middle of every week. This might have been, it is true, but the enthusiasm of a curiosity-hunter, ready to put up with a host of disagreeables for the sake of having at her house the original Dr. Johnson, whom anybody in England would gladly pay to see. But it is clear that her connoisseurship was of a finer type. She understood—her anecdotes prove it—that Dr. Johnson was somehow a rare, an important, an impressive human being whose friendship might be a burden but was certainly an honour. And it was not by any means so easy to know this then as it is now. What one knew then was that Dr. Johnson was coming to dinner. And when Dr. Johnson came to dinner one had to ask one's self who was coming too? For if it was a Cambridge man there might be an outburst. If it was a Whig there would certainly be a scene. If it was a Scotsman anything might happen. Such were his whims and prejudices. Next one would have to bethink one, what food had been ordered for dinner? For the food never went uncriticised; and even when one had provided him with young peas from the garden, one must not praise them. Were not the young peas charming, Mrs. Thrale asked once? and he turned upon her, after gobbling down masses of pork and veal pie with lumps of sugar in it, and snapped "Perhaps they would be so—to a pig." Then what would the talk be about—that was another cause for anxiety. If it got upon painting or music he was apt to dismiss it with scorn, for both arts were indifferent to him. Then if a traveller told a tale he was sure to pooh-pooh it, because he believed nothing that he had not seen himself. Then if any one were to express sympathy in his presence it might well draw down upon one a rebuke for insincerity:

> When, one day, I lamented the loss of a cousin killed in America: "Prithee, my dear," said he, "have done with canting: how would the world be the worse for it, I may ask, if all your relations were at once spitted like larks, and roasted for Presto's supper?"

In short, the meal would be strewn with difficulties; the whole affair might run upon the rocks at any moment.

Had Mrs. Thrale been a shallow curiosity-hunter she would have shown him for a season or so and then let him drop. But Mrs. Thrale realised even at the moment that one must submit to be snubbed and bullied and irritated and offended by Dr. Johnson because—well, what was the force that sent an impudent and arrogant young man like Boswell slinking back to his chair like a beaten boy when Johnson bade him? Why did she herself sit up till four in the morning pouring out tea for him? There was a force in him that awed even a competent woman of the world, that subdued even a thick-skinned, conceited boy. He had a right to scold Mrs. Thrale for inhumanity, when she knew that he spent only seventy pounds a year on himself and with the rest of his income supported a houseful of decrepit and ungrateful lodgers. If he gobbled at table and tore the peaches from the wall, he went back punctually to London to see that his wretched inmates had their three good meals over the week-end. Moreover, he was a warehouse of knowledge. If the dancing-master talked about dancing, Johnson could out-talk him. He could keep one amused by the hour with his tales of the underworld, of the topers and scally-wags who haunted his lodgings and claimed his bounty. He said things casually that one never forgot. But what was perhaps more engaging than all this learning and virtue, was his love of pleasure, his detestation of the mere bookworm, his passion for life and society. And then, as a woman would, Mrs. Thrale loved him for his courage—that he had separated two fierce dogs that were tearing each other to pieces in Mr. Beauclerc's sitting-room; that he had thrown a man, chair and all, into the pit of a theatre; that, blind and twitching as he was, he rode to hounds on Brightelmstone Downs, and followed the hunt as if he had been a gay dog instead of a huge and melancholy old man. Moreover, there was a natural affinity between them. She drew him out: she made him say what without her he would never have said; indeed, he had confessed to her some painful secret of his youth which she never revealed to anybody. Above all, they shared the same passion. Of talk they could neither of them ever have enough.

Thus Mrs. Thrale could always be counted on to produce Dr. Johnson; and it was, of course, Dr. Johnson whom Mr. Greville most particularly wished to meet. As it happened, Dr. Burney had renewed his acquaintance with Dr. Johnson after many years, when he went to Streatham to give his first music lesson, and Dr. Johnson had been there, "wearing his mildest aspect." For he remembered Dr. Burney with kindness. He remembered a letter that Dr. Burney had written to him in praise of the dictionary; he remembered, too, that Dr. Burney having called upon him, years ago, had found him out, had dared to cut some bristles from the hearth broom to send to an admirer. When he met Dr. Burney again at Streatham, he had instantly taken a liking to him; soon he was brought by Mrs. Thrale to see Dr. Burney's books; it was quite easy, therefore, for Dr. Burney to arrange that on a certain night in the early spring of 1777 or 1778, Mr. Greville's great wish to meet Dr. Johnson and Mrs. Thrale should be gratified. A day was fixed and the engagement was made.

Whatever the day was it must have been marked in the host's calendar with a note of interrogation. Anything might happen. Any extreme of splendour or disaster might spring from the meeting of so many marked and distinguished characters. Dr. Johnson was formidable. Mr. Greville was domineering. Mrs. Greville was a celebrity in one way; Mrs. Thrale was a celebrity in another. Then it was an occasion. Everybody felt it to be so. Wits would be on the strain; expectation on tiptoe. Dr. Burney foresaw these difficulties and took steps to avert them, but there was, one vaguely feels, something a little obtuse about Dr. Burney. The eager, kind, busy man, with his head full of music and his desk stuffed with notes, lacked discrimination. The precise outline of people's characters was covered with a rambling pink haze. To his innocent mind music was the universal specific. Everybody must share his own enthusiasm for music. If there was going to be any difficulty, music could solve it. He therefore asked Signor Piozzi to be of the party.

The night arrived and the fire was lit. The chairs were placed and the company arrived. As Dr. Burney had foreseen, the awkwardness was great. Things indeed seemed to go wrong from the start. Dr. Johnson had come in his worsted wig, very clean and prepared evidently for enjoyment. But after one look at him, Mr. Greville seemed to decide that there was something formidable about the old man; it would be better not to compete; it would be better to play the fine gentleman, and leave it to literature to make the first advances. Murmuring, apparently, something about having the toothache, Mr. Greville "assumed his most supercilious air of distant superiority and planted himself, immovable as a noble statue, upon the hearth." He said nothing. Then Mrs. Greville, though longing to distinguish herself, judged it proper for Dr. Johnson to begin, so that she said nothing. Mrs. Thrale, who might have been expected to break up the solemnity, felt, it seemed, that the party was not her party and, waiting for the principals to engage, resolved to say nothing either.

Mrs. Crewe, the Grevilles' daughter, lovely and vivacious as she was, had come to be entertained and instructed and therefore very naturally she, too, said nothing. Nobody said anything. Complete silence reigned. Here was the very moment for which Dr. Burney in his wisdom had prepared. He nodded to Signor Piozzi; and Signor Piozzi stepped to the instrument and began to sing. Accompanying himself on the pianoforte, he sang an *aria parlante*. He sang beautifully, he sang his best. But far from breaking the awkwardness and loosing the tongues, the music increased the constraint. Nobody spoke. Everybody waited for Dr. Johnson to begin. There, indeed, they showed their fatal ignorance, for if there was one thing that Dr. Johnson never did, it was to begin. Somebody had always to start a topic before he consented to pursue it or to demolish it. Now he waited in silence to be challenged. But he waited in vain. Nobody spoke. Nobody dared speak. The roulades of Signor Piozzi continued uninterrupted. As he saw his chance of a pleasant evening's talk drowned in the rattle of a piano, Dr. Johnson sank into silent abstraction and sat with his back to the piano gazing at the fire. The *aria parlante* continued uninterrupted. At last the strain became unendurable. At last Mrs. Thrale could stand it no longer. It was the attitude of Mr. Greville, apparently, that roused her resentment. There he stood on the hearth in front of the fire "staring around him at the whole company in curious silence sardonically." What right had he, even if he were the descendant of the friend of Sir Philip Sidney, to despise the company and absorb the fire? Her own pride of ancestry suddenly asserted itself. Did not the blood of Adam of Salzburg run in her veins? Was it not as blue as that of the Grevilles and far more sparkling? Giving rein to the spirit of recklessness which sometimes bubbled in her, she rose, and stole on tiptoe to the pianoforte. Signor Piozzi was still singing and accompanying himself dramatically as he sang. She began a ludicrous mimicry of his gestures: she shrugged her shoulders, she cast up her eyes, she reclined her head on one side just as he did. At this singular display the company began to titter—indeed, it was a scene that was to be described "from coterie to coterie throughout London, with comments and sarcasms of endless variety." People who saw Mrs. Thrale at her mockery that night never forgot that this was the beginning of that criminal affair, the first scene of that "most extraordinary drama" which lost Mrs. Thrale the respect of friends and children, which drove her in ignominy from England, and scarcely allowed her to show herself in London again—this was the beginning of her most reprehensible, her most unnatural passion for one who was not only a musician but a foreigner. But all this still lay on the laps of the gods. Nobody yet knew of what iniquity the vivacious lady was capable. She was still the respected wife of a wealthy brewer. Happily, Dr. Johnson was staring at the fire, and knew nothing of the scene at the piano. But Dr. Burney put a stop to the laughter instantly. He was shocked that a guest, even if a foreigner and a musician, should be ridiculed behind his back, and stealing to Mrs. Thrale he whispered kindly but with authority in her ear that if she had no taste for music herself she should consider the feelings of those who had. Mrs. Thrale took the rebuke with admirable sweetness, nodded her acquiescence, and returned to her chair. But she had done her part. After that nothing more could be expected from her. Let them now do what they chose—she washed her hands of it, and seated herself "like a pretty little Miss," as she said afterwards, to endure what yet remained to be endured "of one of the most humdrum evenings that she had ever passed."

If no one had dared to tackle Dr. Johnson in the beginning it was scarcely likely that they would dare now. He had apparently decided that the evening was a failure so far as talk was concerned. If he had not come dressed in his best clothes he might have had a book in his pocket which he could have pulled out and read. As it was, nothing but the resources of his own mind were left him; but these were huge; and these he explored as he sat with his back to the piano looking the very image of gravity, dignity, and composure.

At last the *aria parlante* came to an end. Signor Piozzi

indeed, finding nobody to talk to, fell asleep in his solitude. Even Dr. Burney by this time must have been aware that music is not an infallible specific; but there was nothing for it now. Since people would not talk, the music must continue. He called upon his daughters to sing a duet. And then, when that was over, there was nothing for it but that they must sing another. Signor Piozzi still slept, or still feigned sleep. Dr. Johnson explored still further the magnificent resources of his own mind. Mr. Greville still stood superciliously upon the hearth-rug. And the night was cold.

But it was a grave mistake to suppose that because Dr. Johnson was apparently lost in thought, and certainly almost blind, he was not aware of anything, particularly of anything reprehensible, that was taking place in the room. His "starts of vision" were always astonishing and almost always painful. So it was on the present occasion. He suddenly woke up. He suddenly roused himself. He suddenly uttered the words for which the company had been waiting all the evening.

"If it were not for depriving the ladies of the fire," he said, looking fixedly at Mr. Greville, "I should like to stand upon the hearth myself!" The effect of the outburst was prodigious. The Burney children said afterwards that it was as good as a comedy. The descendant of the friend of Sir Philip Sidney quailed before the Doctor's glance. All the blood of all the Brookes rallied itself to overcome the insult. The son of a bookseller should be taught his place. Greville did his best to smile—a faint, scoffing smile. He did his best to stand where he had stood the whole evening. He stood smiling, he stood trying to smile, for two or perhaps for three minutes more. But when he looked round the room and saw all eyes cast down, all faces twitching with amusement, all sympathies plainly on the side of the bookseller's son, he could stand there no longer. Fulke Greville slunk away, sloping even his proud shoulders, to a chair. But as he went, he rang the bell "with force." He demanded his carriage.

"The party then broke up; and no one from amongst it ever asked, or wished for its repetition."

❃

Jack Mytton

❃

Are you curious to know what sort of person your neighbour is in a deck-chair on Brighton pier? Watch, then, which column of *The Times*—she has brought it, rolled like a French roll, and it lies on the top of her bag—she reads first. Politics, presumably, or an article upon a temple in Jerusalem? Not a bit of it—she reads the sporting news. Yet one could have sworn, to look at her—boots, stockings, and all—that she was a public servant of some sort; with an Act of Parliament, a blue-book or two, and a frugal lunch of biscuits and bananas in her bag. If for a moment she basks on Brighton pier while Madame Rosalba, poised high on a platform above the sea, dives for coins or soup-plates it is only to refresh herself before renewing her attack upon the iniquities of our social system. Yet she begins by reading the sporting news.

Perhaps there is nothing so strange in it after all. The great English sports are pursued almost as fiercely by sedentary men who cannot sit a donkey, and by quiet women who cannot drown a mouse, as by the booted and spurred. They hunt in imagination. They follow the fortunes of the Berkeley, the Cattistock, the Quorn, and the Belvoir upon phantom hunters. They roll upon their lips the odd-sounding, beautifully crabbed English place-names—Humblebee, Doddles Hill, Caroline Bog, Winniats Brake. They imagine as they read (hanging to a strap in the Underground or propping the paper against a sub-urban teapot) now a "slow, twisting hunt," now a "brilliant gallop." The rolling meadows are in their eyes; they hear the thunder and the whimper of horses and hounds; the shapely slopes of Leicestershire unfold before them, and in imagination they ride home again, when evening falls, soothed and satisfied, and watch the lights coming out in farmhouse windows. Indeed the English sporting writers, Beckford, St. John, Surtees, Nimrod, make no mean reading. In their slapdash, gentlemanly way they have ridden their pens as boldly as they have ridden their horses. They have had their effect upon the language. This riding and tumbling, this being blown upon and rained upon and splashed from head to heels with mud, have worked themselves into the very texture of English prose and given it that leap and dash, that stripping of images from flying hedge and tossing tree which distinguish it not indeed above the French but so emphatically from it. How much English poetry depends upon English hunting this is not the place to enquire. That Shakespeare was a bold if erratic horseman scarcely needs proving. Therefore that an Englishwoman should choose to read the sporting news rather than the political gossip need cause us no surprise; nor need we condemn her if, when she has folded up her paper, she takes from her bag not a blue-book but a red book and proceeds, while Madame Rosalba dives and the band blares and the green waters of the English channel sparkle and sway between the chinks of the pier, to read the Life of Jack Mytton.

Jack Mytton was by no means an estimable character. Of an old Shropshire family (the name was Mutton once; so Brontë was Prunty), he had inherited a fine property and a large income. The little boy who was born in the year 1796 should have carried on the tradition of politics and sport which his ancestors had pursued respectably for five centuries before him. But families have their seasons, like the year. After months of damp and drizzle, growth and prosperity, there come the wild equinoctial gales, a roaring in the trees all day, fruit destroyed and blossom wasted. Lightning strikes the house and its rooftree goes up in fire. Indeed, Nature and society between them had imposed upon the Mytton of 1796 a burden which might have crushed a finer spirit—a body hewn from the solid rock, a fortune of almost indestructible immensity. Nature and society dared him, almost, to defy them. He accepted the challenge. He went shooting in the thinnest silk stockings, he let the rain pelt on his bare skin, he swam rivers, charged gates, crouched naked on the snow, but still his body remained obdurate and upright. He had his breeches made without pockets; wads of bank-notes were picked up in the woods, but still his fortune survived. He begot children and tossed them in the air and pelted them with oranges; he married wives whom he tormented and imprisoned until one died and the other snatched her chance and ran away. While he shaved, a glass of port stood by his side, and as the day wore on he worked through five or six bottles of wine and sopped them up with pound upon pound of filberts. There was an extremity about his behaviour which raises it from the particular to the general. The shaggy body of primeval man, with all his appetites and aptitudes, seemed to have risen from his grave under the barrows, where the great stones were piled on top of him, where once he sacrificed rams and did homage to the rising sun, to carouse with tippling fox-hunters of the time of George the Fourth. His limbs themselves seemed carved from more primitive materials than modern men's. He had neither beauty of countenance nor grace of manner, yet he bore himself, for all his violence of body and mind, with an air of natural breeding which one can imagine in a savage stepping on his native turf. When he talked, says Nimrod, which he did sparely, he said, in a very few words, things which made everybody laugh; but, unequally gifted as he was, acute in some senses, dull in others, he had a deafness which made him unwieldy in general society.

What, then, could a primeval man do, who was born in England in the reign of George the Fourth? He could take bets and make them. Was it a watery winter's night? He would drive his gig across country under the moon. Was it freezing? He would make his stable-boys hunt rats upon skates. Did some moderately cautious guest admit that he had never been upset in a gig? Mytton at once ran the wheel up the bank and flung them both into the road. Put any obstacle in his way and he leapt it, swam it, smashed it, somehow surmounted it, at the cost of a broken bone or a broken carriage. To yield to danger or to own to pain were both unthinkable. And so the Shropshire peasantry were amazed (as we see them in Alken's and Rawlins's pictures) by the apparition of a gentleman setting his tandem at a gate, riding a bear round his drawing-room, beating a bulldog with naked fists, lying between the hoofs of a nervous horse, riding with broken ribs unmurmuring when every jar was agony. They were amazed; they were scandalised; his eccentricities and infidelities and generosities were the talk of every inn and farmhouse for miles; yet somehow no bailiff in the four counties would arrest him. They looked up at him as one looks at something removed from ordinary duties and joys—a monument, a menace—with contempt and pity and some awe.

But Jack Mytton himself—what was he feeling meanwhile? The thrill of perfect satisfaction, the delight of joys snatched unhesitatingly without compunction? The barbarian surely should have been satisfied. But the by no means introspective mind of Nimrod was puzzled. "Did the late Mr. Mytton really enjoy life amidst all this profusion of expenditure?" No; Nimrod was of opinion that he did not. He had everything that the human heart could desire, but he lacked "the art of enjoyment." He was bored. He was unhappy. "There was that about him which resembled the restlessness of the hyena." He hurried from thing to thing, determined to taste and enjoy, but somehow blunted and bruised his pleasures as he touched them. Two hours before his own exquisite dinner he devoured fat bacon and strong ale at a farmhouse, and then blamed his cook. Still, without an appetite, he would eat; still he would drink, only instead of port it must be brandy to lash his flagging palate into sensation. A "sort of destroying spirit egged him on." He was magnificent, wasteful, extravagant in every detail. ". . . it was his largeness of heart that ruined Mr. Mytton," said Nimrod, "added to the lofty pride which disdained the littleness of prudence."

By the time he was thirty, at any rate, Jack Mytton had done two things that to most men would have been impossible: he had almost ruined his health; he had almost spent his money. He had to leave the ancestral home of the Myttons. But it was no primeval man, glowing with health, bristling with energy, but a "round-shouldered, tottering old-young man bloated by drink" who joined the company of shady adventurers whose necessities obliged them to live at Calais. Even in that society his burden was upon him; still he must shine; still he must excel. No one should call him Johnny Mytton with impunity. Four horses must draw Mr. Mytton the three hundred yards to his rooms or he preferred to walk. And then the hiccough attacked him. Seizing his bedroom candle, he set a light to his shirt and staggered, burning and blazing, to show his friends how Jack Mytton cured the hiccough. What more could human beings ask of him? To what further frenzies would the gods dare their victim? Now that he had burnt himself alive, it seemed as if he had discharged his obligation to society and could lay the primeval man to rest. He might perhaps allow that other spirit, the civilised gentleman who was so incongruously coupled with the barbarian, to come to the surface. He had once learnt Greek. Now as he lay burnt and bloated in bed he quoted Sophocles—"the beautiful passage . . . wherein Oedipus recommends his children to the care of Creon." He remembered the Greek anthology. When they moved him to the seaside he began to pick up shells, and could hardly sit out dinner in his eagerness to be at the work of brushing them "with a nail brush dipped in vinegar." "He to whom the whole world had appeared insufficient to afford pleasure . . . was now completely happy." But alas, shells and Sophocles, peace and happiness, were whelmed in the general dissolution which could not be delayed. The King's Bench prison seized him, and there, corrupt in body, ruined in fortune, worn out in mind, he died at the age of thirty-eight. And his wife cried that she could not "help loving him with all his faults," and four horses drew him to the grave, and three thousand poor people sobbed for the loss of one who had somehow acted out for the benefit of the crowd an odious, monstrous part, laid on him by the gods, for the edification of mankind and their pleasure too, but for his own unutterable misery.

For the truth is we like these exhibitions of human nature. We like to see exalted above us some fox-hunter, like Jack Mytton, burning himself alive to cure the hiccough, some diver like Madame Rosalba, who, mounting higher and higher, wraps herself about in sacking, and then, with a look of indifference and satiety as if she had renounced and suffered and dedicated herself to some insane act of defiance for no pleasure of her own, dives into the Channel and brings up a twopenny-halfpenny soup-plate between her teeth. The lady on the pier feels gratified. It is because of this, she says, that I love my kind.

❋

De Quincey's Autobiography

❋

It must often strike the reader that very little criticism worthy of being called so has been written in English of prose—our great critics have given the best of their minds to poetry. And the reason perhaps why prose so seldom calls out the higher faculties of the critic, but invites him to argue a case or to discuss the personality of the writer—to take a theme from the book and make his criticism an air played in variation on it—is to be sought in the prose-writer's attitude to his own work. Even if he writes as an artist, without a practical end in view, still he treats prose as a humble beast of burden which must accommodate all sorts of odds and ends; as an impure substance in which dust and twigs and flies find lodgment. But more often than not the prose-writer has a practical aim in view, a theory to argue, or a cause to plead, and with it adopts the moralist's view that the remote, the difficult, and the complex are to be abjured. His duty is to the present and the living. He is proud to call himself a journalist. He must use the simplest words and express himself as clearly as possible in order to reach the greatest number in the plainest way. Therefore he cannot complain of the critics if his writing, like the irritation in the oyster, serves only to breed other art; nor be surprised if his pages, once they have delivered their message, are thrown on the rubbish heap like other objects that have served their turn.

But sometimes we meet even in prose with writing that seems inspired by other aims. It does not wish to argue or to convert or even to tell a story. We can draw all our pleasure from the words themselves; we have not to enhance it by reading between the lines or by making a voyage of discovery into the psychology of the writer. De Quincey, of course, is one of these rare beings. When we bring his work to mind we recall it by some passage of stillness and completeness, like the following:

> "*Life is Finished!*" was the secret misgiving of my heart; for the heart of infancy is as apprehensive as that of maturest wisdom in relation to any capital wound inflicted on the happiness. "*Life is Finished! Finished it is!*" was the hidden meaning that, half-unconsciously to myself, lurked within my sighs; and, as bells heard from a distance on a summer evening seem charged at times with an articulate form of words, some monitory message, that rolls round unceasingly, even so for me some noiseless and subterraneous voice seemed to chant continually a secret word, made audible only to my own heart—that "now is the blossoming of life withered for ever."

Such passages occur naturally, for they consist of visions and dreams, not of actions or of dramatic scenes, in his autobiographic sketches. And yet we are not made to think of him, De Quincey, as we read. If we try to analyse our sensations we shall find that we are worked upon as if by music—the senses are stirred rather than the brain. The rise and fall of the sentence immediately soothes us to a mood and removes us to a distance in which the near fades and detail is extinguished. Our minds, thus widened and lulled to a width of apprehension, stand open to receive one by one in slow and stately procession the ideas which De Quincey wishes us to receive; the golden fullness of life; the pomps of the heaven above; the glory of the flowers below, as he stands "between an open window and a dead body on a summer's day." The theme is supported and amplified and varied. The idea of hurry and trepidation, of reaching towards something that for ever flies, intensifies the impression of stillness and eternity. Bells heard on summer evenings, palm trees waving, sad winds that blow for ever keep us by successive waves of emotion in the same mood. The emotion is never stated; it is suggested and brought slowly by repeated images before us until it stays, in all its complexity, complete.

The effect is one that is very rarely attempted in prose and is rarely appropriate to it because of this very quality of finality. It does not lead anywhere. We do not add to our sense of high summer and death and immortality any consciousness of who is hearing, seeing, and feeling. De Quincey wished to shut out from us everything save the picture "of a solitary infant, and its solitary combat with grief—a mighty darkness, and a sorrow without a voice," to make us fathom and explore the depths of that single emotion. It is a state which is general and not particular. Therefore De Quincey was at odds with the aims of the prose-writer and his morality. His reader was to be put in possession of a meaning of that complex kind which is largely a sensation. He had to become fully aware not merely of the fact that a child was standing by a bed, but of stillness, sunlight, flowers, the passage of time and the presence of death. None of this could be conveyed by simple words in their logical order; clarity and simplicity would merely travesty and deform such a meaning. De Quincey, of course, was fully aware of the gulf that lay between him as a writer who wished to convey such ideas and his contemporaries. He turned from the neat precise speech of his time to Milton and Jeremy Taylor and Sir Thomas Browne; from them he learnt the roll of the long sentence that sweeps its coils in and out, that piles its summit higher and higher. Then followed a discipline exacted, most drastically, by the fineness of his own ear—the weighing of cadences, the consideration of pauses; the effect of repetitions and consonances and assonances—all this was part of the duty of a writer who wishes to put a complex meaning fully and completely before his reader.

When, therefore, we come to consider critically one of the passages that has made so deep an impression we find that it has been produced much as a poet like Tennyson would produce it. There is the same care in the use of sound; the same variety of measure; the length of the sentence is varied and its weight shifted. But all these measures are diluted to a lower degree of strength and their force is spread over a much greater space, so that the transition from the lowest compass to the highest is by a gradation of shallow steps and we reach the utmost heights without violence. Hence the difficulty of stressing the particular quality of any single line as in a poem and the futility of taking one passage apart from the context, since its effect is compound of suggestions that have been received sometimes several pages earlier. Moreover, De Quincey, unlike some of his masters, was not at his best in sudden majesty of phrase; his power lay in suggesting large and generalised visions; landscapes in which nothing is seen in detail; faces without features; the stillness of midnight or summer; the tumult and trepidation of flying multitudes; anguish that for ever falls and rises and casts its arms upwards in despair.

But De Quincey was not merely the master of separate passages of beautiful prose; if that had been so his achievement would have been far less than it is. He was also a writer of narrative, an autobiographer, and one, if we consider that he wrote in the year 1833, with very peculiar views of the art of autobiography. In the first place he was convinced of the enormous value of candour.

> If he were really able to pierce the haze which so often envelops, even to himself, his own secret springs of action and reserve, there cannot be a life moving at all under intellectual impulses that would not, through that single force of absolute frankness, fall within the reach of a deep, solemn, and sometimes even of a thrilling interest.

He understood by autobiography the history not only of the external life but of the deeper and more hidden emotions. And he realised the difficulty of making such a confession: ". . . vast numbers of people, though liberated from all reasonable motive of self-restraint, *cannot* be confidential—have it not in their power to lay aside reserve." Aerial chains, invisible spells, bind and freeze the free spirit of communication. "It is because a man cannot see and measure these mystical forces which palsy him that he cannot deal with them effectually." With such perceptions and intentions it is strange that De

Quincey failed to be among the great autobiographers of our literature. Certainly he was not tongue-tied or spellbound. Perhaps one of the reasons that led him to fail in his task of self-delineation was not the lack of expressive power, but the superfluity. He was profusely and indiscriminately loquacious. Discursiveness—the disease that attacked so many of the nineteenth-century English writers—had him in her coils. But while it is easy to see why the works of Ruskin or Carlyle are huge and formless—every kind of heterogeneous object had to be found room for somehow, somewhere—De Quincey had not their excuse. The burden of the prophet was not laid upon him. He was, moreover, the most careful of artists. Nobody tunes the sound and modulates the cadence of a sentence more carefully and more exquisitely. But strangely enough, the sensibility which was on the alert to warn him instantly if a sound clashed or a rhythm flagged failed him completely when it came to the architecture of the whole. Then he could tolerate a disproportion and profusion that make his book as dropsical and shapeless as each sentence is symmetrical and smooth. He is indeed, to use the expressive word coined by his brother to describe De Quincey's tendency as a small boy "to plead some distinction or verbal demur," the prince of Pettifogulisers. Not only did he find "in everybody's words an unintentional opening left for double interpretations"; he could not tell the simplest story without qualifying and illustrating and introducing additional information until the point that was to be cleared up has long since become extinct in the dim mists of the distance.

Together with this fatal verbosity and weakness of architectural power, De Quincey suffered too as an autobiographer from a tendency to meditative abstraction. "It was my disease," he said, "to meditate too much and to observe too little." A curious formality diffuses his vision to a general vagueness, lapsing into a colourless monotony. He shed over everything the lustre and the amenity of his own dreaming, pondering absent-mindedness. He approached even the two disgusting idiots with their red eyes with the elaboration of a great gentleman who has by mistake wandered into a slum. So too he slipped mellifluously across all the fissures of the social scale—talking on equal terms with the young aristocrats at Eton or with the working-class family as they chose a joint of meat for their Sunday dinner. De Quincey indeed prided himself upon the ease with which he passed from one sphere to another: ". . . from my very earliest youth," he observed, "it has been my pride to converse familiarly, *more Socratico*, with all human beings, man, woman, and child, that chance might fling in my way." But as we read his descriptions of these men, women, and children we are led to think that he talked to them so easily because to him they differed so little. The same manner served equally for them all. His relations even with those with whom he was most intimate, whether it was Lord Altamont, his schoolboy friend, or Ann the prostitute, were equally ceremonial and gracious. His portraits have the flowing contours, the statuesque poses, the undifferentiated features of Scott's heroes and heroines. Nor is his own face exempted from the general ambiguity. When it came to telling the truth about himself he shrank from the task with all the horror of a well-bred English gentleman. The candour which fascinates us in the confessions of Rousseau—the determination to reveal the ridiculous, the mean, the sordid in himself—was abhorrent to him. "Nothing indeed is more revolting to English feelings," he wrote, "than the spectacle of a human being obtruding on our notice his moral ulcers and scars."

Clearly, therefore, De Quincey as an autobiographer labours under great defects. He is diffuse and redundant; he is aloof and dreamy and in bondage to the old pruderies and conventions. At the same time he was capable of being transfixed by the mysterious solemnity of certain emotions; of realising how one moment may transcend in value fifty years. He was able to devote to their analysis a skill which the professed analysts of the human heart—

the Scotts, the Jane Austens, the Byrons—did not then possess. We find him writing passages which, in their self-consciousness, are scarcely to be matched in the fiction of the nineteenth century:

> And, recollecting it, I am struck with the truth, that far more of our deepest thoughts and feelings pass to us through perplexed combinations of *concrete* objects, pass to us as *involutes* (if I may coin that word) in compound experiences incapable of being disentangled, than ever reach us *directly* and in their own abstract shapes. . . . Man is doubtless *one* by some subtle *nexus*, some system of links, that we cannot perceive, extending from the new-born infant to the superannuated dotard: but, as regards many affections and passions incident to his nature at different stages, he is *not* one, but an intermitting creature, ending and beginning anew; the unity of man, in this respect, is co-extensive only with the particular stage to which the passion belongs. Some passions, as that of sexual love, are celestial by one-half of their origin, animal and earthly by the other half. These will not survive their own appropriate stage. But love, which is *altogether* holy, like that between two children, is privileged to revisit by glimpses the silence and the darkness of declining years. . . .

When we read such passages of analysis, when such states of mind seem in retrospect to be an important element in life and so to deserve scrutiny and record, the art of autobiography as the eighteenth century knew it is changing its character. The art of biography also is being transformed. Nobody after that could maintain that the whole truth of life can be told without "piercing the haze"; without revealing "his own secret springs of action and reserve." Yet external events also have their importance. To tell the whole story of a life the autobiographer must devise some means by which the two levels of existence can be recorded—the rapid passage of events and actions; the slow opening up of single and solemn moments of concentrated emotion. It is the fascination of De Quincey's pages that the two levels are beautifully, if unequally, combined. For page after page we are in company with a cultivated gentleman who describes with charm and eloquence what he has seen and known—the stage coaches, the Irish rebellion, the appearance and conversation of George the Third. Then suddenly the smooth narrative parts asunder, arch opens beyond arch, the vision of something for ever flying, for ever escaping, is revealed, and time stands still.

❋

Four Figures

❋

I

COWPER AND LADY AUSTEN

It happened, of course, many years ago, but there must have been something remarkable about the meeting, since people still like to bring it before their eyes. An elderly gentleman was looking out of his window in a village street in the summer of 1781 when he saw two ladies go into a draper's shop opposite. The look of one of them interested him very much, and he seems to have said so, for soon a meeting was arranged.

A quiet and solitary life that must have been, in which a gentleman stood in the morning looking out of the window, in which the sight of an attractive face was an event. Yet perhaps it was an event partly because it revived some half-forgotten but still pungent memories. For Cowper had not always looked at the world from the windows of a house in a village street. Time was when the sight of ladies of fashion had been familar enough. In his younger days he had been very foolish. He had flirted and giggled; he had gone smartly dressed to Vauxhall and Marylebone Gardens. He had taken his work at the Law Courts with a levity that alarmed his friends—for he had nothing whatever to live upon. He had fallen in love with his cousin Theodora Cowper. Indeed, he had been a thoughtless, wild young man. But suddenly in the heyday of his youth, in the midst of his gaiety, something terrible had happened. There lurked beneath that levity and perhaps inspired it a morbidity that sprang from some defect of person, a dread which made action, which made marriage, which made any public exhibition of himself insupportable. If goaded to it, and he was now committed to a public career in the House of Lords, he must fly, even into the jaws of death. Rather than take up his appointment he would drown himself. But a man sat on the quay when he came to the water's edge; some invisible hand mysteriously forced the laudanum from his lips when he tried to drink it; the knife which he pressed to his heart broke; and the garter with which he tried to hang himself from the bed-post let him fall. Cowper was condemned to live.

When, therefore, that July morning he looked out of the window at the ladies shopping, he had come through gulfs of despair, but he had reached at last not only the haven of a quiet country town, but a settled state of mind, a settled way of life. He was domesticated with Mrs. Unwin, a widow six years his elder. By letting him talk, and listening to his terrors and understanding them, she had brought him very wisely, like a mother, to something like peace of mind. They had lived side by side for many years in methodical monotony. They began the day by reading the Scriptures together; they then went to church; they parted to read or walk; they met after dinner to converse on religious topics or to sing hymns together; then again they walked if it were fine, or read and talked if it were wet, and at last the day ended with more hymns and more prayers. Such for many years had been the routine of Cowper's life with Mary Unwin. When his fingers found their way to a pen they traced the lines of a hymn, or if they wrote a letter it was to urge some misguided mortal, his brother John, for instance, at Cambridge, to seek salvation before it was too late. Yet this urgency was akin perhaps to the old levity; it, too, was an attempt to ward off some terror, to propitiate some deep unrest that lurked at the bottom of his soul. Suddenly the peace was broken. One night in February 1773 the enemy rose; it smote once and for ever. An awful voice called out to Cowper in a dream. It proclaimed that he was damned, that he was outcast, and he fell prostrate before it. After that he could not pray. When the others said grace at table, he took up his knife and fork as a sign that he had no right to join their prayers. Nobody, not even Mrs. Unwin, understood the terrific import of the dream. Nobody realised why he was unique; why he was singled out from all mankind and stood alone in his damnation. But that loneliness had a strange effect—since he was no longer capable of help or direction he was free. The Reverend John Newton could no longer guide his pen or inspire his muse. Since doom had been pronounced and damnation was inevitable, he might sport with hares, cultivate cucumbers, listen to village gossip, weave nets, make tables; all that could be hoped was to while away the dreadful years without the ability to enlighten others or to be helped himself. Never had Cowper written more enchantingly, more gaily, to his friends than now that he knew himself condemned. It was only at moments, when he wrote to Newton or to Unwin, that terror raised its horrid head above the surface and that he cried aloud: "My days are spent in vanity. . . . Nature revives again; but a soul once slain lives no more." For the most part, as he idled his time away in pleasant pastimes, as he looked with amusement at what passed in the street below, one might think him the happiest of men. There was Geary Ball going to the "Royal Oak" to drink his dram—that happened as regularly as Cowper brushed his teeth; but behold—two ladies were going into the draper's shop opposite. That was an event.

One of the ladies he knew already—she was Mrs. Jones, the wife of a neighbouring clergyman. But the other was a stranger. She was arch and sprightly, with dark hair and round dark eyes. Though a widow—she had been the wife of a Sir Robert Austen—she was far from old and not at all solemn. When she talked, for she and Cowper were soon drinking tea together, "she laughs and makes laugh, and keeps up a conversation without seeming to labour at it." She was a lively, well-bred woman who had lived much in France, and, having seen much of the world, "accounts it a great simpleton as it is."

Such were Cowper's first impressions of Ann Austen. Ann's first impressions of the queer couple who lived in the large house in the village street were even more enthusiastic. But that was natural—Ann was an enthusiast by nature. Moreover, though she had seen a great deal of the world and had a town house in Queen Anne Street, she had no friends or relations in that world much to her liking. Clifton Reynes, where her sister lived, was a rude, rough English village where the inhabitants broke into the house if a lady were left unprotected. Lady Austen was dissatisfied; she wanted society, but she also wanted to be settled and to be serious. Neither Clifton Reynes nor Queen Anne Street gave her altogether what she wanted. And then in the most opportune way—quite by chance—she met a refined, well-bred couple who were ready to appreciate what she had to give and ready to invite her to share the quiet pleasures of the countryside which were so dear to them. She could heighten those pleasures deliciously. She made the days seem full of movement and laughter. She organised picnics—they went to the Spinnie and ate their dinner in the root-house and drank their tea on the top of a wheelbarrow. And when autumn came and the evenings drew in, Ann Austen enlivened them too; she it was who stirred William to write a poem about a sofa and told him, just as he was sinking into one of his fits of melancholy, the story of John Gilpin, so that he leapt out of bed, shaking with laughter. But beneath her sprightliness they were glad to find that she was seriously inclined. She longed for peace and quietude, "for with all the gaiety," Cowper wrote, "she is a great thinker."

And with all that melancholy, to paraphase his words, Cowper was a man of the world. As he said himself, he was not by nature a recluse. He was no lean and solitary hermit. His limbs were sturdy; his cheeks were ruddy; he was growing plump. In his younger days he, too, had known the world, and provided, of course, that you have seen through it, there is something to be said for having known it. Cowper, at any rate, was a little proud of his gentle birth. Even at Olney he kept certain standards of gentility. He must have an elegant box for his snuff and silver buckles for his shoes; if he wanted a hat it must be "not a round slouch, which I abhor, but a smart, well-cocked, fashionable affair." His letters preserve this serenity, this good sense, this sidelong, arch humour embalmed in page after page of beautiful clear prose. As the post went only three times a week he had plenty of time to smooth out every little crease in daily life to perfection. He had time to tell how a farmer was thrown from his cart and one of the pet hares had escaped; Mr. Grenville had called; they had been caught in a shower and Mrs. Throckmorton had asked them to come into the house—some little thing of the kind happened every week very aptly for his purpose. Or if nothing happened and it was true that the days went by at Olney "shod with felt," then he was able to let his mind play with rumours that reached him from the outer world. There was talk of flying. He would write a few pages on the subject of flying and its impiety; he would express his opinion of the wickedness, for Englishwomen at any rate, of painting the cheeks. He would discourse upon Homer and Virgil and perhaps attempt a few translations himself. And when the days were dark and even he could no longer trudge through the mud, he would open one of his favourite travellers and dream that he was voyaging with Cook or with Anson, for he travelled widely in imagination, though in body he moved no further than from Buckingham to Sussex and from Sussex back to Buckingham again.

His letters preserve what must have made the charm of his company. It is easy to see that his wit, his stories, his sedate, considerate ways, must have made his morning visits—and he had got into the habit of visiting Lady Austen at eleven every morning—delightful. But there was more in his society than that—there was some charm, some peculiar fascination, that made it indispensable. His cousin Theodora had loved him—she still loved him anonymously; Mrs. Unwin loved him; and now Ann Austen was beginning to feel something stronger than friendship rise within her. That strain of intense and perhaps inhuman passion which rested with tremulous ecstasy like that of a hawk moth over a flower, upon some tree, some hillside—did that not tensify the quiet of the country morning, and give to intercourse with him some keener interest than belonged to the society of other men? "The very stones in the garden walls are my intimate acquaintance," he wrote. "Everything I see in the fields is to me an object, and I can look at the same rivulet, or at a handsome tree, every day of my life with new pleasure." It is this intensity of vision that gives his poetry, with all its moralising and didacticism, its unforgettable qualities. It is this that makes passages in *The Task* like clear windows let into the prosaic fabrics of the rest. It was this that gave the edge and zest to his talk. Some finer vision suddenly seized and possessed him. It must have given to the long winter evenings, to the early morning visits, an indescribable combination of pathos and charm. Only, as Theodora could have warned Ann Austen, his passion was not for men and women; it was an abstract ardour; he was a man singularly without thought of sex.

Already early in their friendship Ann Austen had been warned. She adored her friends, and she expressed her adoration with the enthusiasm that was natural to her. At once Cowper wrote to her kindly but firmly admonishing her of the folly of her ways. "When we embellish a creature with colours taken from our fancy," he wrote, "we make it an idol . . . and shall derive nothing from it but a painful conviction of our error." Ann read the letter, flew into a rage, and left the country in a huff. But the breach was soon healed; she worked him ruffles; he acknowledged them with a present of his book. Soon she had embraced Mary Unwin and was back again on more intimate terms than ever. In another month indeed, with such rapidity did her plans take effect, she had sold the lease of her town house, taken part of the vicarage next door to Cowper, and declared that she had now no home but Olney and no friends but Cowper and Mary Unwin. The door between the gardens was opened; the two families dined together on alternate nights; William called Ann sister; and Ann called William brother. What arrangement could have been more idyllic? "Lady Austen and we pass our days alternately at each other's chateau. In the morning I walk with one or other of the ladies, and in the afternoon wind thread," wrote Cowper, playfully comparing himself to Hercules and Samson. And then the evening came, the winter evening which he loved best, and he dreamt in the firelight and watched the shadows dance uncouthly and the sooty films play upon the bars until the lamp was brought, and in that level light he had out his netting, or wound silk, and then, perhaps, Ann sang to the harpsichord and Mary and William played battledore and shuttlecock together. Secure, innocent, peaceful, where then was that "thistly sorrow" that grows inevitably, so Cowper said, beside human happiness? Where would discord come, if come it must? The danger lay perhaps with the women. It might be that Mary would notice one evening that Ann wore a lock of William's hair set in diamonds. She might find a poem to Ann in which he expressed more than a brotherly affection. She would grow jealous. For Mary Unwin was no country simpleton, she was a well-read woman with "the manners of a Duchess"; she had nursed and consoled William for years before Ann came to flutter the "still life" which they both loved best. Thus the two ladies would compete; discord would enter at that point. Cowper would be forced to choose between them.

But we are forgetting another presence at that innocent evening's entertainment. Ann might sing; Mary might play; the fire might burn brightly and the frost and the wind outside make the fireside calm all the sweeter. But there was a shadow among them. In that tranquil room a gulf opened. Cowper trod on the verge of an abyss. Whispers mingled with the singing, voices hissed in his ear words of doom and damnation. He was haled by a terrible voice to perdition. And then Ann Austen expected him to make love to her! Then Ann Austen wanted him to marry her! The thought was odious; it was indecent; it was intolerable. He wrote her another letter, a letter to which there could be no reply. In her bitterness Ann burnt it.

She left Olney and no word ever passed between them again. The friendship was over.

And Cowper did not mind very much. Everybody was extremely kind to him. The Throckmortons gave him the key of their garden. An anonymous friend—he never guessed her name—gave him fifty pounds a year. A cedar desk with silver handles was sent him by another friend who wished also to remain unknown. The kind people at Olney supplied him with almost too many tame hares. But if you are damned, if you are solitary, if you are cut off from God and man, what does human kindness avail? "It is all vanity. . . . Nature revives again; but a soul once slain lives no more." He sank from gloom to gloom, and died in misery.

As for Lady Austen, she married a Frenchman. She was happy—so people said.

II

BEAU BRUMMELL

When Cowper, in the seclusion of Olney, was roused to anger by the thought of the Duchess of Devonshire and predicted a time when "instead of a girdle there will be a rent, and instead of beauty, baldness," he was acknowledging the power of the lady whom he thought so despicable. Why, otherwise, should she haunt the damp solitudes of Olney? Why should the rustle of her silken skirts disturb those gloomy meditations? Undoubtedly the Duchess was a good haunter. Long after those words were written, when she was dead and buried beneath a tinsel coronet, her ghost mounted the stairs of a very different dwelling-place. An old man was sitting in his arm-chair at Caen. The door opened, and the servant announced, "The Duchess of Devonshire." Beau Brummell at once rose, went to the door and made a bow that would have graced the Court of St. James's. Only, unfortunately, there was nobody there. The cold air blew up the staircase of an Inn. The Duchess was long dead, and Beau Brummell, in his old age and imbecility, was dreaming that he was back in London again giving a party. Cowper's curse had come true for both of them. The Duchess lay in her shroud, and Brummell, whose clothes had been the envy of kings, had now only one pair of much-mended trousers, which he hid as best he could under a tattered cloak. As for his hair, that had been shaved by order of the doctor.

But though Cowper's sour predictions had thus come to pass, both the Duchess and the dandy might claim that they had had their day. They had been great figures in their time. Of the two, perhaps Brummell might boast the more miraculous career. He had no advantage of birth, and but little of fortune. His grandfather had let rooms in St. James's Street. He had only a moderate capital of thirty thousand pounds to begin with, and his beauty, of figure rather than of face, was marred by a broken nose. Yet without a single noble, important, or valuable action to his credit he cuts a figure; he stands for a symbol; his ghost walks among us still. The reason for this eminence is now a little difficult to determine. Skill of hand and nicety of judgment were his, of course, otherwise he would not have brought the art of tying neck-cloths to perfection. The story is, perhaps, too well known—how he drew his head far back and sunk his chin slowly down so that the cloth wrinkled in perfect symmetry, or if one wrinkle were too deep or to shallow, the cloth was thrown into a basket and the attempt renewed, while the Prince of Wales sat, hour after hour, watching. Yet skill of hand and nicety of judgment were not enough. Brummell owed his ascendency to some curious combination of wit, of taste, of insolence, of independence—for he was never a toady—which it were too heavy handed to call a philosophy of life, but served the purpose. At any rate, ever since he was the most popular boy at Eton coolly jesting when they were for throwing a bargee into the river, "My good fellows, don't send him into the river; the man is evidently in a high state of perspiration, and it almost amounts to a certainty that he will catch cold," he floated buoyantly and gaily and without apparent effort to the top of whatever society he found himself among. Even when he was a captain in the Tenth Hussars and so scandalously inattentive to duty that he only knew his troop by "the very large blue nose" of one of the men, he was liked and tolerated. When he resigned his commission, for the regiment was to be sent to Manchester—and "I really could not go—think, your Royal Highness, Manchester!"—he had only to set up house in Chesterfield Street to become the head of the most jealous and exclusive society of his time. For example, he was at Almack's one night talking to Lord ——. The Duchess of —— was there, escorting her young daughter, Lady Louisa. The Duchess caught sight of Mr. Brummell, and at once warned her daughter that if that gentleman near the door came and spoke to them she was to be careful to impress him favourably, "for," and she sank her voice to a whisper, "he is the celebrated Mr. Brummell." Lady Louisa might well have wondered why a Mr. Brummell was celebrated, and why a Duke's daughter need take care to impress a Mr. Brummell. And then directly he began to move towards them the reason of her mother's warning became apparent. The grace of his carriage was so astonishing; his bows were so exquisite. Everybody looked overdressed or badly dressed—some, indeed, looked positively dirty beside him. His clothes seemed to melt into each other with the perfection of their cut and the quiet harmony of their colour. Without a single point of emphasis everything was distinguished—from his bow to the way he opened his snuff-box, with his left hand invariably. He was the personification of freshness and cleanliness and order. One could well believe that he had his chair brought into his dressing-room and was deposited at Almack's without letting a puff of wind disturb his curls or a spot of mud stain his shoes. When he actually spoke to her, Lady Louisa would be at first enchanted—no one was more agreeable, more amusing, had a manner that was more flattering and enticing—and then she would be puzzled. It was quite possible that before the evening was out he would ask her to marry him, and yet his manner of doing it was such that the most ingenuous débutante could not believe that he meant it seriously. His odd grey eyes seemed to contradict his lips;

they had a look in them which made the sincerity of his compliments very doubtful. And then he said very cutting things about other people. They were not exactly witty; they were certainly not profound; but they were so skilful, so adroit—they had a twist in them which made them slip into the mind and stay there when more important phrases were forgotten. He had downed the Regent himself with his dexterous "Who's your fat friend?" and his method was the same with humbler people who snubbed him or bored him. "Why, what could I do, my good fellow, but cut the connection? I discovered that Lady Mary actually ate cabbage!"—so he explained to a friend his failure to marry a lady. And, again, when some dull citizen pestered him about his tour to the North, "Which of the lakes do I admire?" he asked his valet. "Windermere, sir." "Ah, yes—Windermere, so it is—Windermere." That was his style, flickering, sneering, hovering on the verge of insolence, skimming the edge of nonsense, but always keeping within some curious mean, so that one knew the false Brummell story from the true by its exaggeration. Brummell could never have said, "Wales, ring the bell," any more than he could have worn a brightly coloured waistcoat or a glaring necktie. That "certain exquisite propriety" which Lord Byron remarked in his dress, stamped his whole being, and made him appear cool, refined, and debonair among the gentlemen who talked only of sport, which Brummell detested, and smelt of the stable, which Brummell never visited. Lady Louisa might well be on tenter-hooks to impress Mr. Brummell favourably. Mr. Brummell's good opinion was of the utmost importance in the world of Lady Louisa.

And unless that world fell into ruins his rule seemed assured. Handsome, heartless, and cynical, the Beau seemed invulnerable. His taste was impeccable, his health admirable; and his figure as fine as ever. His rule had lasted many years and survived many vicissitudes. The French Revolution had passed over his head without disordering a single hair. Empires had risen and fallen while he experimented with the crease of a neck-cloth and criticised the cut of a coat. Now the battle of Waterloo had been fought and peace had come. The battle left him untouched; it was the peace that undid him. For some time past he had been winning and losing at the gaming-tables. Harriette Wilson had heard that he was ruined, and then, not without disappointment, that he was safe again. Now, with the armies disbanded, there was let loose upon London a horde of rough, ill-mannered men who had been fighting all those years and were determined to enjoy themselves. They flooded the gaming-houses. They played very high. Brummell was forced into competition. He lost and won and vowed never to play again, and then he did play again. At last his remaining ten thousand pounds was gone. He borrowed until he could borrow no more. And finally, to crown the loss of so many thousands, he lost the six-penny-bit with a hole in it which had always brought him good luck. He gave it by mistake to a hackney coachman: that rascal Rothschild got hold of it, he said, and that was the end of his luck. Such was his own account of the affair—other people put a less innocent interpretation on the matter. At any rate there came a day, 16th May 1816, to be precise—it was a day upon which everything was precise—when he dined alone off a cold fowl and a bottle of claret at Watier's, attended the opera, and then took coach for Dover. He drove rapidly all through the night and reached Calais the day after. He never set foot in England again.

And now a curious process of disintegration set in. The peculiar and highly artificial society of London had acted as a preservative; it had kept him in being; it had concentrated him into one single gem. Now that the pressure was removed, the odds and ends, so trifling separately, so brilliant in combination, which had made up the being of the Beau, fell asunder and revealed what lay beneath. At first his lustre seemed undiminished. His old friends crossed the water to see him and made a point of standing him a dinner and leaving a little present behind them at his bankers. He held his usual levee at his lodgings; he spent the usual hours washing and dressing; he rubbed his teeth with a red root, tweezed out hairs with a silver tweezer, tied his cravat to admiration, and issued at four precisely as perfectly equipped as if the Rue Royale had been St. James's Street and the Prince himself had hung upon his arm. But the Rue Royale was not St. James's Street; the old French Countess who spat on the floor was not the Duchess of Devonshire; the good bourgeois who pressed him to dine off goose at four was not Lord Alvanley; and though he soon won for himself the title of Roi de Calais, and was known to workmen as "George, ring the bell," the praise was gross, the society coarse, and the amusements of Calais very slender. The Beau had to fall back upon the resources of his own mind. These might have been considerable. According to Lady Hester Stanhope, he might have been, had he chosen, a very clever man; and when she told him so, the Beau admitted that he had wasted his talents because a dandy's way of life was the only one "which could place him in a prominent light, and enable him to separate himself from the ordinary herd of men, whom he held in considerable contempt." That way of life allowed of verse-making—his verses, called "The Butterfly's Funeral," were much admired; and of singing, and of some dexterity with the pencil. But now, when the summer days were so long and so empty, he found that such accomplishments hardly served to while away the time. He tried to occupy himself with writing his memoirs; he bought a screen and spent hours pasting it with pictures of great men and beautiful ladies whose virtues and frailties were symbolised by hyenas, by wasps, by profusions of cupids, fitted together with extraordinary skill; he collected Buhl furniture; he wrote letters in a curiously elegant and elaborate style to ladies. But these occupations palled. The resources of his mind had been whittled away in the course of years; now they failed him. And then the crumbling process went a little farther, and another organ was laid bare—the heart. He who had played at love all these years and kept so adroitly beyond the range of passion, now made violent advances to girls who were young enough to be his daughters. He wrote such passionate letters to Mademoiselle Ellen of Caen that she did not know whether to laugh or to be angry. She was angry, and the Beau, who had tyrannised over the daughters of dukes, prostrated himself before her in despair. But it was too late—the heart after all these years was not a very engaging object even to a simple country girl, and he seems at last to have lavished his affections upon animals. He mourned his terrier Vick for three weeks; he had a friendship with a mouse; he became the champion of all the neglected cats and starving dogs in Caen. Indeed, he said to a lady that if a man and a dog were drowning in the same pond he would prefer to save the dog—if, that is, there were nobody looking. But he was still persuaded that everybody was looking; and his immense regard for appearances gave him a certain stoical endurance. Thus, when paralysis struck him at dinner he left the table without a sign; sunk deep in debt as he was, he still picked his way over the cobbles on the points of his toes to preserve his shoes, and when the terrible day came and he was thrown into prison he won the admiration of murderers and thieves by appearing among them as cool and courteous as if about to pay a morning call. But if he were to continue to act his part, it was essential that he should be supported—he must have a sufficiency of boot polish, gallons of eau-de-Cologne, and three changes of linen every day. His expenditure upon these items was enormous. Generous as his old friends were, and persistently as he supplicated them, there came a time when they could be squeezed no longer. It was decreed that he was to content himself with one change of linen daily, and his allowance was to admit of necessaries only. But how could a Brummell exist upon necessaries only? The demand was absurd. Soon afterwards he showed his sense of the gravity of the situation by mounting a black silk neck-cloth. Black silk neck-cloths had always been his aversion. It was a signal of despair, a sign that the end was in sight. After that everything that had supported him and kept him in being dissolved. His self-respect vanished. He would dine with any one who would pay the bill. His memory weakened and he told the same story over and over again till even the burghers of Caen were bored. Then his manners degenerated. His extreme cleanliness lapsed into carelessness, and then into positive filth. People objected to his presence in the dining-room of the hotel. Then his mind went—he thought that the Duchess of Devonshire was coming up the stairs when it was only the wind. At last but one passion remained intact among the crumbled debris of so many—an immense greed. To buy Rheims biscuits he sacrificed the greatest treasure that remained to him—he sold his snuff-box. And then nothing was left but a heap of disagreeables, a mass of corruption, a senile and disgusting old man fit only for the charity of nuns and the protection of an asylum. There the clergyman begged him to pray. " 'I do try,' he said, but he added something which made me doubt whether he understood me." Certainly, he would try; for the clergyman wished it and he had always been polite. He had been polite to thieves and to duchesses and to God Himself. But it was no use trying any longer. He could believe in nothing now except a hot fire, sweet biscuits, and another cup of coffee if he asked for it. And so there was nothing for it but that the Beau who had been compact of grace and sweetness should be shuffled into the grave like any other ill-dressed, ill-bred, unneeded old man. Still, one must remember that Byron, in his moments of dandyism, "always pronounced the name of Brummell with a mingled emotion of respect and jealousy."

[Note.—Mr. Berry of St. James's Street has courteously drawn my attention to the fact that Beau Brummell certainly visited England in 1822. He came to the famous wine-shop on 26th July 1822 and was weighed as usual. His weight was then 10 stones 13 pounds. On the previous occasion, 6th July 1815, his weight was 12 stones 10 pounds. Mr. Berry adds that there is no record of his coming after 1822.]

III
MARY WOLLSTONECRAFT

Great wars are strangely intermittent in their effects. The French Revolution took some people and tore them asunder; others it passed over without disturbing a hair of their heads. Jane Austen, it is said, never mentioned it; Charles Lamb ignored it; Beau Brummell never gave the matter a thought. But to Wordsworth and to Godwin it was the dawn; unmistakably they saw

> France standing on the top of golden hours,
> And human nature seeming born again.

Thus it would be easy for a picturesque historian to lay side by side the most glaring contrasts—here in Chesterfield Street was Beau Brummell letting his chin fall carefully upon his cravat and discussing in a tone studiously free from vulgar emphasis the proper cut of the lapel of a coat; and here in Somers Town was a party of ill-dressed, excited young men, one with a head too big for his body and a nose too long for his face, holding forth day by day over the tea-cups upon human perfectibility, ideal unity, and the rights of man. There was also a woman present with very bright eyes and a very eager tongue, and the young men, who had middle-class names, like Barlow and Holcroft and Godwin, called her simply "Wollstonecraft," as if it did not matter whether she were married or unmarried, as if she were a young man like themselves.

Such glaring discords among intelligent people—for Charles Lamb and Godwin, Jane Austen and Mary Wollstonecraft were all highly intelligent—suggest how much influence circumstances have upon opinions. If Godwin had been brought up in the precincts of the Temple and had drunk deep of antiquity and old letters at Christ's Hospital, he might never have cared a straw for the future of man and his rights in general. If Jane Austen had lain as a child on the landing to prevent her father from thrashing her mother, her soul might have burnt with such a passion against tyranny that all her novels might have been consumed in one cry for justice.

Such had been Mary Wollstonecraft's first experience of the joys of married life. And then her sister Everina had been married miserably and had bitten her wedding ring to pieces in the coach. Her brother had been a burden on her; her father's farm had failed, and in order to start that disreputable man with the red face and the violent temper and the dirty hair in life again she had gone into bondage among the aristocracy as a governess—in short, she had never known what happiness was, and, in its default, had fabricated a creed fitted to meet the sordid misery of real human life. The staple of her doctrine was that nothing mattered save independence. "Every obligation we receive from our fellow-creatures is a new shackle, takes from our native freedom, and debases the mind." Independence was the first necessity for a woman; not grace or charm, but energy and courage and the power to put her will into effect were her necessary qualities. It was her highest boast to be able to say, "I never yet resolved to do anything of consequence that I did not adhere readily to it." Certainly Mary could say this with truth. When she was a little more than thirty she could look back upon a series of actions which she had carried out in the teeth of opposition. She had taken a house by prodigious efforts for her friend Fanny, only to find that Fanny's mind was changed and she did not want a house after all. She had started a school. She had persuaded Fanny into marrying Mr. Skeys. She had thrown up her school and gone to Lisbon alone to nurse Fanny when she died. On the voyage back she had forced the captain of the ship to rescue a wrecked French vessel by threatening to expose him if he refused. And when, overcome by a passion for Fuseli, she declared her wish to live with him and was refused flatly by his wife, she had put her principle of decisive action instantly into effect, and had gone to Paris determined to make her living by her pen.

The Revolution thus was not merely an event that had happened outside her; it was an active agent in her own blood. She had been in revolt all her life—against tyranny, against law, against convention. The reformer's love of humanity, which has so much of hatred in it as well as love, fermented within her. The outbreak of revolution in France expressed some of her deepest theories and convictions, and she dashed off in the heat of that extraordinary moment those two eloquent and daring books—the *Reply to Burke* and the *Vindication of the Rights of Woman*, which are so true that they seem now to contain nothing new in them—their originality has become our commonplace. But when she was in Paris lodging by herself in a great house, and saw with her own eyes the King whom she despised driving past surrounded by National Guards and holding himself with greater dignity than she expected, then, "I can scarcely tell you why," the tears came to her eyes. "I am going to bed," the letter ended, "and, for the first time in my life, I cannot put out the candle." Things were not so simple after all. She could not understand even her own feelings. She saw the most cherished of her convictions put into practice—and her eyes filled with tears. She had won fame and independence and the right to live her own life—and she wanted something different. "I do not want to be loved like a goddess," she wrote, "but I wish to be necessary to you." For Imlay, the fascinating American to whom her letter was addressed, had been very good to her. Indeed, she had fallen passionately in love with him. But it was one of her theories that love should be free—"that mutual affection was marriage and that the marriage tie should not bind after the death of love, if love should die." And yet at the same time that she wanted freedom she wanted certainty. "I like the word affection," she wrote, "because it signifies something habitual."

The conflict of all these contradictions shows itself in her face, at once so resolute and so dreamy, so sensual and so intelligent, and beautiful into the bargain with its great coils of hair and the large bright eyes that Southey thought the most expressive he had ever seen. The life of such a woman was bound to be tempestuous. Every day she made theories by which life should be lived; and every day she came smack against the rock of other people's prejudices. Every day too—for she was no pedant, no cold-blooded theorist—something was born in her that thrust aside her theories and forced her to model them afresh. She acted upon her theory that she had no legal claim upon Imlay; she refused to marry him; but when he left her alone week after week with the child she had borne him her agony was unendurable.

Thus distracted, thus puzzling even to herself, the plausible and treacherous Imlay cannot be altogether blamed for failing to follow the rapidity of her changes and the alternate reason and unreason of her moods. Even friends whose liking was impartial were disturbed by her discrepancies. Mary had a passionate, an exuberant, love of Nature, and yet one night when the colours in the sky were so exquisite that Madeleine Schweizer could not help saying to her, "Come, Mary—come, nature lover—and enjoy this wonderful spectacle—this constant transition from colour to colour." Mary never took her eyes off the Baron de Wolzogen. "I must confess," wrote Madame Schweizer, "that this erotic absorption made such a disagreeable impression on me, that all my pleasure vanished." But if the sentimental Swiss was disconcerted by Mary's sensuality, Imlay, the shrewd man of business, was exasperated by her intelligence. Whenever he saw her he yielded to her charm, but then her quickness, her penetration, her uncompromising idealism harassed him. She saw through his excuses; she met all his reasons; she was even capable of managing his business. There was no peace with her—he must be off again. And then her letters followed him, torturing him with their sincerity and their insight. They were so outspoken; then pleaded so passionately to be told the truth; they showed such a contempt for soap and alum and wealth and comfort; they repeated, as he suspected, so truthfully that he had only to say the word, "and you shall never hear of me more," that he could not endure it. Tickling minnows he had hooked a dolphin, and the creature rushed him through the waters till he was dizzy and only wanted to escape. After all, though he had played at theory-making too, he was a business man, he depended upon soap and alum; "the secondary pleasures of life," he had to admit, "are very necessary to my comfort." And among them was one that for ever evaded Mary's jealous scrutiny. Was it business, was it politics, was it a woman that perpetually took him away from her? He shillied and shallied; he was very charming when they met; then he disappeared again. Exasperated at last, and half insane with suspicion, she forced the truth from the cook. A little actress in a strolling company was his mistress, she learnt. True to her own creed of decisive action, Mary at once soaked her skirts so that she might sink unfailingly, and threw herself from Putney Bridge. But she was rescued; after unspeakable agony she recovered, and then her "unconquerable greatness of mind," her girlish creed of independence, asserted itself again, and she determined to make another bid for happiness and to earn her living without taking a penny from Imlay for herself or their child.

It was in this crisis that she again saw Godwin, the little man with the big head, whom she had met when the French Revolution was making the young men in Somers Town think that a new world was being born. She met him—but that is a euphemism, for in fact Mary Wollstonecraft actually visited him in his own house. Was it the effect of the French Revolution? Was it the blood she had seen spilt on the pavement and the cries of the furious crowd that had run in her ears that made it seem a matter of no importance whether she put on her cloak and went to visit Godwin in Somers Town, or waited in Judd Street West for Godwin to come to her? And what strange upheaval of human life was it that inspired that curious man, who was so queer a mixture of meanness and magnanimity, of coldness and deep feeling—for the memoir of his wife could not have been written without unusual depth of heart—to hold the view that she did right—that he respected Mary for trampling upon the idiotic convention by which women's lives were tied down? He held the most extraordinary views on many subjects, and upon the relations of the sexes in particular. He thought that reason should influence even the love between men and women. He thought that there was something spiritual in their relationship. He had written that "marriage is a law, and the worst of all laws . . . marriage is an affair of property, and the worst of all properties." He held the belief that if two people of the opposite sex like each other, they should live together without any ceremony, or, for living together is apt to blunt love, twenty doors off, say, in the same street. And he went further; he said that if another man liked your wife "this will create no difficulty. We may all enjoy her conversation, and we shall all be wise enough to consider the sensual intercourse a very trivial object." True, when he wrote those words he had never been in love; now for the first time he was to experience that sensation. It came very quietly and naturally, growing "with equal advances in the mind of each" from those talks in Somers Town, from those discussions upon everything under the sun which they held so improperly alone in his rooms. "It was friendship melting into love . . . ," he wrote. "When, in the course of things, the disclosure came, there was nothing in a manner for either party to disclose to the other." Certainly they were in agreement upon the most essential points; they were both of opinion, for instance, that marriage was unnecessary. They would continue to live apart. Only when Nature again intervened, and Mary found herself with child, was it worth while to lose valued friends, she asked, for the sake of a theory? She thought not, and they were married. And then that other theory—that it is best for husband and wife to live apart—was not that also incompatible with other feelings that were coming to birth in her? "A husband is a convenient part of the furniture of the house," she wrote. Indeed, she discovered that she was passionately domestic. Why not, then, revise that theory too, and share the same roof? Godwin should have a room some doors off to work in; and they should dine out separately if they liked—their work, their friends, should be separate. Thus they settled it, and the plan worked admirably. The arrangement combined "the novelty and lively sensation of a visit with the more delicious and heartfelt pleasures of domestic life." Mary admitted that she was happy; Godwin confessed that, after all one's philosophy, it was "extremely gratifying" to find that "there is some one who takes an interest in one's happiness." All sorts of powers and emotions were liberated in Mary by her new satisfaction. Trifles gave her an exquisite pleasure—the sight of Godwin and Imlay's child playing together; the thought of their own child who was to be born; a day's jaunt into the country. One day, meeting Imlay in the New Road, she greeted him without bitterness. But, as Godwin wrote, "Ours is not an idle happiness, a paradise of selfish and transitory pleasures." No, it too was an experiment, as Mary's life had been an experiment from the start, an attempt to make human conventions conform more closely to human needs. And their marriage was only a beginning; all sorts of things were to follow after. Mary was going to have a child. She was going to write a book to be called *The Wrongs of Women.* She was going to reform education. She was going to come down to dinner the day after her child was born. She was going to employ a midwife and not a doctor at her confinement—but that experiment was her last. She died in child-birth. She whose sense of her own existence was so intense, who had cried out even in her misery, "I cannot bear to think of being no more—of losing myself—nay, it appears to me impossible that I should cease to exist," died at the age of thirty-six. But she has her revenge. Many millions have died and been forgotten in the hundred and thirty years that have passed since she was buried; and yet as we read her letters and listen to her arguments and consider her experiments, above all that most fruitful experiment, her relation with Godwin, and realise the high-handed and hot-blooded manner in which she cut her way to the quick of life, one form of immortality is hers undoubtedly: she is alive and active, she argues and experiments, we hear her voice and trace her influence even now among the living.

IV
DOROTHY WORDSWORTH

Two highly incongruous travellers, Mary Wollstonecraft and Dorothy Wordsworth, followed close upon each other's footsteps. Mary was in Altona on the Elbe in 1795 with her baby; three years later Dorothy came there with her brother and Coleridge. Both kept a record of their travels; both saw the same places, but the eyes with which they saw them were very different. Whatever Mary saw served to start her mind upon some theory, upon the effect of government, upon the state of the people, upon the mystery of her own soul. The beat of the oars on the waves made her ask, "Life, what are you? Where goes this breath? This *I* so much alive? In what element will it mix, giving and receiving fresh energy?" And sometimes she forgot to look at the sunset and looked instead at the Baron Wolzogen. Dorothy, on the other hand, noted what was before her accurately, literally, and with prosaic precision. "The walk very pleasing between Hamburgh and Altona. A large piece of ground planted with trees, and intersected by gravel walks. . . . The ground on the opposite side of the Elbe appears marshy." Dorothy never railed against "the cloven hoof of despotism." Dorothy never asked "men's questions" about exports and imports; Dorothy never confused her own soul with the sky. This "*I* so much alive" was ruthlessly subordinated to the trees and the grass. For if she let "I" and its rights and its wrongs and its passions and its suffering get between her and the object, she would be calling the moon "the Queen of the Night"; she would be talking of dawn's "orient beams"; she would be soaring into reveries and rhapsodies and forgetting to find the exact phrase for the ripple of moonlight upon the lake. It was like "herrings in the water"—she could not have said that if she had been thinking about herself. So while Mary dashed her head against wall after wall, and cried out, "Surely something resides in this heart that is not perishable—and life is more than a dream," Dorothy went on methodically at Alfoxden noting the approach of spring. "The sloe in blossom, the hawthorn green, the larches in the park changed from black to green, in two or three days." And next day, 14th April 1798, "the evening very stormy, so we staid indoors. Mary Wollstonecraft's life, &c., came." And the day after they walked in the squire's grounds and noticed that "Nature was very successfully striving to make beautiful what art had deformed—ruins, hermitages, &c., &c." There is no reference to Mary Wollstonecraft; it seems as if her life and all its storms had been swept away in one of those compendious et ceteras, and yet the next sentence reads like an unconscious comment. "Happily we cannot shape the huge hills, or carve out the valleys according to our fancy." No, we cannot reform, we must not rebel; we can only accept and try to understand the message of Nature. And so the notes go on.

Spring passed; summer came; summer turned to autumn; it was winter, and then again the sloes were in blossom and the hawthorns green and spring had come. But it was spring in the North now, and Dorothy was living alone with her brother in a small cottage at Grasmere in the midst of the hills. Now after the hardships and separations of youth they were together under their own roof; now they could address themselves undisturbed to the absorbing occupation of living in the heart of Nature and trying, day by day, to read her meaning. They had money enough at last to let them live together without the need of earning a penny. No family duties or professional tasks distracted them. Dorothy could ramble all day on the hills and sit up talking to Coleridge all night without being scolded by her aunt for unwomanly behaviour. The hours were theirs from sunrise to sunset, and could be altered to suit the season. If it was fine, there was no need to come in; if it was wet, there was no need to get up. One could go to bed at any hour. One could let the dinner cool if the cuckoo were shouting on the hill and William had not found the exact epithet he wanted. Sunday was a day like any other. Custom, convention, everything was subordinated to the absorbing, exacting, exhausting task of living in the heart of Nature and writing poetry. For exhausting it was. William would make his head ache in the effort to find the right word. He would go on hammering at a poem until Dorothy was afraid to suggest an alteration. A chance phrase of hers would run in his head and make it impossible for him to get back into the proper mood. He would come down to breakfast and sit "with his shirt neck unbuttoned, and his waistcoat open," writing a poem on a Butterfly which some story of hers had suggested, and he would eat nothing, and then he would begin altering the poem and again would be exhausted.

It is strange how vividly all this is brought before us considering that the diary is made of brief notes such as any quiet woman might make of her garden's changes and her brother's moods and the progress of the seasons. It was warm and mild, she notes, after a day of rain. She met a cow in a field. "The cow looked at me, and I looked at the cow, and whenever I stirred the cow gave over eating." She met an old man who walked with two sticks—for days on end she met nothing more out of the way than a cow eating and an old man walking. And her motives for writing are common enough—"because I will not quarrel with myself, and because I shall give William pleasure by it when he comes home again." It is only gradually that the difference between this rough notebook and others discloses itself; only by degrees that the brief notes unfurl in the mind and open a whole landscape before us, that the plain statement proves to be aimed so directly at the object that if we look exactly along the line that it points we shall see precisely what she saw. "The moonlight lay upon the hills like snow." "The air was become still, the lake of a bright slate colour, the hills darkening. The bays shot into the low fading shores. Sheep resting. All things quiet." "There was no one waterfall above another—it was the sound of waters in the air—the voice of the air." Even in such brief notes one feels the suggestive power which is the gift of the poet rather than of the naturalist, the power which, taking only the simplest facts, so orders them that the whole scene comes before us, heightened and composed, the lake in its quiet, the hills in their splendour. Yet she was no descriptive writer in the usual sense. Her first concern was to be truthful—grace and symmetry must be made subordinate to truth. But then truth is sought because to falsify the look of the stir of the breeze on the lake is to tamper with the spirit which inspires appearances. It is that spirit which goads her and urges her and keeps her faculties for ever on the stretch. A sight or a sound would not let her be till she had traced her perception along its course and fixed it in words, though they might be bald, or in an image, though it might be angular. Nature was a stern taskmistress. The exact prosaic detail must be rendered as well as the vast and visionary outline. Even when the distant hills trembled before her in the glory of a dream she must note with literal accuracy "the glittering silver line on the ridge of the backs of the sheep," or remark how "the crows at a little distance from us became white as silver as they flew in the sunshine, and when they went still further, they looked like shapes of water passing over the green fields." Always trained and in use, her powers of observation became in time so expert and so acute that a day's walk stored her mind's eye with a vast assembly of curious objects to be sorted at leisure. How strange the sheep looked mixed with the soldiers at Dumbarton Castle! For some reason the sheep looked their real size, but the soldiers looked like puppets. And then the movements of the sheep were so natural and fearless, and the motion of the dwarf soldiers was so restless and apparently without meaning. It was extremely queer. Or lying in bed she would look up at the ceiling and think how the varnished beams were "as glossy as black rocks on a sunny day cased in ice." Yes, they

> crossed each other in almost as intricate and fantastic a manner as I have seen the underboughs of a large beech-tree withered by the depth of the shade above. . . . It was like what I should suppose an underground cave or temple to be, with a dripping or moist roof, and the moonlight entering in upon it by some means or other, and yet the colours were more like melted gems. I lay looking up till the light of the fire faded away. . . . I did not sleep much.

Indeed, she scarcely seemed to shut her eyes. They looked and they looked, urged on not only by an indefatigable curiosity but also by reverence, as if some secret of the utmost importance lay hidden beneath the surface. Her pen sometimes stammers with the intensity of the emotion that she controlled as De Quincey said that her tongue stammered with the conflict between her ardour and her shyness when she spoke. But controlled she was. Emotional and impulsive by nature, her eyes "wild and starting," tormented by feelings which almost mastered her, still she must control, still she must repress, or she would fail in her task—she would cease to see. But if one subdued oneself, and resigned one's private agitations, then, as if in reward, Nature would bestow an exquisite satisfaction. "Rydale was very beautiful, with spear-shaped streaks of polished steel. . . . It calls home the heart to quietness. I had been very melancholy," she wrote. For did not Coleridge come walking over the hills and tap at the cottage door late at night—did she not carry a letter from Coleridge hidden safe in her bosom?

Thus giving to Nature, thus receiving from Nature, it seemed, as the arduous and ascetic days went by, that Nature and Dorothy had grown together in perfect sympathy—a sympathy not cold or vegetable or inhuman because at the core of it burnt that other love for "my beloved," her brother, who was indeed its heart and inspiration. William and Nature and Dorothy herself, were they not one being? Did they not compose a trinity, self-contained and self-sufficient and independent whether indoors or out? They sit indoors. It was

> about ten o'clock and a quiet night. The fire flickers and the watch ticks. I hear nothing but the breathing of my Beloved as he now and then pushes his book forward, and turns over a leaf.

And now it is an April day, and they take the old cloak and lie in John's grove out of doors together.

> William heard me breathing, and rustling now and then, but we both lay still and unseen by one another. He thought that it would be sweet thus to lie in the grave, to hear the peaceful sounds of the earth, and just to know that our dear friends were near. The lake was still; there was a boat out.

It was a strange love, profound, almost dumb, as if brother and sister had grown together and shared not the speech but the mood, so that they hardly knew which felt, which spoke, which saw the daffodils or the sleeping city; only Dorothy stored the mood in prose, and later William came and bathed in it and made it into poetry. But one could not act without the other. They must feel, they must think, they must be together. So now, when they had lain out on the hillside they would rise and go home and make tea, and Dorothy would write to Coleridge, and they would sow the scarlet beans together, and William would work at his "Leech Gatherer," and Dorothy would copy the lines for him. Rapt but controlled, free yet strictly ordered, the homely narrative moves naturally from ecstasy on the hills to baking bread and ironing linen and fetching William his supper in the cottage.

The cottage, though its garden ran up into the fells, was on the highroad. Through her parlour window Dorothy looked out and saw whoever might be passing—a tall beggar woman perhaps with her baby on her back; an old soldier; a coroneted landau with touring ladies peering inquisitively inside. The rich and the great she would let pass—they interested her no more than cathedrals or picture galleries or great cities; but she could never see a beggar at the door without asking him in and questioning him closely. Where had he been? What had he seen? How many children had he? She searched into the lives of the poor as if they held in them the same secret as the hills. A tramp eating cold bacon over the kitchen fire might have been a starry night, so closely she watched him; so clearly she noted how his old coat was patched "with three bell-shaped patches of darker blue behind, where the buttons had been," how his beard of a fortnight's growth was like "grey *plush*." And then as they rambled on with their tales of seafaring and the pressgang and the Marquis of Granby, she never failed to capture the one phrase that sounds on in the mind after the story is forgotten, "What, you are stepping westward?" "To be sure there is great promise for virgins in Heaven." "She could trip lightly by the graves of those who died when they were young." The poor had their poetry as the hills had theirs. But it was out of doors, on the road or on the moor, not in the cottage parlour, that her imagination had freest play. Her happiest moments were passed tramping beside a jibbing horse on a wet Scottish road without certainty of bed or supper. All she knew was that there was some sight ahead, some grove of trees to be noted, some waterfall to be inquired into. On they tramped hour after hour in silence for the most part, though Coleridge, who was of the party, would suddenly begin to debate aloud the true meaning of the words majestic, sublime, and grand. They had to trudge on foot because the horse had thrown the cart over a bank and the harness was only mended with string and pocket-handkerchiefs. They were hungry, too, because Wordsworth had dropped the chicken and the breed into the lake, and they had nothing else for dinner. They were uncertain of the way, and did not know where they would find lodging: all they knew was that there was a waterfall ahead. At last Coleridge could stand it no longer. He had rheumatism in the joints; the Irish jaunting car provided no shelter from the weather; his companions were silent and absorbed. He left them. But William and Dorothy tramped on. They looked like tramps themselves. Dorothy's cheeks were brown as a gipsy's, her clothes were shabby, her gait was rapid and ungainly. But still she was indefatigable; her eye never failed her; she noticed everything. At last they reached the waterfall. And then all Dorothy's powers fell upon it. She searched out its character, she noted its resemblances, she defined its differences, with all the ardour of a discoverer, with all the exactness of a naturalist, with all the rapture of a lover. She possessed it at last—she had laid it up in her mind for ever. It had become one of those "inner visions" which she could call to mind at any time in their distinctness and in their particularity. It would come back to her long years afterwards when she was old and her mind had failed her; it would come back stilled and heightened and mixed with all the happiest memories of her past—with the thought of Racedown and Alfoxden and Coleridge reading "Christabel," and her beloved, her brother William. It would bring with it what no human being could give, what no human relation could offer—consolation and quiet. If, then, the passionate cry of Mary Wollstonecraft had reached her ears—"Surely something resides in this heart that is not perishable—and life is more than a dream"—she would have had no doubt whatever as to her answer. She would have said quite simply, "We looked about us, and felt that we were happy."

❋

William Hazlitt

❋

Had one met Hazlitt no doubt one would have liked him on his own principle that "We can scarcely hate any one we know." But Hazlitt has been dead now a hundred years, and it is perhaps a question how far we can know him well enough to overcome those feelings of dislike, both personal and intellectual, which his writings still so sharply arouse. For Hazlitt—it is one of his prime merits—was not one of those non-committal writers who shuffle off in a mist and die of their own insignificance. His essays are emphatically himself. He has no reticence and he has no shame. He tells us exactly what he thinks, and he tells us—the confidence is less seductive—exactly what he feels. As of all men he had the most intense consciousness of his own existence, since never a day passed without inflicting on him some pang of hate or of jealousy, some thrill of anger or of pleasure, we cannot read him for long without coming in contact with a very singular character—ill conditioned yet high minded; mean yet noble; intensely egotistical yet inspired by the most genuine passion for the rights and liberties of mankind.

Soon, so thin is the veil of the essay as Hazlitt wore it, his very look comes before us. We see him as Coleridge saw him, "browhanging, shoe-contemplative, strange." He comes shuffling into the room, he looks nobody straight in the face, he shakes hands with the fin of a fish; occasionally he darts a malignant glance from his corner. "His manners are 99 in a 100 singularly repulsive," Coleridge said. Yet now and again his face lit up with intellectual beauty, and his manner became radiant with sympathy and understanding. Soon, too, as we read on, we become familiar with the whole gamut of his grudges and his grievances. He lived, one gathers, mostly at inns. No woman's form graced his board. He had quarrelled with all his old friends, save perhaps with Lamb. Yet his only fault had been that he had stuck to his principles and "not become a government tool." He was the object of malignant persecution—Blackwood's reviewers called him "pimply Hazlitt," though his cheek was pale as alabaster. These lies, however, got into print, and then he was afraid to visit his friends because the footman had read the newspaper and the housemaid tittered behind his back. He had —no one could deny it—one of the finest minds, and he wrote indisputably the best prose style of his time. But what did that avail with women? Fine ladies have no respect for scholars, nor chambermaids either—so the growl and plaint of his grievances keeps breaking through, disturbing us, irritating us; and yet there is something so independent, subtle, fine, and enthusiastic about him—when he can forget himself he is so rapt in ardent speculation about other things—that dislike crumbles and turns to something much warmer and more complex. Hazlitt was right:

> It is the mask only that we dread and hate; the man may have something human about him! The notions in short which we entertain of people at a distance, or from partial representation, or from guess-work, are simple, uncompounded ideas, which answer to nothing in reality; those which we derive from experience are mixed modes, the only true and, in general, the most favourable ones.

Certainly no one could read Hazlitt and maintain a simple and uncompounded idea of him. From the first he was a twy-minded man—one of those divided natures which are inclined almost equally to two quite opposite careers. It is significant that his first impulse was not to essay-writing but to painting and philosophy. There was something in the remote and silent art of the painter that offered a refuge to his tormented spirit. He noted enviously how happy the old age of painters was—"their minds keep alive to the last"; he turned longingly to the calling that takes one out of doors, among fields and woods, that deals with bright pigments, and has solid brush and canvas for its tools and not merely black ink and white paper. Yet at the same time he was bitten by an abstract curiosity that would not let him rest in the contemplation of concrete beauty. When he was a boy of fourteen he heard his father, the good Unitarian minister, dispute with an old lady of the congregation as they were coming out of Meeting as to the limits of religious toleration, and, he said, "it was this circumstance that decided the fate of my future life." It set him off "forming in my head . . . the following system of political rights and general jurisprudence." He wished "to be satisfied of the reason of things." The two ideals were ever after to clash. To be a thinker and to express in the plainest and most accurate of terms "the reason of things," and to be a painter gloating over blues and crimsons, breathing fresh air and living sensually in the emotions—these were two different, perhaps incompatible ideals, yet like all Hazlitt's emotions both were tough and each strove for mastery. He yielded now to one, now to the other. He spent months in Paris copying pictures at the Louvre. He came home and toiled laboriously at the portrait of an old woman in a bonnet day after day, seeking by industry and pains to discover the secret of Rembrandt's genius; but he lacked some quality—perhaps it was invention—and in the end cut the canvas to ribbons in a rage or turned it against the wall in despair. At the same time he was writing the *Essay on the Principles of Human Action* which he preferred to all his other works. For there he wrote plainly and truthfully, without glitter or garishness, without any wish to please or to make money, but solely to gratify the urgency of his own desire for truth. Naturally, "the book dropped still-born from the press." Then, too, his political hopes, his belief that the age of freedom had come and that the tyranny of kingship was over, proved vain. His friends deserted to the Government, and he was left to uphold the doctrines of liberty, fraternity, and revolution in that perpetual minority which requires so much self-approval to support it.

Thus he was a man of divided tastes and of thwarted ambition; a man whose happiness, even in early life, lay behind. His mind had set early and bore for ever the stamp of first impressions. In his happiest moods he looked not forwards but backwards—to the garden where he had played as a child, to the blue hills of Shropshire and to all those landscapes which he had seen when hope was still his, and peace brooded upon him and he looked up from his painting or his book and saw the fields and woods as if they were the outward expression of his own inner quietude. It is to the books that he read then that he returns—to Rousseau and to Burke and to the *Letters of Junius*. The impression that they made upon his youthful imagination was never effaced and scarcely overlaid; for after youth was over he ceased to read for pleasure, and youth and the pure and intense pleasures of youth were soon left behind.

Naturally, given his susceptibility to the charms of the other sex, he married; and naturally, given his consciousness of his own "misshapen form made to be mocked," he married unhappily. Miss Sarah Stoddart pleased him when he met her at the Lambs by the common sense with which she found the kettle and boiled it when Mary absent-mindedly delayed. But of domestic talents she had none. Her little income was insufficient to meet the burden of married life, and Hazlitt soon found that instead of spending eight years in writing eight pages he must turn journalist and write articles upon politics and plays and pictures and books of the right length, at the right moment. Soon the mantelpiece of the old house at York Street where Milton had lived was scribbled over with ideas for essays. As the habit proves, the house was not a tidy house, nor did geniality and comfort excuse the lack of order. The Hazlitts were to be found eating breakfast at two in the afternoon, without a fire in the grate or a curtain to the window. A valiant walker and a clear-sighted woman, Mrs. Hazlitt had no delusions about her husband. He was not faithful to her, and she faced the fact with admirable common sense. But "he said that I had always despised him and his abilities," she noted in her diary, and that was carrying common sense too far. The prosaic marriage came lamely to an end. Free at last from the encumbrance of home and husband, Sarah Hazlitt pulled on her boots and set off on a walking tour through Scotland, while Hazlitt, incapable of attachment or comfort, wandered from inn to inn, suffered tortures of humiliation and disillusionment, but, as he drank cup after cup of very strong tea and made love to the inn-keeper's daughter, he wrote those essays that are of course among the very best that we have.

That they are not quite the best—that they do not haunt the mind and remain entire in the memory as the essays of Montaigne or Lamb haunt the mind—is also true. He seldom reaches the perfection of these great writers or their unity. Perhaps it is the nature of these short pieces that they need unity and a mind at harmony with itself. A little jar there makes the whole composition tremble. The essays of Montaigne, Lamb, even Addison, have the reticence which springs from composure, for with all their familiarity they never tell us what they wish to keep hidden. But with Hazlitt it is different. There is always something divided and discordant even in his finest essays, as if two minds were at work who never succeed save for a few moments in making a match of it. In the first place there is the mind of the inquiring boy who wishes to be satisfied of the reason of things—the mind of the thinker. It is the thinker for the most part who is allowed the choice of the subject. He chooses some abstract idea, like Envy, or Egotism, or Reason and Imagination. He treats it with energy and independence. He explores its ramifications and scales its narrow paths as if it were a mountain road and the ascent both difficult and inspiring. Compared with this athletic progress, Lamb's seems the flight of a butterfly cruising capriciously among the flowers and perching for a second incongruously here upon a barn, there upon a wheelbarrow. But every sentence in Hazlitt carries us forward. He has his end in view and, unless some accident intervenes, he strides towards it in that "pure conversational prose style" which, as he points out, is so much more difficult to practise than fine writing.

There can be no question that Hazlitt the thinker is an admirable companion. He is strong and fearless; he knows his mind and he speaks his mind forcibly yet brilliantly too, for the readers of newspapers are a dull-eyed race who must be dazzled in order to make them see. But besides Hazlitt the thinker there is Hazlitt the artist. There is the sensuous and emotional man, with his feeling for colour and touch, with his passion for prize-fighting and Sarah Walker, with his sensibility to all those emotions which disturb the reason and make it often seem futile enough to spend one's time slicing things up finer and finer with the intellect when the body of the world is so firm and so warm and demands so imperatively to be pressed to the heart. To know the reason of things is a poor substitute for being able to feel them. And Hazlitt felt with the intensity of a poet. The most abstract of his essays will suddenly glow red-hot or white-hot if something reminds him of his past. He will drop his fine analytic pen and paint a phrase or two with a full brush brilliantly and beautifully if some landscape stirs his imagination or some book brings back the hour when he first read it. The famous passages about reading *Love for Love* and drinking coffee from a silver pot, and reading *La Nouvelle Héloïse* and eating a cold chicken are known to all, and yet how oddly they often break into the context, how violently we are switched from reason to rhapsody—how embarrassingly our austere thinker falls upon our shoulders and demands our sympathy! It is this disparity and the sense of two forces in conflict that trouble the serenity and cause the inconclusiveness of some of Hazlitt's finest essays. They set out to give us a proof and they end by giving us a picture. We are about to plant our feet upon the solid rock of Q.E.D., and behold the rock turns to quagmire and we are knee-deep in mud and water and flowers. "Faces pale as the primrose with hyacinthine locks" are in our eyes; the woods of Tuderly breathe their mystic voices in our ears. Then suddenly we are recalled, and the thinker, austere, muscular, and sardonic, leads us on to analyse, to dissect, and to condemn.

Thus if we compare Hazlitt with the other great masters in his line it is easy to see where his limitations lie. His range is narrow and his sympathies few if intense. He does not open the doors wide upon all experience like Montaigne, rejecting nothing, tolerating everything, and watching the play of the soul with irony and detachment. On the contrary, his mind shut hard with egotistic tenacity upon his first impressions and froze them to unalterable convictions. Nor was it for him to make play, like Lamb, with the figures of his friends, creating them afresh in fantastic flights of imagination and reverie. His characters are seen with the same quick sidelong glance full of shrewdness and suspicion which he darted upon people in the flesh. He does not use the essayist's licence to circle and meander. He is tethered by his egotism and by his convictions to one time and one place and one being. We never forget that this is England in the early days of the nineteenth century; indeed, we feel ourselves in the Southampton Buildings or in the inn parlour that looks over the downs and on to the high road at Winterslow. He has an extraordinary power of making us contemporary with himself. But as we read on through the many volumes which he filled with so much energy and yet with so little love of his task, the comparison with the other essayists drops from us. These are not essays, it seems, independent and self-sufficient, but fragments broken off from some larger book—some searching inquiry into the reason for human actions or into the nature of human institutions. It is only accident that has cut them short, and only deference to the public taste that has decked them out with gaudy images and bright colours. The phrase which occurs in one form or another so frequently and indicates the structure which if he were free he would follow—"I will here try to go more at large into the subject and then give such instances and illustrations of it as occur to me"—could by no possibility occur in the *Essays of Elia* or *Sir Roger de Coverley*. He loves to grope among the curious depths of human psychology and to track down the reason of things. He excels in hunting out the obscure causes that lie behind some common saying or sensation, and the drawers of his mind are well stocked with illustrations and arguments. We can believe him when he says that for twenty years he had thought hard and suffered acutely. He is speaking of what he knows from experience when he exclaims, "How many ideas and trains of sentiment, long and deep and intense, often pass through the mind in only one day's thinking or reading!" Convictions are his life-blood; ideas have formed in him like stalactites, drop by drop, year by year. He has sharpened them in a thousand solitary walks; he has tested them in argument after argument, sitting in his corner, sardonically observant, over a late supper at the Southampton Inn. But he has not changed them. His mind is his own and it is made up.

Thus however threadbare the abstraction—*Hot and Cold*, or *Envy*, or *The Conduct of Life*, or *The Picturesque and the Ideal*—he has something solid to write about. He never lets his brain slacken or trusts to his great gift of picturesque phrasing to float him over a stretch of shallow thought. Even when it is plain from the savagery and contempt with which he attacks his task that he is out of the mood and only keeps his mind to the grindstone by strong tea and sheer force of will we still find him mordant and searching and acute. There is a stir and trouble, a vivacity and conflict in his essays as if the very contrariety of his gifts kept him on the stretch. He is always hating, loving, thinking, and suffering. He could never come to terms with authority or doff his own idiosyncrasy in deference to opinion. Thus chafed and goaded the level of his essays is extraordinarily high. Often dry, garish in their bright imagery, monotonous in the undeviating energy of their rhythm—for Hazlitt believed too implicitly in his own saying, "mediocrity, insipidity, want of character, is the great fault," to be an easy writer to read for long at a stretch—there is scarcely an essay without its stress of thought, its thrust of insight, its moment of penetration. His pages are full of fine sayings and unexpected turns and independence and originality. "All that is worth remembering of life is the poetry of it." "If the truth were known, the most disagreeable people are the most amiable." "You will hear more good things on the outside of a stage-coach from London to Oxford, than if you were to pass a twelve-month with the under-graduates or heads of colleges of that famous University." We are constantly plucked at by sayings that we would like to put by to examine later.

But besides the volumes of Hazlitt's essays there are the volumes of Hazlitt's criticism. In one way or another, either as lecturer or reviewer, Hazlitt strode through the greater part of English literature and delivered his opinion of the majority of famous books. His criticism has the rapidity and the daring, if it has also the looseness and the roughness, which arise from the circumstances in which it was written. He must cover a great deal of ground, make his points clear to an audience not of readers but of listeners, and has time only to point to the tallest towers and the brightest pinnacles in the landscape. But even in his most perfunctory criticism of books we feel that faculty for seizing on the important and indicating the main outline which learned critics often lose and timid critics never acquire. He is one of those rare critics who have thought so much that they can dispense with reading. It matters very little that Hazlitt had read only one poem by Donne; that he found Shakespeare's sonnets unintelligible; that he never read a book through after he was thirty; that he came indeed to dislike reading altogether. What he had read he had read with fervour. And since in his view it was the duty of a critic to "reflect the colours, the light and shade, the soul and body of a work," appetite, gusto, enjoyment were far more important than analytic subtlety or prolonged and extensive study. To communicate his own fervour was his aim. Thus he first cuts out with vigorous and direct strokes the figure of one author and contrasts it with another, and next builds up with the freest use of imagery and colour the brilliant ghost that the book has left glimmering in his mind. The poem is re-created in glowing phrases—"A rich distilled perfume emanates from it like the breath of genius; a golden cloud envelops it; a honeyed paste of poetic diction encrusts it, like the candied coat of the auricula." But since the analyst in Hazlitt is never far from the surface, this painter's imagery is kept in check by a nervous sense of the hard and lasting in literature, of what a book means and where it should be placed, which models his enthusiasm and gives it angle and outline. He singles out the peculiar quality of his author and stamps it vigorously. There is the "deep, internal, sustained sentiment" of Chaucer; "Crabbe is the only poet who has attempted and succeeded in the *still life* of tragedy." There is nothing flabby, weak, or merely ornamental in his criticism of Scott—sense and enthusiasm run hand in hand. And if such criticism is the reverse of final, if it is initiatory and inspiring rather than conclusive and complete, there is something to be said for the critic who starts the reader on a journey and fires him with a phrase to shoot off on adventures of his own. If one needs an incentive to read Burke, what is better than "Burke's style was forked and playful like the lightning, crested like the serpent"? Or again, should one be trembling on the brink of a dusty folio, the following passage is enough to plunge one in midstream:

It is delightful to repose on the wisdom of the ancients; to have some great name at hand, besides one's own initials always staring one in the face; to travel out of one's self into the Chaldee, Hebrew, and Egyptian characters; to have the palm-trees waving mystically in the margin of the page, and the camels moving slowly on in the distance of three thousand years. In that dry desert of learning, we gather strength and patience, and a strange and insatiable thirst of knowledge. The ruined monuments of antiquity are also there, and the fragments of buried cities (under which the adder lurks) and cool springs, and green sunny spots, and the whirlwind and the lion's roar, and the shadow of angelic wings.

Needless to say that is not criticism. It is sitting in an armchair and gazing into the fire, and building up image after image of what one has seen in a book. It is loving and taking the liberties of a lover. It is being Hazlitt.

But it is likely that Hazlitt will survive not in his lectures, nor in his travels, nor in his *Life of Napoleon*, nor in his *Conversations of Northcote*, full as they are of energy and integrity, of broken and fitful splendour and shadowed with the shape of some vast unwritten book that looms on the horizon. He will live in a volume of essays in which is distilled all those powers that are dissipated and distracted elsewhere, where the parts of his complex and tortured spirit come together in a truce of amity and concord. Perhaps a fine day was needed, or a game of fives or a long walk in the country, to bring about this consummation. The body has a large share in everything that Hazlitt writes. Then a mood of intense and spontaneous reverie came over him; he soared into what Patmore called "a calm so pure and serene that one did not like to interrupt it." His brain worked smoothly and swiftly and without consciousness of its own operations; the pages dropped without an erasure from his pen. Then his mind ranged in a rhapsody of well-being over books and love, over the past and its beauty, the present and its comfort, and the future that would bring a partridge hot from the oven or a dish of sausages sizzling in the pan.

> I look out of my window and see that a shower has just fallen: the fields look green after it, and a rosy cloud hangs over the brow of the hill; a lily expands its petals in the moisture, dressed in its lovely green and white; a shepherd-boy has just brought some pieces of turf with daisies and grass for his young mistress to make a bed for her skylark, not doomed to dip his wings in the dappled dawn—my cloudy thoughts draw off, the storm of angry politics has blown over—Mr. Blackwood, I am yours—Mr. Croker, my service to you—Mr. T. Moore, I am alive and well.

There is then no division, no discord, no bitterness. The different faculties work in harmony and unity. Sentence follows sentence with the healthy ring and chime of a blacksmith's hammer on the anvil; the words glow and the sparks fly; gently they fade and the essay is over. And as his writing had such passages of inspired description, so, too, his life had its seasons of intense enjoyment. When he lay dying a hundred years ago in a lodging in Soho his voice rang out with the old pugnacity and conviction: "Well, I have had a happy life." One has only to read him to believe it.

*

Geraldine and Jane

*

Geraldine Jewsbury would certainly not have expected anybody at this time of day to bother themselves about her novels. If she had caught one pulling the down from the shelf in some library she would have expostulated. "They're such nonsense, my dear," she would have said. And then one likes to fancy that she would have burst out in that irresponsible, unconventional way of hers against libraries and literature and love and life and all the rest of it with a "Damn it all!" or a "Confound it!" for Geraldine was fond of swearing.

The odd thing about Geraldine Jewsbury, indeed, was the way in which she combined oaths and endearments, sense and effervescence, daring and gush: ". . . defenceless and tender on the one hand, and strong enough to cleave the very rocks on the other"—that is how Mrs. Ireland, her biographer, puts it; or again: "Intellectually she was a man, but the heart within her was as womanly as ever daughter of Eve could boast." Even to look at there was, it would seem, something incongruous, queer, provocative about her. She was very small and yet boyish; very ugly yet attractive. She dressed very well, wore her reddish hair in a net, and ear-rings made in the form of miniature parrots swung in her ears as she talked. There, in the only portrait we have of her, she sits reading, with her face half-turned away, defenceless and tender at the moment rather than cleaving the very rocks.

But what had happened to her before she sat at the photographer's table reading her book it is impossible to say. Until she was twenty-nine we know nothing of her except that she was born in the year 1812, was the daughter of a merchant, and lived in Manchester, or near it. In the first part of the nineteenth century a woman of twenty-nine was no longer young; she had lived her life or she had missed it. And though Geraldine, with her unconventional ways, was an exception, still it cannot be doubted that something very tremendous had happened in those dim years before we know her. Something had happened in Manchester. An obscure male figure looms in the background—a faithless but fascinating creature who had taught her that life is treacherous, life is hard, life is the very devil for a woman. A dark pool of experience had formed in the back of her mind into which she would dip for the consolation or for the instruction of others. "Oh! it is too frightful to talk about. For two years I lived only in short respites from this blackness of darkness," she exclaimed from time to time. There had been seasons "like dreary, calm November days when there is but one cloud, but that one covers the whole heaven." She had struggled, "but struggling is no use." She had read Cudworth though. She had written an essay upon materialism before giving way. For, though the prey to so many emotions, she was also oddly detached and speculative. She liked to puzzle her head with questions about "matter and spirit and the nature of life" even while her heart was bleeding. Upstairs there was a box full of extracts, abstracts, and conclusions. Yet what conclusion could a woman come to? Did anything avail a woman when love had deserted her, when her lover had played her false? No. It was useless to struggle; one had better let the wave engulf one, the cloud close over one's head. So she meditated, lying often on a sofa with a piece of knitting in her hands and a green shade over her eyes. For she suffered from a variety of ailments—sore eyes, colds, nameless exhaustion; and Greenheys, the suburb outside Manchester, where she kept house for her brother, was very damp. "Dirty, half-melted snow and fog, a swampy meadow, set off by a creeping cold damp"—that was the view from her window. Often she could hardly drag herself across the room. And then there were incessant interruptions: somebody had come unexpectedly for dinner; she had to jump up and run into the kitchen and cook a fowl with her own hands. That done, she would put on her green shade and peer at her book again, for she was a great reader. She read metaphysics, she read travels, she read old books and new books—and especially the wonderful books of Mr. Carlyle.

Early in the year 1841 she came to London and secured an introduction to the great man whose works she so much admired. She met Mrs. Carlyle. They must have become intimate with great rapidity. In a few weeks Mrs. Carlyle was "dearest Jane." They must have discussed everything. They must have talked about life and the past and the present, and certain "individuals" who were sentimentally interested or were not sentimentally interested in Geraldine. Mrs. Carlyle, so metropolitan, so brilliant, so deeply versed in life and scornful of its humbugs, must have captivated the young woman from Manchester completely, for directly Geraldine returned to Manchester she began writing long letters to Jane which echo and continue the intimate conversations of Cheyne Row. "A man who has had *le plus grand succès* among women, and who was the most passionate and poetically refined lover in his manners and conversation you would wish to find, once said to me . . ." So she would begin. Or she would reflect:

> It may be that we women are made as we are in order that they may in some sort fertilise the world. We shall go on loving, they [the men] will go on struggling and toiling, and we are all alike mercifully allowed to die—after a while. I don't know whether you will agree to this, and I cannot see to argue, for my eyes are very bad and painful.

Probably Jane agreed to very little of all this. For Jane was eleven years the elder. Jane was not given to abstract reflections upon the nature of life. Jane was the most caustic, the most concrete, the most clear-sighted of women. But it is perhaps worth noting that when she first fell in with Geraldine she was beginning to feel those premonitions of jealousy, that uneasy sense that old relationships had shifted and that new ones were forming themselves, which had come to pass with the establishment of her husband's fame. No doubt, in the course of those long talks in Cheyne Row, Geraldine had received certain confidences, heard certain complaints, and drawn certain conclusions. For besides being a mass of emotion and sensibility, Geraldine was a clever, witty woman who thought for herself and hated what she called "respectability" as much as Mrs. Carlyle hated what she called "humbug." In addition, Geraldine had from the first the strangest feelings about Mrs. Carlyle. She felt "vague undefined yearnings to be yours in some way." "You will let me be yours and think of me as such, will you not?" she urged again and again. "I think of you as Catholics think of their saints," she said: ". . . you will laugh, but I feel towards you much more like a lover than a female friend!" No doubt Mrs. Carlyle did laugh, but also she could scarcely fail to be touched by the little creature's adoration.

Thus when Carlyle himself early in 1843 suggested unexpectedly that they should ask Geraldine to stay with them, Mrs. Carlyle, after debating the question with her usual candour, agreed. She reflected that a little of Geraldine would be "very enlivening," but, on the other hand, much of Geraldine would be very exhausting. Geraldine dropped hot tears on to one's hands; she watched one; she fussed one; she was always in a state of emotion. Then "with all her good and great qualities" Geraldine had in her "a born spirit of intrigue" which might make mischief between husband and wife, though not in the usual way, for, Mrs. Carlyle reflected, her husband "had the habit" of preferring her to other women, "and habits are much stronger in him than passions." On the other hand, she herself was getting lazy intellectually; Geraldine loved talk and clever talk; with all her aspirations and enthusiasms it would be a kindness to let the young woman marooned in Manchester come to Chelsea; and so she came.

She came on the 1st or 2nd of February, and she stayed till the Saturday, the 11th of March. Such were visits in the year 1843. And the house was very small, and the servant was inefficient. Geraldine was always there. All the morning she scribbled letters. All the afternoon she lay fast asleep on the sofa in the drawing-room. She dressed herself in a low-necked dress to receive visitors on Sunday. She talked too much. As for her reputed intellect, "she is sharp as a meat axe, but as narrow." She flattered. She wheedled. She was insincere. She flirted. She swore. Nothing would make her go. The charges against her rose in a crescendo of irritation. Mrs. Carlyle almost had to turn her out of the house. At last they parted; and Geraldine, as she got into the cab, was in floods of tears, but Mrs. Carlyle's eyes were dry. Indeed, she was immensely relieved to see the last of her visitor. Yet when Geraldine had driven off and she found herself alone she was not altogether easy in her mind. She knew that her behaviour to a guest whom she herself had invited had been far from perfect. She had been "cold, cross, ironical, disobliging." Above all, she was angry with herself for having taken Geraldine for a *confidante*. "Heaven grant that the consequences may be only *boring*—not *fatal*," she wrote. But it is clear that she was very much out of temper; and with herself as much as with Geraldine.

Geraldine, returned to Manchester, was well aware that something was wrong. Estrangement and silence fell between them. People repeated malicious stories which she half believed. But Geraldine was the least vindictive of women—"very noble in her quarrels," as Mrs. Carlyle herself admitted—and, if foolish and sentimental, neither conceited nor proud. Above all, her love for Jane was sincere. Soon she was writing to Mrs. Carlyle again "with an assiduity and disinterestedness that verge on the superhuman," as Jane commented with a little exasperation. She was worrying about Jane's health and saying that she did not want witty letters, but only dull letters telling the truth about Jane's state. For—it may have been one of those things that made her so trying as a visitor—Geraldine had not stayed for four weeks in Cheyne Row without coming to conclusions which it is not likely that she kept entirely to herself. "You have no one who has any sort of consideration for you," she wrote. "You have had patience and endurance till I am sick of the virtues, and what have they done for you? Half-killed you." "Carlyle," she burst out, "is much too grand for everyday life. A sphinx does not fit in comfortably to our parlour life arrangements." But she could do nothing. "The more one loves, the more helpless one feels," she moralised. She could only watch from Manchester the bright kaleidoscope of her friend's existence and compare it with her own prosaic life, all made up of little odds and ends; but somehow, obscure though her own life was, she no longer envied Jane the brilliance of her lot.

So they might have gone on corresponding in a desultory way at a distance—and "I am tired to death of writing letters into space," Geraldine exclaimed; "one only writes after a long separation, to oneself, instead of one's friend"—had it not been for the Mudies. The Mudies and Mudieism, as Geraldine called it, played a vast, if almost unrecorded, part in the obscure lives of Victorian gentlewomen. In this case the Mudies were two girls, Elizabeth and Juliet: "flary, staring, and conceited, stolid-looking girls," Carlyle called them, the daughters of a Dundee schoolmaster, a respectable man who had written books on natural history and died, leaving a foolish widow and little or no provision for his family. Somehow the Mudies arrived in Cheyne Row inconveniently, if one may hazard a guess, just as dinner was on the table. But the Victorian lady never minded that—she put herself to any inconvenience to help the Mudies. The question at once presented itself to Mrs. Carlyle, what could be done for them? Who knew of a place? who had influence with a rich man? Geraldine flashed into her mind. Geraldine was always wishing she could be of use. Geraldine might fairly be asked if there were situations to be had for the Mudies in Manchester. Geraldine acted with a promptitude that was much to her credit. She "placed" Juliet at once. Soon she had heard of another place for Elizabeth. Mrs. Carlyle, who was in the Isle of Wight, at once procured stays, gown, and petticoat for Elizabeth, came up to London, took Elizabeth all the way across London to Euston Square at half past seven in the evening, put her in charge of a benevolent-looking, fat old man, saw that a letter to Geraldine was pinned to her stays, and returned home, exhausted, triumphant, yet, as happens often with the devotees of Mudieism, a prey to secret misgivings. Would the Mudies be happy? Would they thank her for what she had done? A few days later the inevitable bugs appeared in Cheyne Row, and were ascribed, with or without reason, to Elizabeth's shawl. What was far worse, Elizabeth herself appeared four months later, having proved herself "wholly inapplicable to any practical purpose," having "sewed a *black* apron with *white* thread," and, on being mildly scolded, having "thrown herself on the kitchen floor and kicked and screamed." "Of course, her immediate dismissal is the result." Elizabeth vanished—to sew more black aprons with white thread, to kick and scream and be dismissed—who knows what happened eventually to poor Elizabeth Mudie? She disappears from the world altogether, swallowed up in the dark shades of her sisterhood. Juliet, however, remained. Geraldine made Juliet her charge. She superintended and advised. The first place was unsatisfactory. Geraldine engaged herself to find another. She went off and sat in the hall of a "very stiff old lady" who wanted a maid. The very stiff old lady said she would want Juliet to clear-starch collars, to iron cuffs, and to wash and iron petticoats. Juliet's heart failed her. All this clear-starching and ironing, she exclaimed, were beyond her. Off went Geraldine again, late in the evening, and saw the old lady's daughter. It was arranged that the petticoats should be "put out" and only the collars and frills left for Juliet to iron. Off went Geraldine and arranged with her own milliner to give her lessons in quilling and trimming. And Mrs. Carlyle wrote kindly to Juliet and sent her a packet. So it went on with more places and more bothers, and more old ladies, and more interviews till Juliet wrote a novel, which a gentleman praised very highly, and Juliet told Miss Jewsbury that she was annoyed by another gentleman who followed her home from church; but still she was a very nice girl, and everybody spoke well of her until the year 1849, when suddenly, without any reason given, silence descends upon the last of the Mudies. It covers, one cannot doubt, another failure. The novel, the stiff old lady, the gentleman, the caps, the petticoats, the clear-starching—what was the cause of her downfall? Nothing is known. "The wretched stalking blockheads," wrote Carlyle, "stalked fatefully, in spite of all that could be done and said, steadily downwards towards perdition and sank altogether out of view." For all her endeavours Mrs. Carlyle had to admit that Mudieism was always a failure.

But Mudieism had unexpected results. Mudieism brought Jane and Geraldine together again. Jane could not deny that "the fluff of feathers" whom she had served up, as her way was, in so many a scornful phrase for Carlyle's amusement, had "taken up the matter with an enthusiasm even surpassing my own." She had grit in her as well as fluff. Thus when Geraldine sent her the manuscript of her first novel, *Zoe*, Mrs. Carlyle bestirred herself to find a publisher ("for," she wrote, "what is to become of her when she is old without ties, without purposes?") and with surprising success. Chapman & Hall at once agreed to publish the book, which, their reader reported, "had taken hold of him with a grasp of iron." The book had been long on the way. Mrs. Carlyle herself had been consulted at various stages of its career. She had read the first sketch "with a feeling little short of terror! So much power of genius rushing so recklessly into unknown space." But she had also been deeply impressed.

> Geraldine in particular shows herself here a far more profound and daring speculator than ever I had fancied her. I do not believe there is a woman alive at the present day, not even Georges Sand herself, that could have written some of the best passages in this book . . . but they must not publish it—decency forbids!

There was, Mrs. Carlyle complained, an indecency or "want of reserve in the spiritual department," which no respectable public would stand. Presumably Geraldine consented to make alterations, though she confessed that she "had no vocation for propriety as such"; the book was rewritten, and it appeared at last in February 1845. The usual buzz and conflict of opinion at once arose. Some were enthusiastic, others were shocked. The "old and young roués of the Reform Club almost go off into hysterics over—its *indecency*." The publisher was a little alarmed; but the scandal helped the sale, and Geraldine became a lioness.

And now, of course, as one turns the pages of the three little yellowish volumes, one wonders what reason there was for approval or disapproval, what spasm of indignation or admiration scored that pencil mark, what mysterious emotion pressed violets, now black as ink, between the pages of the love scenes. Chapter after chapter glides amiably, fluently past. In a kind of haze we catch glimpses of an illegitimate girl called Zoe; of an enigmatic Roman Catholic priest called Everhard; of a castle in the country; of ladies lying on sky-blue sofas; of gentlemen reading aloud; of girls embroidering hearts in silk. There is a conflagration. There is an embrace in a wood. There is incessant conversation. There is a moment of terrific emotion when the priest exclaims, "Would that I had never been born!" and proceeds to sweep a letter from the Pope asking him to edit a translation of the principal works of the Fathers of the first four centuries and a parcel containing a gold chain from the University of Göttingen into a drawer because Zoe has shaken his faith. But what indecency there was pungent enough to shock the roués of the Reform Club, what genius there was brilliant enough to impress the shrewd intellect of Mrs. Carlyle, it is impossible to guess. Colours that were fresh as roses eighty years ago have faded to a feeble pink; nothing remains of all those scents and savours but a faint perfume of faded violets, of stale hair-oil, we know not which. What miracles, we exclaim, are within the power of a few years to accomplish! But even as we exclaim, we see, far away, a trace perhaps of what they meant. The passion, in so far as it issues from the lips of living people, is completely spent. The Zoes, the Clothildes, the Everhards moulder on their perches; but, nevertheless, there is somebody in the room with them; an irresponsible spirit, a daring and agile woman, if one considers that she is cumbered with crinoline and stays; an absurd sentimental creature, languishing, expatiating, but for all that still strangely alive. We catch a sentence now and then rapped out boldly, a thought subtly conceived. "How much better to do right without religion!" "Oh! if they really believed all they preach, how would any priest or preacher be able to sleep in his bed!" "Weakness is the only state for which there is no hope." "To love rightly is the highest morality of which mankind is capable." Then how she hated the "compacted, plausible theories of men"! And what is life? For what end was it given us? Such questions, such convictions, still hurtle past the heads of the stuffed figures mouldering on their perches. They are dead, but Geraldine Jewsbury herself still survives, independent, courageous, absurd, writing page after page without stopping to correct, and coming out with her views upon love, morality, religion, and the relations of the sexes, whoever may be within hearing, with a cigar between her lips.

Some time before the publication of *Zoe*, Mrs. Carlyle had forgotten, or overcome, her irritation with Geraldine, partly because she had worked so zealously in the cause of the Mudies, partly also because by Geraldine's painstaking she was "almost over-persuaded back into my old illusion that she has some sort of strange, passionate . . .. incomprehensible *attraction* towards me." Not only was she drawn back into correspondence—after all her vows to the contrary she again stayed under the same roof with Geraldine, at Seaforth House near Liverpool, in July 1844. Not many days had passed before Mrs. Carlyle's "illusion" about the strength of Geraldine's affection for her proved to be no illusion but a monstrous fact. One morning there was some slight tiff between them: Geraldine sulked all day; at night Geraldine came to Mrs. Carlyle's bedroom and made a scene which was "a revelation to me, not only of Geraldine, but of human nature! Such mad, lover-like jealousy on the part of one woman towards another it had never entered into my heart to conceive." Mrs. Carlyle was angry and outraged and contemptuous. She saved up a full account of the scene to entertain her husband with. A few days later she turned upon Geraldine in public and sent the whole company into fits of laughter by saying: "I wondered she should expect me to behave decently to her after she had for a whole evening been making love before my very face to *another man!*" The trouncing must have been severe, the humiliation painful. But Geraldine was incorrigible. A year later she was again sulking and raging and declaring that she had a right to rage because "she loves me better than all the rest of the world"; and Mrs. Carlyle was getting up and saying, "Geraldine, until you can behave like a gentlewoman . . ." and leaving the room. And again there were tears and apologies and promises to reform.

Yet though Mrs. Carlyle scolded and jeered, though they were estranged, and though for a time they ceased to write to each other, still they always came together again. Geraldine, it is abundantly clear, felt that Jane was in every way wiser, better, stronger that she was. She depended on Jane. She needed Jane to keep her out of scrapes; for Jane never got into scrapes herself. But though Jane was so much wiser and cleverer than Geraldine, there were times when the foolish and irresponsible one of the two became the counsellor. Why, she asked, waste your time in mending old clothes? Why not work at something that will really employ your energies? Write, she advised her. For Jane, who was so profound, so far-seeing, could, Geraldine was convinced, write something that would help women in "their very complicated duties and difficulties." She owed a duty to her sex. But, the bold woman proceeded, "do not go to Mr. Carlyle for sympathy, do not let him dash you with cold water. You must respect your own work, and your own motives"—a piece of advice that Jane, who was afraid to to accept the dedication of Geraldine's new novel *The Half Sisters*, lest Mr. Carlyle might object, would have done well to follow. The little creature was in some ways the bolder and the more independent of the two.

She had, morever, a quality that Jane with all her brilliancy lacked—an element of poetry, a trace of the speculative imagination. She browsed upon old books and copied out romantic passages about the palm trees and cinnamon of Arabia and sent them to lie, incongruously enough, upon the breakfast table in Cheyne Row. Jane's genius, of course, was the very opposite; it was positive, direct, and practical. Her imagination concentrated itself upon people. Her letters owe their incomparable brilliancy to the hawk-like swoop and descent of her mind upon facts. Nothing escapes her. She sees through clear water down to the rocks at the bottom. But the intangible eluded her; she dismissed the poetry of Keats with a sneer; something of the narrowness and something of the prudery of a Scottish country doctor's daughter clung to her. Though infinitely the less masterly, Geraldine was sometimes the broader minded.

Such sympathies and antipathies bound the two women together with an elasticity that made for permanence. The tie between them could stretch and stretch indefinitely without breaking. Jane knew the extent of Geraldine's folly; Geraldine had felt the full lash of Jane's tongue. They had learnt to tolerate each other. Naturally, they quarrelled again; but their quarrels were different now; they were quarrels that were bound to be made up. And when after her brother's marriage in 1854 Geraldine moved to London, it was to be near Mrs. Carlyle at Mrs. Carlyle's own wish. The woman who in 1843 would never be a friend of hers again was now the most intimate friend she had in the world. She was to lodge two streets off; and perhaps two streets off was the right space to put between them. The emotional friendship was full of misunderstandings at a distance; it was intolerably exacting under the same roof. But when they lived round the corner their relationship broadened and simplified; it became a natural intercourse whose ruffles and whose calms were based upon the depths of intimacy. They went about together. They went to hear *The Messiah*; and, characteristically, Geraldine wept at the beauty of the music and Jane had much ado to prevent herself from shaking Geraldine for crying and from crying herself at the ugliness of the chorus women. They went to Norwood for a jaunt, and Geraldine left a silk handkerchief and an aluminum brooch ("a love token from Mr. Barlow") in the hotel and a new silk parasol in the waiting-room. Also Jane noted with sardonic satisfaction that Geraldine, in an attempt at economy, bought two second-class tickets, while the cost of a return ticket first class was precisely the same.

Meanwhile Geraldine lay on the floor and generalised and speculated and tried to formulate some theory of life from her own tumultuous experience. "How loathsome" (her language was always apt to be strong—she knew that she "sinned against Jane's notions of good taste" very often), how loathsome the position of women was in many ways! How she herself had been crippled and stunted! How her blood boiled in her at the power that men had over women! She would like to kick certain gentlemen—"the lying hypocritical beggars! Well, it's no good swearing—only, I am angry and it eases my mind."

And then her thoughts turned to Jane and herself and to the brilliant gifts—at any rate, Jane had brilliant gifts—which had borne so little visible result. Nevertheless, except when she was ill,

> I do not think that either you or I are to be called failures. We are indications of a development of womanhood which as yet is not recognised. It has, so far, no ready-made channels to run in, but still we have looked and tried, and found that the present rules for woman will not hold us—that something better and stronger is needed. . . . There are women to come after us, who will approach nearer the fullness of the measure of the stature of a woman's nature. I regard myself as a mere faint indication, a rudiment of the idea, of certain higher qualities and possibilities that lie in women, and all the eccentricities and mistakes and miseries and absurdities I have made are only the consequences of an imperfect formation, an immature growth.

So she theorised, so she speculated; and Mrs. Carlyle listened, and laughed, and contradicted no doubt, but with more of sympathy than of derision: she could have wished that Geraldine were more precise; she could have wished her to moderate her language. Carlyle might come in at any moment; and if there was one creature that Carlyle hated, it was a strong-minded woman of the George Sand species. Yet she could not deny that there was an element of truth in what Geraldine said; she had always thought that Geraldine "was born to spoil a horn or make a spoon." Geraldine was no fool in spite of appearances.

But what Geraldine thought and said; how she spent her mornings; what she did in the long evenings of the London winter—all, in fact, that constituted her life at Markham Square—is but slightly and doubtfully known to us. For, fittingly enough, the bright light of Jane extinguished the paler and more flickering fire of Geraldine. She had no need to write to Jane any more. She was in and out of the house—now writing a letter for Jane because Jane's fingers were swollen, now taking a letter to the post and forgetting, like the scatter-brained romantic creature she was, to post it. A crooning domestic sound like the purring of a kitten or the humming of a tea-kettle seems to rise, as we turn the pages of Mrs. Carlyle's letters, from the intercourse of the two incompatible but deeply attached women. So the years passed. At length, on Saturday, 21st April 1866, Geraldine was to help Jane with a tea-party. Mr. Carlyle was in Scotland, and Mrs. Carlyle hoped to get through some necessary civilities to admirers in his absence. Geraldine was actually dressing for the occasion when Mr. Froude appeared suddenly at her house. He had just had a message from Cheyne Row to say that "something had happened to Mrs. Carlyle." Geraldine flung on her cloak. They hastened together to St. George's Hospital. There, writes Froude, they saw Mrs. Carlyle beautifully dressed as usual

> as if she had sat upon the bed after leaving the brougham, and had fallen back upon it asleep. . . . The brilliant mockery, the sad softness with which the mockery alternated, both were alike gone. The features lay composed in a stern majestic calm. . . . [Geraldine] could not speak.

Nor indeed can we break that silence. It deepened. It became complete. Soon after Jane's death she went to live at Sevenoaks. She lived there alone for twenty-two years. It is said that she lost her vivacity. She wrote no more books. Cancer attacked her and she suffered much. On her deathbed she began tearing up Jane's letters, as Jane had wished, and she had destroyed all but one before she died. Thus, just as her life began in obscurity, so it ended in obscurity. We know her well only for a few years in the middle. But let us not be too sanguine about "knowing her well." Intimacy is a difficult art, as Geraldine herself reminds us.

> Oh, my dear [she wrote to Mrs. Carlyle], if you and I are drowned, or die, what would become of us if any superior person were to go and write our "life and errors"? What a precious mess a "truthful person" would go and make of us, and how very different to what we really are or were!

The echo of her mockery, ungrammatical, colloquial, but as usual with the ring of truth in it, reaches us from where she lies in Lady Morgan's vault in the Brompton cemetery.

*

"*Aurora Leigh*"

*

By one of those ironies of fashion that might have amused the Brownings themselves, it seems likely that they are now far better known in the flesh than they have ever been in the spirit. Passionate lovers, in curls and side whiskers, oppressed, defiant, eloping—in this guise thousands of people must know and love the Brownings who have never read a line of their poetry. They have become two of the most conspicuous figures in that bright and animated company of authors who, thanks to our modern habit of writing memoirs and printing letters and sitting to be photographed, live in the flesh, not merely as of old in the word; are known by their hats, not merely by their poems. What damage the art of photography has inflicted upon the art of literature has yet to be reckoned. How far we are going to read a poet when we can read about a poet is a problem to lay before biographers. Meanwhile, nobody can deny the power of the Brownings to excite our sympathy and rouse our interest. "Lady Geraldine's Courtship" is glanced at perhaps by two professors in American universities once a year; but we all know how Miss Barrett lay on her sofa; how she escaped from the dark house in Wimpole Street one September morning; how she met health and happiness, freedom, and Robert Browning in the church round the corner.

But fate has not been kind to Mrs. Browning as a writer. Nobody reads her, nobody discusses her, nobody troubles to put her in her place. One has only to compare her reputation with Christina Rossetti's to trace her decline. Christina Rossetti mounts irresistibly to the first place among English women poets. Elizabeth, so much more loudly applauded during her lifetime, falls farther and farther behind. The primers dismiss her with contumely. Her importance, they say, "has now become merely historical. Neither education nor association with her husband ever succeeded in teaching her the value of words and a sense of form." In short, the only place in the mansion of literature that is assigned her is downstairs in the servants' quarters, where, in company with Mrs. Hemans, Eliza Cook, Jean Ingelow, Alexander Smith, Edwin Arnold, and Robert Montgomery she bangs the crockery about and eats vast handfuls of peas on the point of her knife.

If, therefore, we take *Aurora Leigh* from the shelf it is not so much in order to read it as to muse with kindly condescension over this token of bygone fashion, as we toy with the fringes of our grandmothers' mantles and muse over the alabaster models of the Taj Mahal which once adorned their drawing-room tables. But to the Victorians, undoubtedly, the book was very dear. Thirteen editions of *Aurora Leigh* had been demanded by the year 1873. And, to judge from the dedication, Mrs. Browning herself was not afraid to say that she set great store by it—"the most mature of my works," she calls it, "and the one into which my highest convictions upon Life and Art have entered." Her letters show that she had had the book in mind for many years. She was brooding over it when she first met Browning, and her intention with regard to it forms almost the first of those confidences about their work which the lovers delighted to share.

> . . . my chief *intention* [she wrote] just now is the writing of a sort of novel-poem . . . running into the midst of our conventions, and rushing into drawing-rooms and the like, "where angels fear to tread"; and so, meeting face to face and without mask the Humanity of the age, and speaking the truth of it out plainly. That is my intention.

But for reasons which later became clear, she hoarded her intention throughout the ten astonishing years of escape and happiness; and when at last the book appeared in 1856 she might well feel that she had poured into it the best that she had to give. Perhaps the hoarding and the saturation which resulted have something to do with the surprise that awaits us. At any rate we cannot read the first twenty pages of *Aurora Leigh* without becoming aware that the Ancient Mariner who lingers, for unknown reasons, at the porch of one book and not of another has us by the hand, and makes us listen like a three years child while Mrs. Browning pours out in nine volumes of blank verse the story of Aurora Leigh. Speed and energy, forthrightness and complete self-confidence—these are the qualities that hold us enthralled. Floated off our feet by them, we learn how Aurora was the child of an Italian mother "whose rare blue eyes were shut from seeing her when she was scarcely four years old." Her father was "an austere Englishman, Who, after a dry lifetime spent at home In college-learning, law and parish talk, Was flooded with a passion unaware," but died, too, and the child was sent back to England to be brought up by an aunt. The aunt, of the well-known family of the Leighs, stood upon the hall step of her country house dressed in black to welcome her. Her somewhat narrow forehead was braided tight with brown hair pricked with grey; she had a close, mild mouth; eyes of no colour; and cheeks like roses pressed in books, "Kept more for ruth than pleasure, —if past bloom, Past fading also." The lady had lived a quiet life, exercising her Christian gifts upon knitting stockings and stitching petticoats "because we are of one flesh, after all, and need one flannel." At her hand Aurora suffered the education that was thought proper for women. She learnt a little French, a little algebra; the internal laws of the Burmese empire; what navigable river joins itself to Lara; what census of the year five was taken at Klagenfurt; also how to draw nereids neatly draped, to spin glass, to stuff birds, and model flowers in wax. For the Aunt liked a woman to be womanly. Of an evening she did cross-stitch and, owing to some mistake in her choice of silk, once embroidered a shepherdess with pink eyes. Under this torture of women's education, the passionate Aurora exclaimed, certain women have died; others pine; a few have, as Aurora had, "relations with the unseen," survive, and walk demurely, and are civil to their cousins and listen to the vicar and pour out tea. Aurora herself was blessed with a little room. It was green papered, had a green carpet and there were green curtains to the bed, as if to match the insipid greenery of the English countryside. There she retired; there she read. "I had found the secret of a garret room Piled high with cases in my father's name, Piled high, packed large, where, creeping in and out . . . like some small nimble mouse between the ribs of a mastodon" she read and read. The mouse indeed (it is the way with Mrs. Browning's mice) took wings and soared, for "It is rather when We gloriously forget ourselves and plunge Soul-forward, headlong into a book's profound, Impassioned for its beauty and salt of truth—'Tis then we get the right good from a book." And so she read and read, until her cousin Romney called to walk with her, or the painter, Vincent Carrington "whom men judge hardly as bee-bonneted Because he holds that paint a body well you paint a soul by implication," tapped on the window.

This hasty abstract of the first volume of *Aurora Leigh* does it of course no sort of justice; but having gulped down the original much as Aurora herself advises, soul-forward, headlong, we find ourselves in a state where some attempt at the ordering of our multitudinous impressions becomes imperative. The first of these impressions and the most pervasive is the sense of the writer's presence. Through the voice of Aurora the character, the circumstances, the idiosyncracies of Elizabeth Barrett Browning ring in our ears. Mrs. Browning could no more conceal herself than she could control herself, a sign no doubt of imperfection in an artist, but a sign also that life has impinged upon art more than life should. Again and again in the pages we have read, Aurora the fictitious seems to be throwing light upon Elizabeth the actual. The idea of the poem, we must remember, came to her in the early forties when the connexion between a woman's art and a woman's life was unnaturally close, so that it is impossible for the most austere of critics not sometimes to touch the flesh when his eyes should be fixed upon the page. And as everybody knows, the life of Elizabeth Barrett was of a nature to affect the most authentic and individual of gifts. Her mother had died when she was a child; she had read profusely and privately; her favourite brother was drowned; her health broke down; she had been immured by the tyranny of her father in almost conventual seclusion in a bedroom in Wimpole Street. But instead of rehearsing the well-known facts, it is better to read in her own words her own account of the effect they had upon her.

> I have lived only inwardly [she wrote] or with *sorrow*, for a strong emotion. Before this seclusion of my illness, I was secluded still, and there are few of the youngest women in the world who have not seen more, heard more, known more, of society, than I, who am scarcely to be called young now. I grew up in the country—I had no social opportunities, had my heart in books and poetry, and my experience in reveries. And so time passed and passed—and afterwards, when my illness came . . . and no prospect (as appeared at one time) of ever passing the threshold of one room again; why then, I turned to thinking with some bitterness . . . that I had stood blind in this temple I was about to leave—that I had seen no Human nature, that my brothers and sisters of the earth were *names* to me, that I had beheld no great mountain or river, nothing in fact. . . . And do you also know what a disadvantage this ignorance is to my art? Why, if I live on and yet do not escape from this seclusion, do you not perceive that I labour under signal disadvantages—that I am, in a manner as a *blind poet?* Certainly, there is compensation to a degree. I have had much of the inner life, and from the habit of self-consciousness and self-analysis, I make great guesses at Human nature in the main. But how willingly I would as a poet exchange some of this lumbering, ponderous, helpless knowledge of books, for some experience of life and man, for some . . .

She breaks off, with three little dots, and we may take advantage of her pause to turn once more to *Aurora Leigh*.

What damage had her life done her as a poet? A great one, we cannot deny. For it is clear, as we turn the pages of *Aurora Leigh* or of the *Letters*—one often echoes the other—that the mind which found its natural expression in this swift and chaotic poem about real men and women was not the mind to profit by solitude. A lyrical, a scholarly, a fastidious mind might have used seclusion and solitude to perfect its powers. Tennyson asked no better than to live with books in the heart of the country. But the mind of Elizabeth Barrett was lively and secular and satirical. She was no scholar. Books were to her not an end in themselves but a substitute for living. She raced through folios because she was forbidden to scamper on the grass. She wrestled with Aeschylus and Plato because it was out of the question that she should argue about politics with live men and women. Her favourite reading as an invalid was Balzac and George Sand and other "immortal improprieties" because "they kept the colour in my life to some degree." Nothing is more striking when at last she broke the prison bars than the fervour with which she flung herself into the life of the moment. She loved to sit in a café and watch people passing; she loved the arguments, the politics, and the strife of the modern world. The past and its ruins, even the past of Italy and Italian ruins, interested her much less than the theories of Mr. Hume the medium, or the politics of Napoleon, Emperor of the French. Italian pictures, Greek poetry roused in her a clumsy and conventional enthusiasm in strange contrast with the original independence of her mind when it applied itself to actual facts.

Such being her natural bent, it is not surprising that even in the depths of her sick-room her mind turned to modern life as a subject for poetry. She waited, wisely, until her escape had given her some measure of knowledge and proportion. But it cannot be doubted that the long years of seclusion had done her irreparable damage as an artist. She had lived shut off, guessing at what was outside, and inevitably magnifying what was within. The loss of Flush, the spaniel, affected her as the loss of a child might have affected another woman. The tap of ivy on the pane became the thrash of trees in a gale. Every sound was enlarged, every incident exaggerated, for the silence of the sick-room was profound and the monotony of Wimpole Street was intense. When at last she was able to "rush into drawing-rooms and the like and meet face to face without mask the Humanity of the age and speak the truth of it out plainly," she was too weak to stand the shock. Ordinary daylight, current gossip, the usual traffic of human beings left her exhausted, ecstatic, and dazzled into a state where she saw so much and felt so much that she did not altogether know what she felt or what she saw.

Aurora Leigh, the novel-poem, is not, therefore, the masterpiece that it might have been. Rather it is a masterpiece in embryo; a work whose genius floats diffused and fluctuating in some pre-natal stage waiting the final stroke of creative power to bring it into being. Stimulating and boring, ungainly and eloquent, monstrous and exquisite all by turns, it overwhelms and bewilders; but, nevertheless, it still commands our interest and inspires our respect. For it becomes clear as we read that, whatever Mrs. Browning's faults, she was one of those rare writers who risk themselves adventurously and disinterestedly in an imaginative life which is independent of their private lives and demands to be considered apart from personalities. Her "intention" survives; the interest of her theory redeems much that is faulty in her practice. Abridged and simplified from Aurora's argument in the fifth book, that theory runs something like this. The true work of poets, she said, is to present their own age, not Charlemagne's. More passion takes place in drawing-rooms than at Roncesvalles with Roland and his knights. "To flinch from modern varnish, coat or flounce, Cry out for togas and the picturesque, Is fatal—foolish too." For living art presents and records real life, and the only life we can truly know is our own. But what form, she asks, can a poem on modern life take? The drama is impossible, for only servile and docile plays have any chance of success. Moreover, what we (in 1846) have to say about life is not fit for "boards, actors, prompters, gas-light, and costume; our stage is now the soul itself." What then can she do? The problem is difficult, performance is bound to fall short of endeavour; but she has at least wrung her life-blood on to every page of her book, and, for the rest "Let me think of forms less, and the external. Trust the spirit . . . Keep up the fire and leave the generous flames to shape themselves." And so the fire blazed and the flames leapt high.

The desire to deal with modern life in poetry was not confined to Miss Barrett. Robert Browning said that he had had the same ambition all his life. Coventry Patmore's "Angel in the House" and Clough's "Bothie" were both attempts of the same kind and preceded *Aurora Leigh* by some years. It was natural enough. The novelists were dealing triumphantly with modern life in prose. *Jane Eyre*, *Vanity Fair*, *David Copperfield*, *Richard Feverel* all trod fast on each other's heels between the years 1847 and 1860. The poets may well have felt, with Aurora Leigh, that modern life had an intensity and a meaning of its own. Why should these spoils fall solely into the laps of the prose writers? Why should the poet be forced back to the remoteness of Charlemagne and Roland, to the toga and the picturesque, when the humours and tragedies of village life, drawing-room life, club life, and street life all cried aloud for celebration? It was true that the old form in which poetry had dealt with life—the drama—was obsolete; but was there none other that could take its place? Mrs. Browning, convinced of the divinity of poetry, pondered, seized as much as she could of actual experience, and then at last threw down her challenge to the Brontës and the Thackerays in nine books of blank verse. It was in blank verse that she sang of Shoreditch and Kensington; of my aunt and the vicar; of Romney Leigh and Vincent Carrington; of Marian Erle and Lord Howe; of fashionable weddings and drab suburban streets, and bonnets and whiskers and four-wheeled cabs, and railway trains. The poets can treat of these things, she exclaimed, as well as of knights and dames, moats and drawbridges and castle courts. But can they? Let us see what happens to a poet when he poaches upon a novelist's preserves and gives us not an epic or a lyric but the story of many lives that move and change and are inspired by the interests and passions that are ours in the middle of the reign of Queen Victoria.

In the first place there is the story; a tale has to be told; the poet must somehow convey to us the necessary information that his hero has been asked out to dinner. This is a statement that a novelist would convey as quietly and prosaically as possible; for example, "While I was kissing her glove, sadly enough, a note was brought saying that her father sent his regards and asked me to dine with them next day." That is harmless. But the poet has to write:

> While thus I grieved, and kissed her glove,
> My man brought in her note to say,
> Papa had bid her send his love,
> And would I dine with them next day!

Which is absurd. The simple words have been made to strut and posture and take on an emphasis which makes them ridiculous. Then again, what will the poet do with dialogue? In modern life, as Mrs. Browning indicated when she said that our stage is now the soul, the tongue has superseded the sword. It is in talk that the high moments of life, the shock of character upon character, are defined. But poetry when it tries to follow the words on people's lips is terribly impeded. Listen to Romney in a moment of high emotion talking to his old love Marian about the baby she has borne to another man:

> May God so father me, as I do him,
> And so forsake me, as I let him feel
> He's orphaned haply. Here I take the child
> To share my cup, to slumber on my knee,
> To play his loudest gambol at my foot,
> To hold my finger in the public ways . . .

and so on. Romney, in short, rants and reels like any of those Elizabethan heroes whom Mrs. Browning had warned so imperiously out of her modern living-room. Blank verse has proved itself the most remorseless enemy of living speech. Talk tossed up on the surge and swing of the verse becomes high, rhetorical, impassioned; and as talk, since action is ruled out, must go on and on, the reader's mind stiffens and glazes under the monotony of the rhythm. Following the lilt of her rhythm rather than the emotions of her characters, Mrs. Browning is swept on into generalisation and declamation. Forced by the nature of her medium, she ignores the slighter, the subtler, the more hidden shades of emotion by which a novelist builds up touch by touch a character in prose. Change and development, the effect of one character upon another—all this is abandoned. The poem becomes one long soliloquy, and the only character that is known to us and the only story that is told us are the character and story of Aurora Leigh herself.

Thus, if Mrs. Browning meant by a novel-poem a book in which character is closely and subtly revealed, the relations of many hearts laid bare, and a story unfalteringly unfolded, she failed completely. But if she meant rather to give us a sense of life in general, of people who are unmistakably Victorian, wrestling with the problems of their own time, all brightened, intensified, and compacted by the fire of poetry, she succeeded. Aurora Leigh, with her passionate interest in social questions, her conflict as artist and woman, her longing for knowledge and freedom, is the true daughter of her age. Romney, too, is no less certainly a mid-Victorian gentleman of high ideals who has thought deeply about the social question, and has founded, unfortunately, a phalanstery in Shropshire. The aunt, the antimacassars, and the country house from which Aurora escapes are real enough to fetch high prices in the Tottenham Court Road at this moment. The broader aspects of what it felt like to be a Victorian are seized as surely and stamped as vividly upon us as in any novel by Trollope or Mrs. Gaskell.

And indeed if we compare the prose novel and the novel-poem the triumphs are by no means all to the credit of prose. As we rush through page after page of narrative in which a dozen scenes that the novelist would smooth out separately are pressed into one, in which pages of deliberate description are fused into a single line, we cannot help feeling that the poet has outpaced the prose writer. Her page is packed twice as full as his. Characters, too, if they are not shown in conflict but snipped off and summed up with something of the exaggeration of a caricaturist, have a heightened and symbolical significance which prose with its gradual approach cannot rival. The general aspect of things—market, sunset, church—have a brilliance and a continuity, owing to the compressions and elisions of poetry, which mock the prose writer and his slow accumulations of careful detail. For these reasons *Aurora Leigh* remains, with all its imperfections, a book that still lives and breathes and has its being. And when we think how still and cold the plays of Beddoes or of Sir Henry Taylor lie, in spite of all their beauty, and how seldom in our own day we disturb the repose of the classical dramas of Robert Bridges, we may suspect that Elizabeth Barrett was inspired by a flash of true genius when she rushed into the drawing-room and said that here, where we live and work, is the true place for the poet. At any rate, her courage was justified in her own case. Her bad taste, her tortured ingenuity, her floundering, scrambling, and confused impetuosity have space to spend themselves here without inflicting a deadly wound, while her ardour and abundance, her brilliant descriptive powers, her shrewd and caustic humour infect us with her own enthusiasm. We laugh, we protest, we complain—it is absurd, it is impossible, we cannot tolerate this exaggeration a moment longer—but, nevertheless, we read to the end enthralled. What more can an author ask? But the best compliment that we can pay *Aurora Leigh* is that it makes us wonder why it has left no successors. Surely the street, the drawing-room, are promising subjects; modern life is worthy of the muse. But the rapid sketch that Elizabeth Barrett Browning threw off when she leapt from her couch and dashed into the drawing-room remains unfinished. The conservatism or the timidity of poets still leaves the chief spoils of modern life to the novelist. We have no novel-poem of the age of George the Fifth.

❋

The Niece of an Earl

❋

There is an aspect of fiction of so delicate a nature that less has been said about it than its importance deserves. One is supposed to pass over class distinctions in silence; one person is supposed to be as well born as another; and yet English fiction is so steeped in the ups and downs of social rank that without them it would be unrecognisable. When Meredith, in *The Case of General Ople and Lady Camper*, remarks, "He sent word that he would wait on Lady Camper immediately, and betook himself forthwith to his toilette. She was the niece of an Earl," all of British blood accept the statement unhesitatingly, and know that Meredith is right. A General in those circumstances would certainly have given his coat an extra brush. For though the General might have been, we are given to understand that he was not, Lady Camper's social equal. He received the shock of her rank upon a naked surface. No earldom, baronetage, or knighthood protected him. He was an English gentleman merely, and a poor one at that. Therefore, to British readers even now it seems unquestionably fitting that he should "betake himself to his toilette" before appearing in the lady's presence.

It is useless to suppose that social distinctions have vanished. Each may pretend that he knows no such restrictions, and that the compartment in which he lives allows him the run of the world. But it is an illusion. The idlest stroller down summer streets may see for himself the charwoman's shawl shouldering its way among the silk wraps of the successful; he sees shop-girls pressing their noses against the plate glass of motor-cars; he sees radiant youth and august age waiting their summons within to be admitted to the presence of King George. There is no animosity, perhaps, but there is no communication. We are enclosed, and separate, and cut off. Directly we see ourselves in the looking-glass of fiction we know that this is so. The novelist, and the English novelist in particular, knows and delights, it seems, to know that Society is a nest of glass boxes one separate from another, each housing a group with special habits and qualities of its own. He knows that there are Earls and that Earls have nieces; he knows that there are Generals and that Generals brush their coats before they visit the nieces of Earls. But this is only the A B C of what he knows. For in a few short pages, Meredith makes us aware not only that Earls have nieces, but that Generals have cousins; that the cousins have friends; that the friends have cooks; that the cooks have husbands, and that the husbands of the cooks of the friends of the cousins of the Generals are carpenters. Each of these people lives in a glass box of his own, and has peculiarities of which the novelist must take account. What appears superficially to be the vast equality of the middle classes is, in truth, nothing of the sort. All through the social mass run curious veins and streakings separating man from man and woman from woman; mysterious prerogatives and disabilities too ethereal to be distinguished by anything so crude as a title impede and disorder the great business of human intercourse. And when we have threaded our way carefully through all these grades from the niece of the Earl to the friend of the cousin of the General, we are still faced with an abyss; a gulf yawns before us; on the other side are the working classes. The writer of perfect judgment and taste, like Jane Austen, does no more than glance across the gulf; she restricts herself to her own special class and finds infinite shades within it. But for the brisk, inquisitive, combative writer like Meredith, the temptation to explore is irresistible. He runs up and down the social scale; he chimes one note against another; he insists that the Earl and the cook, the General and the farmer shall speak up for themselves and play their part in the extremely complicated comedy of English civilised life.

It was natural that he should attempt it. A writer touched by the comic spirit relishes these distinctions keenly; they give him something to take hold of; something to make play with. English fiction without the nieces of Earls and the cousins of Generals would be an arid waste. It would resemble Russian fiction. It would have to fall back upon the immensity of the soul and upon the brotherhood of man. Like Russian fiction, it would lack comedy. But while we realise the immense debt that we owe the Earl's niece and the General's cousin, we doubt sometimes whether the pleasure we get from the play of satire on these broken edges is altogether worth the price we pay. For the price is a high one. The strain upon a novelist is tremendous. In two short stories Meredith gallantly attempts to bridge all gulfs, and to take half a dozen different levels in his stride. Now he speaks as an Earl's niece; now as a carpenter's wife. It cannot be said that his daring is altogether successful. One has a feeling (perhaps it is unfounded) that the blood of the niece of an Earl is not quite so tart and sharp as he would have it. Aristocracy is not, perhaps, so consistently high and brusque and eccentric as, from his angle, he would represent it. Yet his great people are more successful than his humble. His cooks are too ripe and rotund; his farmers too ruddy and earthy. He overdoes the pith and the sap; the fist-shaking and the thigh-slapping. He has got too far from them to write of them with ease.

It seems, therefore, that the novelist, and the English novelist in particular, suffers from a disability which affects no other artist to the same extent. His work is influenced by his birth. He is fated to know intimately, and so to describe with understanding, only those who are of his own social rank. He cannot escape from the box in which he has been bred. A bird's-eye view of fiction shows us no gentlemen in Dickens; no working men in Thackeray. One hesitates to call Jane Eyre a lady. The Elizabeths and the Emmas of Miss Austen could not possibly be taken for anything else. It is vain to look for dukes or for dustmen—we doubt that such extremes are to be found anywhere in fiction. We are, therefore, brought to the melancholy and tantalising conclusion not only that novels are poorer than they might be, but that we are very largely prevented—for after all, the novelists, are the great interpreters—from knowing what is happening either in the heights of Society or in its depths. There is practically no evidence available by which we can guess at the feelings of the highest in the land. What does a King feel? What does a Duke think? We cannot say. For the highest in the land have seldom written at all, and have never written about themselves. We shall never know what the Court of Louis XIV looked like to Louis XIV himself. It seems likely indeed that the English aristocracy will pass out of existence, or be merged with the common people, without leaving any true picture of themselves behind.

But our ignorance of the aristocracy is nothing compared with our ignorance of the working classes. At all times the great families of England and France have delighted to have famous men at their tables, and thus the Thackerays and the Disraelis and the Prousts have been familiar enough with the cut and fashion of aristocratic life to write about it with authority. Unfortunately, however, life is so framed that literary success invariably means a rise, never a fall, and seldom, what is far more desirable, a spread in the social scale. The rising novelist is never pestered to come to gin and winkles with the plumber and his wife. His books never bring him into touch with the cat's-meat man, or start a correspondence with the old lady who sells matches and bootlaces by the gate of the British Museum. He becomes rich; he becomes respectable; he buys an evening suit and dines with peers. Therefore, the later works of successful novelists show, if anything, a slight rise in the social scale. We tend to get more and more portraits of the successful and the distinguished. On the other hand, the old rat-catchers and ostlers of Shakespeare's day are shuffled altogether off the scene, or become, what is far more offensive, objects of pity, examples of curiosity. They serve to show up the rich. They serve to point the evils of the social system. They are no longer, as they used to be when Chaucer wrote, simply themselves. For it is impossible, it would seem, for working men to write in their own language about their own lives. Such education as the act of writing implies at once makes them self-conscious, or class-conscious, or removes them from their own class. That anonymity, in the shadow of which writers write most happily, is the prerogatives of the middle class alone. It is from the middle class that writers spring, because it is in the middle class only that the practice of writing is as natural and habitual as hoeing a field or building a house. Thus it must have been harder for Byron to be a poet than Keats; and it is as impossible to imagine that a Duke could be a great novelist as that *Paradise Lost* could be written by a man behind a counter.

But things change; class distinctions were not always so hard and fast as they have now become. The Elizabethan age was far more elastic in this respect than our own; we, on the other hand, are far less hidebound than the Victorians. Thus it may well be that we are on the edge of a greater change than any the world has yet known. In another century or so, none of these distinctions may hold good. The Duke and the agricultural labourer as we know them now may have died out as completely as the bustard and the wild cat. Only natural differences such as those of brain and character will serve to distinguish us. General Ople (if there are still Generals) will visit the niece (if there are still nieces) of the Earl (if there are still Earls) without brushing his coat (if there are still coats). But what will happen to English fiction when it has come to pass that there are neither Generals, nieces, Earls, nor coats, we cannot imagine. It may change its character so that we no longer know it. It may become extinct. Novels may be written as seldom and as unsuccessfully by our descendants as the poetic drama by ourselves. The art of a truly democratic age will be—what?

*

George Gissing

*

"Do you know there are men in London who go the round of the streets selling paraffin oil?" wrote George Gissing in the year 1880, and the phrase because it is Gissing's calls up a world of fog and fourwheelers, of slatternly landladies, of struggling men of letters, of gnawing domestic misery, of gloomy back streets, and ignoble yellow chapels; but also, above this misery, we see tree-crowned heights, the columns of the Parthenon, and the hills of Rome. For Gissing is one of those imperfect novelists through whose books one sees the life of the author faintly covered by the lives of fictitious people. With such writers we establish a personal rather than an artistic relationship. We approach them through their lives as much as through their work, and when we take up Gissing's letters, which have character, but little wit and no brilliance to illumine them, we feel that we are filling in a design which we began to trace out when we read *Demos* and *New Grub Street* and *The Nether World.*

Yet here, too, there are gaps in plenty, and many dark places left unlit. Much information has been kept back, many facts necessarily omitted. The Gissings were poor, and their father died when they were children; there were many of them, and they had to scrape together what education they could get. George, his sister said, had a passion for learning. He would rush off to school with a sharp herring bone in his throat for fear of missing his lesson. He would copy out from a little book called *That's It* the astonishing number of eggs that the tench lays and the sole lays and the carp lays, "because I think it is a fact worthy of attention." She remembers his "overwhelming veneration" for intellect, and how patiently, sitting beside her, the tall boy with the high white forehead and the short-sighted eyes would help her with her Latin, "giving the same explanation time after time without the least sign of impatience."

Partly because he reverenced facts and had no faculty it seems (his language is meagre and unmetaphorical) for impressions, it is doubtful whether his choice of a novelist's career was a happy one. There was the whole world, with its history and its literature, inviting him to haul it into his mind; he was eager; he was intellectual; yet he must sit down in hired rooms and spin novels about "earnest young people striving for improvement in, as it were, the dawn of a new phase of our civilisation."

But the art of fiction is infinitely accommodating, and it was quite ready about the year 1880 to accept into its ranks a writer who wished to be the "mouthpiece of the advanced Radical Party," who was determined to show in his novels the ghastly condition of the poor and the hideous injustice of society. The art of fiction was ready, that is, to agree that such books were novels; but it was doubtful if such novels would be read. Smith Elder's reader summed up the situation tersely enough. Mr. Gissing's novel, he wrote, "is too painful to please the ordinary novel reader, and treats of scenes that can never attract the subscribers to Mr. Mudie's Library." So, dining off lentils and hearing the men cry paraffin for sale in the streets of Islington, Gissing paid for the publication himself. It was then that he formed the habit of getting up at five in the morning in order to tramp half across London in order to coach Mr. M. before breakfast. Often enough Mr. M. sent down word that he was already engaged, and then another page was added to the dismal chronicle of life in modern *Grub Street*—we are faced by another of those problems with which literature is sown so thick. The writer has dined upon lentils; he gets up at five; he walks across London; he finds Mr. M. still in bed, whereupon he stands forth as the champion of life as it is, and proclaims that ugliness is truth, truth ugliness, and that is all we know and all we need to know. But there are signs that the novel resents such treatment. To use a burning consciousness of one's own misery, of the shackles that cut one's own limbs, to quicken one's sense of life in general, as Dickens did, to shape out of the murk which has surrounded one's childhood some resplendent figure such as Micawber or Mrs. Gamp is admirable: but to use personal suffering to rivet the reader's sympathy and curiosity upon your private case is disastrous. Imagination is at its freest when it is most generalised; it loses something of its sweep and power, it becomes petty and personal, when it is limited to the consideration of a particular case calling for sympathy.

At the same time the sympathy which identifies the author with his hero is a passion of great intensity; it makes the pages fly; it lends what has perhaps little merit artistically another and momentarily perhaps a keener edge. Biffen and Reardon had, we say to ourselves, bread and butter and sardines for supper; so had Gissing; Biffen's overcoat had been pawned, and so had Gissing's; Reardon could not write on Sunday; no more could Gissing. We forget whether it was Reardon who loved cats or Gissing who loved barrel organs. Certainly both Reardon and Gissing bought their copies of Gibbon at a second-hand book-stall, and lugged the volumes home one by one through the fog. So we go on capping these resemblances, and each time we succeed, dipping now into the novel, now into the letters, a little glow of satisfaction comes over us, as if novel-reading were a game of skill in which the puzzle set us is to find the face of the writer.

We know Gissing thus as we do not know Hardy or George Eliot. Where the great novelist flows in and out of his characters and bathes them in an element which seems to be common to us all, Gissing remains solitary, self-centred, apart. His is one of those sharp lights beyond whose edges all is vapour and phantom. But mixed with this sharp light is one ray of singular penetration. With all his narrowness of outlook and meagreness of sensibility, Gissing is one of the extremely rare novelists who believes in the power of the mind, who makes his people think. They are thus differently poised from the majority of fictitious men and women. The awful hierarchy of the passions is slightly displaced. Social snobbery does not exist; money is desired almost entirely to buy bread and butter; love itself takes a second place. But the brain works, and that alone is enough to give us a sense of freedom. For to think is to become complex; it is to overflow boundaries, to cease to be a "character," to merge one's private life in the life of politics or art or ideas, to have relationships based partly on them, and not on sexual desire alone. The impersonal side of life is given its due place in the scheme. "Why don't people write about the really important things of life?" Gissing makes one of his characters exclaim, and at the unexpected cry the horrid burden of fiction begins to slip from the shoulders. Is it possible that we are going to talk of other things besides falling in love, important though that is, and going to dinner with Duchesses, fascinating though that is? Here in Gissing is a gleam of recognition that Darwin had lived, that science was developing, that people read books and look at pictures, that once upon a time there was such a place as Greece. It is the consciousness of these things that makes his books such painful reading; it was this that made it impossible for them to "attract the subscribers to Mr. Mudie's Library." They owe their peculiar grimness to the fact that the people who suffer most are capable of making their suffering part of a reasoned view of life. The thought endures when the feeling has gone. Their unhappiness represents something more lasting than a personal reverse; it becomes part of a view of life. Hence when we have finished one of Gissing's novels we have taken away not a character, nor an incident, but the comment of a thoughtful man upon life as life seemed to him.

But because Gissing was always thinking, he was always changing. In that lies much of his interest for us. As a young man he had thought that he would write books to show up the "hideous injustice of our whole system of society." Later his views changed; either the task was impossible, or other tastes were tugging him in a different direction. He came to think, as he believed finally, that "the only thing known to us of absolute value is artistic perfection . . . the works of the artist . . . remain sources of health to the world." So that if one wishes to better the world one must, paradoxically enough, withdraw and spend more and more time fashioning one's sentences to perfection in solitude. Writing, Gissing thought, is a task of the utmost difficulty; perhaps at the end of his life he might be able "to manage a page that is decently grammatical and fairly harmonious." There are moments when he succeeded splendidly. For example, he is describing a cemetery in the East End of London:

> Here on the waste limits of that dread east, to wander among tombs is to go hand-in-hand with the stark and eyeless emblems of mortality; the spirit fails beneath the cold burden of ignoble destiny. Here lie those who were born for toil; who, when toil has worn them to the uttermost, have but to yield their useless breath and pass into oblivion. For them is no day, only the brief twilight of a winter's sky between the former and the latter night. For them no aspiration; for them no hope of memory in the dust; their very children are wearied into forgetfulness. Indistinguishable units in the vast throng that labours but to support life, the name of each, father, mother, child, is but a dumb cry for the warmth and love of which fate so stinted them. The wind wails above their narrow tenements; the sandy soil, soaking in the rain as soon as it has fallen, is a symbol of the great world which absorbs their toil and straightway blots their being.

Again and again such passages of description stand out like stone slabs, shaped and solid, among the untidy litter with which the pages of fiction are strewn.

Gissing, indeed, never ceased to educate himself. While the Baker Street trains hissed their steam under his window, and the lodger downstairs blew his room out, and the landlady was insolent, and the grocer refused to send the sugar so that he had to fetch it himself, and the fog burnt his throat and he caught cold and never spoke to anybody for three weeks, yet must drive his pen through page after page and vacillated miserably from one domestic disaster to another—while all this went on with a dreary monotony, for which he could only blame the weakness of his own character, the columns of the Parthenon, the hills of Rome still rose above the fogs and the fried-fish shops of the Euston Road. He was determined to visit Greece and Rome. He actually set foot in Athens; he saw Rome; he read his Thucydides in Sicily before he died. Life was changing round him; his comment upon life was changing too. Perhaps the old sordidity, the fog and the paraffin and the drunken landlady, was not the only reality; ugliness is not the whole truth; there is an element of beauty in the world. The past, with its literature and its civilisation, solidifies the present. At any rate his books in future were to be about Rome in the time of Totila, not about Islington in the time of Queen Victoria. He was reaching some point in his perpetual thinking where "one has to distinguish between two forms of intelligence"; one cannot venerate the intellect only. But before he could mark down the spot he had reached on the map of thought, he, who had shared so many of his characters' experiences, shared, too, the death he had given to Edwin Reardon. "Patience, patience," he said to the friend who stood by him as he died—an imperfect novelist, but a highly educated man.

*

The Novels of George Meredith

*

Twenty years ago[1] the reputation of George Meredith was at its height. His novels had won their way to celebrity through all sorts of difficulties, and their fame was all the brighter and the more singular for what it had subdued. Then, too, it was generally discovered that the maker of these splendid books was himself a splendid old man. Visitors who went down to Box Hill reported that they were thrilled as they walked up the drive of the little suburban house by the sound of a voice booming and reverberating within. The novelist, seated among the usual knick-knacks of the drawing-room, was like the bust of Euripides to look at. Age had worn and sharpened the fine features, but the nose was still acute, the blue eyes still keen and ironical. Though he had sunk immobile into an arm-chair, his aspect was still vigorous and alert. It was true that he was almost stone-deaf, but this was the least of afflictions to one who was scarcely able to keep pace with the rapidity of his own ideas. Since he could not hear what was said to him, he could give himself whole-heartedly to the delights of soliloquy. It did not much matter, perhaps, whether his audience was cultivated or simple. Compliments that would have flattered a duchess were presented with equal ceremony to a child. To neither could he speak the simple language of daily life. But all the time this highly wrought, artificial conversation, with its crystallised phrases and its high-piled metaphors, moved and tossed on a current of laughter. His

[1] Written in January 1928.

laugh curled round his sentences as if he himself enjoyed their humorous exaggeration. The master of language was splashing and diving in his element of words. So the legend grew; and the fame of George Meredith, who sat with the head of a Greek poet on his shoulders in a suburban villa beneath Box Hill, pouring out poetry and sarcasm and wisdom in a voice that could be heard almost on the highroad, made his fascinating and brilliant books seem more fascinating and brilliant still.

But that is twenty years ago. His fame as a talker is necessarily dimmed, and his fame as a writer seems also under a cloud. On none of his successors is his influence now marked. When one of them whose own work has given him the right to be heard with respect chances to speak his mind on the subject, it is not flattering.

> Meredith [writes Mr. Forster in his *Aspects of Fiction*] is not the great name he was twenty years ago. . . . His philosophy has not worn well. His heavy attacks on sentimentality—they bore the present generation. . . . When he gets serious and noble-minded there is a strident overtone, a bullying that becomes distressing. . . . What with the faking, what with the preaching, which was never agreeable and is now said to be hollow, and what with the home countries posing as the universe, it is no wonder Meredith now lies in the trough.

The criticism is not, of course, intended to be a finished estimate; but in its conversational sincerity it condenses accurately enough what is in the air when Meredith is mentioned. No, the general conclusion would seem to be, Meredith has not worn well. But the value of centenaries lies in the occasion they offer us for solidifying such airy impressions. Talk, mixed with half-rubbed-out memories, forms a mist by degrees though which we scarcely see plain. To open the books again, to try to read them as if for the first time, to try to free them from the rubbish of reputation and accident—that, perhaps, is the most acceptable present we can offer to a writer on his hundredth birthday.

And since the first novel is always apt to be an unguarded one, where the author displays his gifts without knowing how to dispose of them to the best advantage, we may do well to open *Richard Feverel* first. It needs no great sagacity to see that the writer is a novice at his task. The style is extremely uneven. Now he twists himself into iron knots; now he lies flat as a pancake. He seems to be of two minds as to his intention. Ironic comment alternates with long-winded narrative. He vacillates from one attitude to another. Indeed, the whole fabric seems to rock a little insecurely. The baronet wrapped in a cloak; the county family; the ancestral home; the uncles mouthing epigrams in the dining-room; the great ladies flaunting and swimming; the jolly farmers slapping their thighs: all liberally if spasmodically sprinkled with dried aphorisms from a pepper-pot called the Pilgrim's Scrip—what an odd conglomeration it is! But the oddity is not on the surface; it is not merely that whiskers and bonnets have gone out of fashion: it lies deeper, in Meredith's intention, in what he wishes to bring to pass. He has been, it is plain, at great pains to destroy the conventional form of the novel. He makes no attempt to preserve the sober reality of Trollope and Jane Austen; he has destroyed all the usual staircases by which we have learnt to climb. And what is done so deliberately is done with a purpose. This defiance of the ordinary, these airs and graces, the formality of the dialogue with its Sirs and Madams are all there to create an atmosphere that is unlike that of daily life, to prepare the way for a new and an original sense of the human scene. Peacock, from whom Meredith learnt so much, is equally arbitrary, but the virtue of the assumptions he asks us to make is proved by the fact that we accept Mr. Skionar and the rest with natural delight. Meredith's characters in *Richard Feverel*, on the other hand, are at odds with their surroundings. We at once exclaim how unreal they are, how artificial, how impossible. The baronet and the butler, the hero and the heroine, the good woman and the bad woman are mere types of baronets and butler, good women and bad. For what reason, then, has he sacrificed the substantial advantages of realistic common sense—the staircase and the stucco? Because, it becomes clear as we read, he possessed a keen sense not of the complexity of character, but of the splendour of a scene. One after another in this first book he creates a scene to which we can attach abstract names—Youth, The Birth of Love, The Power of Nature. We are galloped to them over every obstacle on the pounding hoofs of rhapsodical prose.

> Away with Systems! Away with a corrupt World! Let us breathe the air of the Enchanted Island! Golden lie the meadows; golden run the streams; red gold is on the pine stems.

We forget that Richard is Richard and that Lucy is Lucy; they are youth; the world runs molten gold. The writer is a rhapsodist, a poet then; but we have not yet exhausted all the elements in this first novel. We have to reckon with the author himself. He has a mind stuffed with ideas, hungry for argument. His boys and girls may spend their time picking daisies in the meadows, but they breathe, however unconsciously, an air bristling with intellectual question and comment. On a dozen occasions these incongruous elements strain and threaten to break apart. The book is cracked through and through with those fissures which come when the author seems to be of twenty minds at the same time. Yet it succeeds in holding miraculously together, not certainly by the depths and originality of its character drawing but by the vigour of its intellectual power and by its lyrical intensity.

We are left, then, with our curiosity aroused. Let him write another book or two; get into his stride; control his crudities: and we will open *Harry Richmond* and see what has happened now. Of all the things that might have happened this surely is the strangest. All trace of immaturity is gone; but with it every trace of the uneasy adventurous mind has gone too. The story bowls smoothly along the road which Dickens has already trodden of autobiographical narrative. It is a boy speaking, a boy thinking, a boy adventuring. For that reason, no doubt, the author has curbed his redundance and pruned his speech. The style is the most rapid possible. It runs smooth, without a kink in it. Stevenson, one feels, must have learnt much from this supple narrative, with its precise adroit phrases, its exact quick glance at visible things.

> Plunged among dark green leaves, smelling wood-smoke, at night; at morning waking up, and the world alight, and you standing high, and marking the hills where you will see the next morning and the next, morning after morning, and one morning the dearest person in the world surprising you just before you wake: I thought this a heavenly pleasure.

It goes gallantly, but a little self-consciously. He hears himself talking. Doubts begin to rise and hover and settle at last (as in *Richard Feverel*) upon the human figures. These boys are no more real boys than the sample apple which is laid on top of the basket is a real apple. They are too simple, too gallant, too adventurous to be of the same unequal breed as David Copperfield, for example. They are sample boys, novelist's specimens; and again we encounter the extreme conventionality of Meredith's mind where we found it, to our surprise, before. With all his boldness (and there is no risk that he will not run with probability) there are a dozen occasions on which a reach-me-down character will satisfy him well enough. But just as we are thinking that the young gentlemen are altogether too pat, and the adventures which befall them altogether too slick, the shallow bath of illusion closes over our heads and we sink with Richmond Roy and the Princess Ottilia into the world of fantasy and romance, where all holds together and we are able to put our imagination at the writer's service without reserve. That such surrender is above all things delightful: that it adds spring-heels to our boots: that it fires the cold scepticism out of us and makes the world glow in lucid transparency before our eyes, needs no showing, as it certainly submits to no analysis. That Meredith can induce such moments proves him possessed of an extraordinary power. Yet it is a capricious power and highly intermittent. For pages all is effort and agony; phrase after phrase is struck and no light comes. Then, just as we are about to drop the book, the rocket roars into the air; the whole scene flashes into light; and the book, years after, is recalled by that sudden splendour.

If, then, this intermittent brilliancy is Meredith's characteristic excellence it is worth while to look into it more closely. And perhaps the first thing that we shall discover is that the scenes which catch the eye and remain in memory are static; they are illuminations, not discoveries; they do not improve our knowledge of the characters. It is significant that Richard and Lucy, Harry and Ottilia, Clara and Vernon, Beauchamp and Renée are presented in carefully appropriate surroundings—on board a yacht, under a flowering cherry tree, upon some river-bank, so that the landscape always makes part of the emotion. The sea or the sky or the wood is brought forward to symbolise what the human beings are feeling or looking.

> The sky was bronze, a vast furnace dome. The folds of light and shadow everywhere were satin rich. That afternoon the bee hummed of thunder and refreshed the ear.

That is a description of a state of mind.

> These winter mornings are divine. They move on noiselessly. The earth is still as if waiting. A wren warbles, and flits through the lank, drenched branches; hillside opens green; everywhere is mist, everywhere expectancy.

That is a description of a woman's face. But only some states of mind and some expressions of face can be described in imagery—only those which are so highly wrought as to be simple and, for that reason, will not submit to analysis. This is a limitation; for though we may be able to see these people, very brilliantly, in a moment of illumination, they do not change or glow; the light sinks and leaves us in darkness. We have no such intuitive knowledge of Meredith's characters as we have of Stendhal's, Tchehov's, Jane Austen's. Indeed, our knowledge of such characters is so intimate that we can almost dispense with "great scenes" altogether. Some of the most emotional scenes in fiction are the quietest. We have been wrought upon by nine hundred and ninety-nine little touches; the thousandth, when it comes, is as slight as the others, but the effect is prodigious. But with Meredith there are no touches; there are hammer-strokes only, so that our knowledge of his characters is partial, spasmodic, and intermittent.

Meredith, then, is not among the great psychologists who feel their way, anonymously and patiently, in and out of the fibres of the mind and make one character differ minutely and completely from another. He is among the poets who identify the character with the passion or with the idea; who symbolise and make abstract. And yet—here lay his difficulty perhaps—he was not a poet-novelist wholly and completely as Emily Brontë was a poet-novelist. He did not steep the world in one mood. His mind was too self-conscious, and too sophisticated to remain lyrical for long. He does not sing only; he dissects. Even in his most lyrical scenes a sneer curls its lash round the phrases and laughs at their extravagance. And as we read on, we shall find that the comic spirit, when it is allowed to dominate the scene, licked the world to a very different shape. *The Egoist* at once modifies our theory that Meredith is pre-eminently the master of great scenes. Here there is none of that precipitate hurry that has rushed us over obstacles to the summit of one emotional peak after another. The case is one that needs argument; argument needs logic; Sir Willoughby, "our original male in giant form," is turned slowly round before a steady fire of scrutiny and criticism which allows no twitch on the victim's part to escape it. That the victim is a wax model and not entirely living flesh and blood is perhaps true. At the same time Meredith pays us a supreme compliment to which as novel-readers we are little accustomed. We are civilised people, he seems to say, watching the comedy of human relations together. Human relations are of profound interest. Men and women are not cats and monkeys, but beings of a larger growth and of a greater range. He imagines us capable of disinterested curiosity in the behaviour of our kind. This is so rare a compliment from a novelist to his reader that we are at first bewildered and then delighted. Indeed his comic spirit is a far more penetrating goddess than his lyrical. It is she who cuts a clear path through the brambles of his manner; she who surprises us again and again by the depth of her observations; she who creates the dignity, the seriousness, and the vitality of Meredith's world. Had Meredith, one is tempted to reflect, lived in an age or in a country where comedy was the rule, he might never have contracted those airs of intellectual superiority, that manner of oracular solemnity which it is, as he points out, the use of the comic spirit to correct.

But in many ways the age—if we can judge so amorphous a shape—was hostile to Meredith, or, to speak more accurately, was hostile to his success with the age we now live in—the year 1928. His teaching seems now too strident and too optimistic and too shallow. It obtrudes; and when philosophy is not consumed in a novel, when we can underline this phrase with a pencil, and cut out that exhortation with a pair of scissors and paste the whole into a system, it is safe to say that there is something wrong with the philosophy or with the novel or with both. Above all, his teaching is too insistent. He cannot, even to hear the profoundest secret, suppress his own opinion. And there is nothing that characters in fiction resent more. If, they seem to argue, we have been called into existence merely to express Mr. Meredith's views upon the universe, we would rather not exist at all. Thereupon they die; and a novel that is full of dead characters, even though it is also full of profound wisdom and exalted teaching, is not achieving its aim as a novel. But here we reach another point upon which the present age may be inclined to have more sympathy with Meredith. When he wrote, in the seventies and eighties of the last century, the novel had reached a stage where it could only exist by moving onward. It is a possible contention that after those two perfect novels, *Pride and Prejudice* and *The Small House at Allington*, English fiction had to escape from the dominion of that perfection, as English poetry had to escape from the perfection of Tennyson. George Eliot, Meredith, and Hardy were all imperfect novelists largely because they insisted upon introducing qualities, of thought and of poetry, that are perhaps incompatible with fiction at its most perfect. On the other hand, if fiction had remained what it was to Jane Austen and Trollope, fiction would by this time be dead. Thus Meredith deserves our gratitude and excites our interest as a great innovator. Many of our doubts about him and much of our inability to frame any definite opinion of his work comes from the fact that it is experimental and thus contains elements that do not fuse harmoniously—the qualities are at odds: the one quality which binds and concentrates has been omitted. To read Meredith, then, to our greatest advantage we must make certain allowances and relax certain standards. We must not expect the perfect quietude of a traditional style nor the triumphs of a patient and pedestrian psychology. On the other hand, his claim, "My method has been to prepare my readers for a crucial exhibition of the personae, and then to give the scene in the fullest of their blood and brain under stress of a fierce situation," is frequently justified. Scene after scene rises on the mind's eye with a flare of fiery intensity. If we are irritated by the dancing-master dandyism which made him write "gave his lungs full play" instead of laughed, or "tasted the swift intricacies of the needle" instead of sewed, we must remember that such phrases prepare the way for the "fierce situations." Meredith is creating the atmosphere from which we shall pass naturally into a highly pitched state of emotion. Where the realistic novelist, like Trollope, lapses into flatness and dullness, the lyrical novelist, like Meredith, becomes meretricious and false; and such falsity is, of course, not only much more glaring than flatness, but it is a greater crime against the phlegmatic nature of prose fiction. Perhaps Meredith had been well advised if he had abjured the novel altogether and kept himself wholly to poetry. Yet we have to remind ourselves that the fault may be ours. Our prolonged diet upon Russian fiction, rendered neutral and negative in translation, our absorption in the convolutions of psychological Frenchmen, may have led us to forget that the English language is naturally exuberant, and the English character full of humours and eccentricities. Meredith's flamboyancy has a great ancestry behind it; we cannot avoid all memory of Shakespeare.

When such questions and qualifications crowd upon

us as we read, the fact may be taken to prove that we are neither near enough to be under his spell nor far enough to see him in proportion. Thus the attempt to pronounce a finished estimate is even more illusive than usual. But we can testify even now that to read Meredith is to be conscious of a packed and muscular mind; of a voice booming and reverberating with its own unmistakable accent even though the partition between us is too thick for us to hear what he says distinctly. Still, as we read we feel that we are in the presence of a Greek god though he is surrounded by the innumerable ornaments of a suburban drawing-room; who talks brilliantly, even if he is deaf to the lower tones of the human voice; who, if he is rigid and immobile, is yet marvellously alive and on the alert. This brilliant and uneasy figure has his place with the great eccentrics rather than with the great masters. He will be read, one may guess, by fits and starts; he will be forgotten and discovered and again discovered and forgotten like Donne, and Peacock, and Gerard Hopkins. But if English fiction continues to be read, the novels of Meredith must inevitably rise from time to time into view; his work must inevitably be disputed and discussed.

*

"I Am Christina Rossetti"

*

On the fifth of this December[1] Christina Rossetti will celebrate her centenary, or, more properly speaking, we shall celebrate it for her, and perhaps not a little to her distress, for she was one of the shyest of women, and to be spoken of, as we shall certainly speak of her, would have caused her acute discomfort. Nevertheless, it is inevitable; centenaries are inexorable; talk of her we must. We shall read her life; we shall read her letters; we shall study her portraits, speculate about her diseases—of which she had a great variety; and rattle the drawers of her writing-table, which are for the most part empty. Let us begin with the biography—for what could be more amusing? As everybody knows, the fascination of reading biographies is irresistible. No sooner have we opened the pages of Miss Sandars's careful and competent book (*Life of Christina Rossetti*, by Mary F. Sandars. [Hutchinson]) than the old illusion comes over us. Here is the past and all its inhabitants miraculously sealed as in a magic tank; all we have to do is to look and to listen and to listen and to look and soon the little figures—for they are rather under life size—will begin to move and to speak, and as they move we shall arrange them in all sorts of patterns of which they were ignorant, for they thought when they were alive that they could go where they liked; and as they speak we shall read into their sayings all kinds of meanings which never struck them, for they believed when they were alive that they said straight off what-

[1] 1930.

ever came into their heads. But once you are in a biography all is different.

Here, then, is Hallam Street, Portland Place, about the year 1830; and here are the Rossettis, an Italian family consisting of father and mother and four small children. The street was unfashionable and the home rather poverty-stricken; but the poverty did not matter, for, being foreigners, the Rossettis did not care much about the customs and conventions of the usual middle-class British family. They kept themselves to themselves, dressed as they liked, entertained Italian exiles, among them organ-grinders and other distressed compatriots, and made ends meet by teaching and writing and other odd jobs. By degrees Christina detached herself from the family group. It is plain that she was a quiet and observant child, with her own way of life already fixed in her head—she was to write—but all the more did she admire the superior competence of her elders. Soon we begin to surround her with a few friends and to endow her with a few characteristics. She detested parties. She dressed anyhow. She liked her brother's friends and little gatherings of young artists and poets who were to reform the world, rather to her amusement, for although so sedate, she was also whimsical and freakish, and liked making fun of people who took themselves with egotistic solemnity. And though she meant to be a poet she had very little of the vanity and stress of young poets; her verses seem to have formed themselves whole and entire in her head, and she did not worry very much what was said of them because in her own mind she knew that they were good. She had also immense powers of admiration—for her mother, for example, who was so quiet, and so sagacious, so simple and so sincere; and for her elder sister Maria, who had no taste for painting or for poetry, but was, for that very reason, perhaps more vigorous and effective in daily life. For example, Maria always refused to visit the Mummy Room at the British Museum because, she said, the Day of Resurrection might suddenly dawn and it would be very unseemly if the corpses had to put on immortality under the gaze of mere sight-seers—

a reflection which had not struck Christina, but seemed to her admirable. Here, of course, we, who are outside the tank, enjoy a hearty laugh, but Christina, who is inside the tank and exposed to all its heats and currents, thought her sister's conduct worthy of the highest respect. Indeed, if we look at her a little more closely we shall see that something dark and hard, like a kernel, had already formed in the centre of Christina Rossetti's being.

It was religion, of course. Even when she was quite a girl her life-long absorption in the relation of the soul with God had taken possession of her. Her sixty-four years might seem outwardly spent in Hallam Street and Endsleigh Gardens and Torrington Square, but in reality she dwelt in some curious region where the spirit strives towards an unseen God—in her case, a dark God, a harsh God—a God who decreed that all the pleasures of the world were hateful to Him. The theatre was hateful, the opera was hateful, nakedness was hateful—when her friend Miss Thompson painted naked figures in her pictures she had to tell Christina that they were fairies, but Christina saw through the imposture—everything in Christina's life radiated from that knot of agony and intensity in the centre. Her belief regulated her life in the smallest particulars. It taught her that chess was wrong, but that whist and cribbage did not matter. But also it interfered in the most tremendous questions of her heart. There was a young painter called James Collinson, and she loved James Collinson and he loved her, but he was a Roman Catholic and so she refused him. Obligingly he became a member of the Church of England, and she accepted him. Vacillating, however, for he was a slippery man, he wobbled back to Rome, and Christina, though it broke her heart and for ever shadowed her life, cancelled the engagement. Years afterwards another, and it seems better founded, prospect of happiness presented itself. Charles Cayley proposed to her. But alas, this abstract and erudite man who shuffled about the world in a state of absent-minded dishabille, and translated the gospel into Iroquois, and asked smart ladies at a party "whether they were interested in the Gulf Stream," and for a present gave Christina a sea mouse preserved in spirits, was, not unnaturally, a free thinker. Him, too, Christina put from her. Though "no woman ever loved a man more deeply," she would not be the wife of a sceptic. She who loved the "obtuse and furry"—the wombats, toads, and mice of the earth—and called Charles Cayley "my blindest buzzard, my special mole," admitted no moles, wombats, buzzards, or Cayleys to her heaven.

So one might go on looking and listening for ever. There is no limit to the strangeness, amusement, and oddity of the past sealed in a tank. But just as we are wondering which cranny of this extraordinary territory to explore next, the principal figure intervenes. It is as if a fish, whose unconscious gyrations we had been watching in and out of reeds, round and round rocks, suddenly dashed at the glass and broke it. A tea-party is the occasion. For some reason Christina went to a party given by Mrs. Virtue Tebbs. What happened there is unknown —perhaps something was said in a casual, frivolous, tea-party way about poetry. At any rate,

> suddenly there uprose from a chair and paced forward into the centre of the room a little woman dressed in black, who announced solemnly, "I am Christina Rossetti!" and having so said, returned to her chair.

With those words the glass is broken. Yes [she seems to say], I am a poet. You who pretend to honour my centenary are no better than the idle people at Mrs. Tebb's tea-party. Here you are rambling among unimportant trifles, rattling my writing-table drawers, making fun of the Mummies and Maria and my love affairs when all I care for you to know is here. Behold this green volume. It is a copy of my collected works. It costs four shillings and sixpence. Read that. And so she returns to her chair.

How absolute and unaccommodating these poets are! Poetry, they say, has nothing to do with life. Mummies and wombats, Hallam Street and omnibuses, James Collinson and Charles Cayley, sea mice and Mrs. Virtue Tebbs, Torrington Square and Endsleigh Gardens, even the vagaries of religious belief are irrelevant, extraneous, superfluous, unreal. It is poetry that matters. The only question of any interest is whether that poetry is good or bad. But this question of poetry, one might point out if only to gain time, is one of the greatest difficulty. Very little of value has been said about poetry since the world began. The judgment of contemporaries is almost always wrong. For example, most of the poems which figure in Christina Rossetti's complete works were rejected by editors. Her annual income from her poetry was for many years about ten pounds. On the other hand, the works of Jean Ingelow, as she noted sardonically, went into eight editions. There were, of course, among her contemporaries one or two poets and one or two critics whose judgment must be respectfully consulted. But what very different impressions they seem to gather from the same works—by what different standards they judge! For instance, when Swinburne read her poetry he exclaimed: "I have always thought that nothing more glorious in poetry has ever been written," and went on to say of her New Year Hymn

> that it was touched as with the fire and bathed as in the light of sunbeams, tuned as to chords and cadences of refluent sea-music beyond reach of harp and organ, large echoes of the serene and sonorous tides of heaven.

Then Professor Saintsbury comes with his vast learning, and examines *Goblin Market*, and reports that

> The metre of the principal poem ["Goblin Market"] may be best described as a dedoggerelised Skeltonic, with the gathered music of the various metrical progress since Spenser, utilised in the place of the wooden rattling of the followers of Chaucer. There may be discerned in it the same inclination towards line irregularity which has broken out, at different times, in the Pindaric of the late seventeeth and earlier eighteenth centuries, and in the rhymelessness of Sayers earlier and of Mr. Arnold later.

And then there is Sir Walter Raleigh:

> I think she is the best poet alive. . . . The worst of it is you cannot lecture on really pure poetry any more than you

can talk about the ingredients of pure water—it is adulterated, methylated, sanded poetry that makes the best lectures. The only thing that Christina makes me want to do, is cry, not lecture.

It would appear, then, that there are at least three schools of criticism: the refluent sea-music school; the line-irregularity school, and the school that bids one not criticise but cry. This is confusing; if we follow them all we shall only come to grief. Better perhaps read for oneself, expose the mind bare to the poem, and transcribe in all its haste and imperfection whatever may be the result of the impact. In this case it might run something as follows: O Christina Rossetti, I have humbly to confess that though I know many of your poems by heart, I have not read your works from cover to cover. I have not followed your course and traced your development. I doubt indeed that you developed very much. You were an instinctive poet. You saw the world from the same angle always. Years and the traffic of the mind with men and books did not affect you in the least. You carefully ignored any book that could shake your faith or any human being who could trouble your instincts. You were wise perhaps. Your instinct was so sure, so direct, so intense that it produced poems that sing like music in one's ears—like a melody by Mozart or an air by Gluck. Yet for all its symmetry, yours was a complex song. When you struck your harp many strings sounded together. Like all instinctives you had a keen sense of the visual beauty of the world. Your poems are full of gold dust and "sweet geraniums' varied brightness"; your eye noted incessantly how rushes are "velvet-headed," and lizards have a "strange metallic mail"—your eye, indeed, observed with a sensual pre-Raphaelite intensity that must have surprised Christina the Anglo-Catholic. But to her you owed perhaps the fixity and sadness of your muse. The pressure of a tremendous faith circles and clamps together these little songs. Perhaps they owe to it their solidity. Certainly they owe to it their sadness—your God was a harsh God, your heavenly crown was set with thorns. No sooner have you feasted on beauty with your eyes than your mind tells you that beauty is vain and beauty passes. Death, oblivion, and rest lap round your songs with their dark wave. And then, incongruously, a sound of scurrying and laughter is heard. There is the patter of animals' feet and the odd guttural notes of rooks and the snufflings of obtuse furry animals grunting and nosing. For you were not a pure saint by any means. You pulled legs; you tweaked noses. You were at war with all humbug and pretence. Modest as you were, still you were drastic, sure of your gift, convinced of your vision. A firm hand pruned your lines; a sharp ear tested their music. Nothing soft, otiose, irrelevant cumbered your pages. In a word, you were an artist. And thus was kept open, even when you wrote idly, tinkling bells for your own diversion, a pathway for the descent of that fiery visitant who came now and then and fused your lines into that indissoluble connection which no hand can put asunder:

> But bring me poppies brimmed with sleepy death
> And ivy choking what it garlandeth
>   And primroses that open to the moon.

Indeed so strange is the constitution of things, and so great the miracle of poetry, that some of the poems you wrote in your little back room will be found adhering in perfect symmetry when the Albert Memorial is dust and tinsel. Our remote posterity will be singing:

> When I am dead, my dearest,

or:

> My heart is like a singing bird,

when Torrington Square is a reef of coral perhaps and the fishes shoot in and out where your bedroom window used to be; or perhaps the forest will have reclaimed those pavements and the wombat and the ratel will be shuffling on soft, uncertain feet among the green undergrowth that will then tangle the area railings. In view of all this, and to return to your biography, had I been present when Mrs.

Virtue Tebbs gave her party, and had a short elderly woman in black risen to her feet and advanced to the middle of the room, I should certainly have committed some indiscretion—have broken a paper-knife or smashed a tea-cup in the awkward ardour of my admiration when she said, "I am Christina Rossetti."

❋

The Novels of Thomas Hardy[1]

❋

When we say that the death of Thomas Hardy leaves English fiction without a leader, we mean that there is no other writer whose supremacy would be generally accepted, none to whom it seems so fitting and natural to pay homage. Nobody of course claimed it less. The unworldly and simple old man would have been painfully embarrassed by the rhetoric that flourishes on such occasions as this. Yet it is no less than the truth to say that while he lived there was one novelist at all events who made the art of fiction seem an honourable calling; while Hardy lived there was no excuse for thinking meanly of the art he practised. Nor was this solely the result of his peculiar genius. Something of it sprang from his character in its modesty and integrity, from his life, lived simply down in Dorsetshire without self-seeking or self-advertisement. For both reasons, because of his genius and because of the dignity with which his gift was used, it was impossible not to honour him as an artist and to feel respect and affection for the man. But it is of the work that we must speak, of the novels that were written so long ago that they seem as detached from the fiction of the moment as Hardy himself was remote from the stir of the present and its littleness.

We have to go back more than a generation if we are to trace the career of Hardy as a novelist. In the year 1871 he was a man of thirty-one; he had written a novel, *Desperate Remedies*, but he was by no means an assured

[1] Written in January 1928.

craftsman. He "was feeling his way to a method," he said himself; as if he were conscious that he possessed all sorts of gifts, yet did not know their nature, or how to use them to advantage. To read that first novel is to share in the perplexity of its author. The imagination of the writer is powerful and sardonic; he is book-learned in a home-made way; he can create characters but he cannot control them; he is obviously hampered by the difficulties of his technique and, what is more singular, he is driven by some sense that human beings are the sport of forces outside themselves, to make use of an extreme and even melodramatic use of coincidence. He is already possessed of the conviction that a novel is not a toy, nor an argument; it is a means of giving truthful if harsh and violent impressions of the lives of men and women. But perhaps the most remarkable quality in the book is the sound that echoes and booms through its pages of a waterfall. It is the first manifestation of the power that was to assume such vast proportions in the later books. He already proves himself a minute and skilled observer of nature; the rain, he knows, falls differently as it falls upon roots or arable; he knows that the wind sounds differently as it passes through the branches of different trees. But he is aware in a larger sense of Nature as a force; he feels in it a spirit that can sympathise or mock or remain the indifferent spectator of human fortunes. Already that sense was his; and the crude story of Miss Aldclyffe and Cytherea is memorable because it is watched by the eyes of the gods, and worked out in the presence of Nature.

That he was a poet should have been obvious; that he was a novelist might still have been held uncertain. But the year after, when *Under the Greenwood Tree* appeared, it was clear that much of the effort of "feeling for a method" had been overcome. Something of the stubborn originality of the earlier book was lost. The second is accomplished, charming, idyllic compared with the first. The writer, it seems, may well develop into one of our English landscape painters, whose pictures are all of cottage gardens and old peasant women, who lingers to collect and preserve from oblivion the old-fashioned ways and words which are rapidly falling into disuse. And yet what kindly lover of antiquity, what naturalist with a microscope in his pocket, what scholar solicitous for the changing shapes of language, ever heard the cry of a small bird killed in the next wood by an owl with such intensity? The cry "passed into the silence without mingling with it." Again we hear, very far away, like the sound of a gun out at sea on a calm summer's morning, a strange and ominous echo. But as we read these early books there is a sense of waste. There is a feeling that Hardy's genius was obstinate and perverse; first one gift would have its way with him and then another. They would not consent to run together easily in harness. Such indeed was likely to be the fate of a writer who was at once poet and realist, a faithful son of field and down, yet tormented by the doubts and despondencies bred of book-learning; a lover of old ways and plain country men, yet doomed to see the faith and flesh of his forefathers turn to thin and spectral transparencies before his eyes.

To this contradiction Nature had added another element likely to disorder a symmetrical development. Some writers are born conscious of everything; others are unconscious of many things. Some, like Henry James and Flaubert, are able not merely to make the best use of the spoil their gifts bring in, but control their genius in the act of creation; they are aware of all the possibilities of every situation, and are never taken by surprise. The unconscious writers, on the other hand, like Dickens and Scott, seem suddenly and without their own consent to be lifted up and swept onwards. The wave sinks and they cannot say what has happened or why. Among them—it is the source of his strength and of his weakness—we must place Hardy. His own word, "moments of vision," exactly describes those passages of astonishing beauty and force which are to be found in every book that he wrote. With a sudden quickening of power which we cannot foretell, nor he, it seems, control, a single scene breaks off from the rest. We see, as if it existed alone and for all time, the wagon with Fanny's dead body inside travelling along the road under the dripping trees; we see the bloated sheep struggling among the clover; we see Troy flashing his sword round Bathsheba where she stands motionless, cutting the lock off her head and spitting the caterpillar on her breast. Vivid to the eye, but not to the eye alone, for every sense participates, such scenes dawn upon us and their splendour remains. But the power goes as it comes. The moment of vision is succeeded by long stretches of plain daylight, nor can we believe that any craft or skill could have caught the wild power and turned it to a better use. The novels therefore are full of inequalities; they are lumpish and dull and inexpressive; but they are never arid; there is always about them a little blur of unconsciousness, that halo of freshness and margin of the unexpressed which often produce the most profound sense of satisfaction. It is as if Hardy himself were not quite aware of what he did, as if his consciousness held more than he could produce, and he left it for his readers to make out his full meaning and to supplement it from their own experience.

For these reasons Hardy's genius was uncertain in development, uneven in accomplishment, but, when the moment came, magnificent in achievement. The moment came, completely and fully, in *Far from the Madding Crowd*. The subject was right; the method was right; the poet and the countryman, the sensual man, the sombre reflective man, the man of learning, all enlisted to produce a book which, however fashions may chop and change, must hold its place among the great English novels. There is, in the first place, that sense of the physical world which Hardy more than any novelist can bring before us; the sense that the little prospect of man's existence is ringed by a landscape which, while it exists apart, yet confers a deep and solemn beauty upon his drama. The dark downland, marked by the barrows of the dead and the huts of shepherds, rises against the sky, smooth as a wave of the sea, but solid and eternal; rolling away to the infinite distance, but sheltering in its folds quiet villages whose smoke rises in frail columns by day, whose lamps burn in the immense darkness by night. Gabriel Oak tending his sheep up there on the back of the world is the eternal shepherd; the stars are ancient beacons; and for ages he has watched beside his sheep.

But down in the valley the earth is full of warmth and life; the farms are busy, the barns stored, the fields loud with the lowing of cattle and the bleating of sheep. Nature is prolific, splendid, and lustful; not yet malignant and still the Great Mother of labouring men. And now for the first time Hardy gives full play to his humour, where it is freest and most rich, upon the lips of country men. Jan Coggan and Henry Fray and Joseph Poorgrass gather in the malt-house when the day's work is over and give vent to that half-shrewd, half-poetic humour which has been brewing in their brains and finding expression over their beer since the pilgrims tramped the Pilgrims' Way; which Shakespeare and Scott and George Eliot all loved to overhear, but none loved better or heard with greater understanding than Hardy. But it is not the part of the peasants in the Wessex novels to stand out as individuals. They compose a pool of common wisdom, of common humour, a fund of perpetual life. They comment upon the actions of the hero and heroine, but while Troy or Oak or Fanny or Bathsheba come in and out and pass away, Jan Coggan and Henry Fray and Joseph Poorgrass remain. They drink by night and they plough the fields by day. They are eternal. We meet them over and over again in the novels, and they always have something typical about them, more of the character that marks a race than of the features which belong to an individual. The peasants are the great sanctuary of sanity, the country the last stronghold of happiness. When they disappear, there is no hope for the race.

With Oak and Troy and Bathsheba and Fanny Robin we come to the men and women of the novels at their full stature. In every book three or four figures predominate, and stand up like lightning conductors to attract the force of the elements. Oak and Troy and Bathsheba; Eustacia, Wildeve, and Venn; Henchard, Lucetta, and Farfrae; Jude, Sue Bridehead, and Phillotson.

There is even a certain likeness between the different groups. They live as individuals and they differ as individuals; but they also live as types and have a likeness as types. Bathsheba is Bathsheba, but she is a woman and sister to Eustacia and Lucetta and Sue; Gabriel Oak is Gabriel Oak, but he is man and brother to Henchard, Venn, and Jude. However lovable and charming Bathsheba may be, still she is weak; however stubborn and ill-guided Henchard may be, still he is strong. This is a fundamental part of Hardy's vision; the staple of many of his books. The woman is the weaker and the fleshlier, and she clings to the stronger and obscures his vision. How freely, nevertheless, in his greater books life is poured over the unalterable frame-work! When Bathsheba sits in the wagon among her plants, smiling at her own loveliness in the little looking-glass, we may know, and it is proof of Hardy's power that we do know, how severely she will suffer and cause others to suffer before the end. But the moment has all the bloom and beauty of life. And so it is, time and time again. His characters, both men and women, were creatures to him of an infinite attraction. For the women he shows a more tender solicitude than for the men, and in them, perhaps, he takes a keener interest. Vain might their beauty be and terrible their fate, but while the glow of life is in them their step is free, their laughter sweet, and theirs is the power to sink into the breast of Nature and become part of her silence and solemnity, or to rise and put on them the movement of the clouds and the wildness of the flowering woodlands. The men who suffer, not like the women through dependence upon other human beings, but through conflict with fate, enlist our sterner sympathies. For such a man as Gabriel Oak we need have no passing fears. Honour him we must, though it is not granted us to love him quite so freely. He is firmly set upon his feet and can give as shrewd a blow, to men at least, as any he is likely to receive. He has a prevision of what is to be expected that springs from character rather than from education. He is stable in his temperament, steadfast in his affections, and capable of open-eyed endurance without flinching. But he, too, is no puppet. He is a homely, hum-drum fellow on ordinary occasions. He can walk the street without making people turn to stare at him. In short, nobody can deny Hardy's power—the true novelist's power—to make us believe that his characters are fellow-beings driven by their own passions and idiosyncrasies, while they have—and this is the poet's gift—something symbolical about them which is common to us all.

And it is when we are considering Hardy's power of creating men and women that we become most conscious of the profound differences that distinguish him from his peers. We look back at a number of these characters and ask ourselves what it is that we remember them for. We recall their passions. We remember how deeply they have loved each other and often with what tragic results. We remember the faithful love of Oak for Bathsheba; the tumultuous but fleeting passions of men like Wildeve, Troy, and Fitzpiers; we remember the filial love of Clym for his mother, the jealous paternal passion of Henchard for Elizabeth Jane. But we do not remember how they have loved. We do not remember how they talked and changed and got to know each other, finely, gradually, from step to step and from stage to stage. Their relationship is not composed of those intellectual apprehensions and subtleties of perception which seem so slight yet are so profound. In all the books love is one of the great facts that mould human life. But it is a catastrophe; it happens suddenly and overwhelmingly, and there is little to be said about it. The talk between the lovers when it is not passionate is practical or philosophic, as though the discharge of their daily duties left them with more desire to question life and its purpose than to investigate each other's sensibilities. Even if it were in their power to analyse their emotions, life is too stirring to give them time. They need all their strength to deal with the downright blows, the freakish ingenuity, the gradually increasing malignity of fate. They have none to spend upon the subtleties and delicacies of the human comedy.

Thus there comes a time when we can say with certainty that we shall not find in Hardy some of the qualities that have given us most delight in the works of other novelists. He has not the perfection of Jane Austen, or the wit of Meredith, or the range of Thackeray, or Tolstoy's amazing intellectual power. There is in the work of the great classical writers a finality of effect which places certain of their scenes, apart from the story, beyond the reach of change. We do not ask what bearing they have upon the narrative, nor do we make use of them to interpret problems which lie on the outskirts of the scene. A laugh, a blush, half a dozen words of dialogue, and it is enough; the source of our delight is perennial. But Hardy has none of this concentration and completeness. His light does not fall directly upon the human heart. It passes over it and out on to the darkness of the heath and upon the trees swaying in the storm. When we look back into the room the group by the fireside is dispersed. Each man or woman is battling with the storm, alone, revealing himself most when he is least under the observation of other human beings. We do not know them as we know Pierre or Natasha or Becky Sharp. We do not know them in and out and all round as they are revealed to the casual caller, to the Government official, to the great lady, to the general on the battlefield. We do not know the complication and involvement and turmoil of their thoughts. Geographically, too, they remain fixed to the same stretch of the English countryside. It is seldom, and always with unhappy results, that Hardy leaves the yeoman or farmer to describe the class above theirs in the social scale. In the drawing-room and clubroom and ballroom, where people of leisure and education come together, where comedy is bred and shades of character revealed, he is awkward and ill at ease. But the opposite is equally true. If we do not know his men and women in their relations to each other, we know them in their relations to time, death, and fate. If we do not see them in quick agitation against the lights and crowds of cities, we see them against the earth, the storm, and the seasons. We know their attitude towards some of the most tremendous problems that can confront mankind. They take on a more than mortal size in memory. We see them, not in detail but enlarged and dignified. We see Tess reading the baptismal service in her nightgown "with an impress of dignity that was almost regal." We see Marty South, "like a being who had rejected with indifference the attribute of sex for the loftier quality of abstract humanism," laying the flowers on Winterbourne's grave. Their speech has a Biblical dignity and poetry. They have a force in them which cannot be defined, a force of love or of hate, a force which in the men is the cause of rebellion against life, and in the women implies an illimitable capacity for suffering, and it is this which dominates the character and makes it unnecessary that we should see the finer features that lie hid. This is the tragic power; and, if we are to place Hardy among his fellows, we must call him the greatest tragic writer among English novelists.

But let us, as we approach the danger-zone of Hardy's philosophy, be on our guard. Nothing is more necessary, in reading an imaginative writer, than to keep at the right distance above his page. Nothing is easier, especially with a writer of marked idiosyncrasy, than to fasten on opinions, convict him of a creed, tether him to a consistent point of view. Nor was Hardy any exception to the rule that the mind which is most capable of receiving impressions is very often the least capable of drawing conclusions. It is for the reader, steeped in the impression to supply the comment. It is his part to know when to put aside the writer's conscious intention in favour of some deeper intention of which perhaps he may be unconscious. Hardy himself was aware of this. A novel "is an impression, not an argument," he has warned us, and, again

> Unadjusted impressions have their value, and the road to a true philosophy of life seems to lie in humbly recording diverse readings of its phenomena as they are forced upon us by chance and change.

Certainly it is true to say of him that, at his greatest, he gives us impressions; at his weakest, arguments. In *The Woodlanders*, *The Return of the Native*, *Far from the Madding Crowd*, and, above all, in *The Mayor of Casterbridge*, we have Hardy's impression of life as it came to him without conscious ordering. Let him once begin to tamper with his direct intuitions and his power is gone. "Did you say the stars were worlds, Tess?" asks little Abraham as they drive to market with their beehives. Tess replies that they are like "the apples on our stubbard-tree, most of them splendid and sound—a few blighted." "Which do we live on—a splendid or a blighted one?" "A blighted one," she replies, or rather the mournful thinker who has assumed her mask speaks for her. The words protrude, cold and raw, like the springs of a machine where we had seen only flesh and blood. We are crudely jolted out of that mood of sympathy which is renewed a moment later when the little cart is run down and we have a concrete instance of the ironical methods which rule our planet.

That is the reason why *Jude the Obscure* is the most painful of all Hardy's books, and the only one against which we can fairly bring the charge of pessimism. In *Jude the Obscure* argument is allowed to dominate impression, with the result that though the misery of the book is overwhelming it is not tragic. As calamity succeeds calamity we feel that the case against society is not being argued fairly or with profound understanding of the facts. Here is nothing of that width and force and knowledge of mankind which, when Tolstoy criticises society, makes his indictment formidable. Here we have revealed to us the petty cruelty of men, not the large injustice of the gods. It is only necessary to compare *Jude the Obscure* with *The Mayor of Casterbridge* to see where Hardy's true power lay. Jude carries on his miserable contest against the deans of colleges and the conventions of sophisticated society. Henchard is pitted, not against another man, but against something outside himself which is opposed to men of his ambition and power. No human being wishes him ill. Even Farfrae and Newson and Elizabeth Jane whom he has wronged all come to pity him, and even to admire his strength of character. He is standing up to fate, and in backing the old Mayor whose ruin has been largely his own fault, Hardy makes us feel that we are backing human nature in an unequal contest. There is no pessimism here. Throughout the book we are aware of the sublimity of the issue, and yet it is presented to us in the most concrete form. From the opening scene in which Henchard sells his wife to the sailor at the fair to his death on Egdon Heath the vigour of the story is superb, its humour rich and racy, its movement large-limbed and free. The skimmity ride, the fight between Farfrae and Henchard in the loft, Mrs. Cuxsom's speech upon the death of Mrs. Henchard, the talk of the ruffians at Peter's Finger with Nature present in the background or mysteriously dominating the foreground, are among the glories of English fiction. Brief and scanty, it may be, is the measure of happiness allowed to each, but so long as the struggle is, as Henchard's was, with the decrees of fate and not with the laws of man, so long as it is in the open air and calls for activity of the body rather than of the brain, there is greatness in the contest, there is pride and pleasure in it, and the death of the broken corn merchant in his cottage on Egdon Heath is comparable to the death of Ajax lord of Salamis. The true tragic emotion is ours.

Before such power as this we are made to feel that the ordinary tests which we apply to fiction are futile enough. Do we insist that a great novelist shall be a master of melodious prose? Hardy was no such thing. He feels his way by dint of sagacity and uncompromising sincerity to the phrase he wants, and it is often of unforgettable pungency. Failing it, he will make do with any homely or clumsy or old-fashioned turn of speech, now of the utmost angularity, now of a bookish elaboration. No style in literature, save Scott's, is so difficult to analyse; it is on the face of it so bad, yet it achieves its aim so unmistakably. As well might one attempt to rationalise the charm of a muddy country road, or of a plain field of roots in winter. And then, like Dorsetshire itself, out of these very elements of stiffness and angularity his prose will put on greatness; will roll with a Latin sonority; will shape itself in a massive and monumental symmetry like that of his own bare downs. Then again, do we require that a novelist shall observe the probabilities, and keep close to reality? To find anything approaching the violence and convolution of

Hardy's plots one must go back to the Elizabethan drama. Yet we accept his story completely as we read it; more than that, it becomes obvious that his violence and his melodrama, when they are not due to a curious peasant-like love of the monstrous for its own sake, are part of that wild spirit of poetry which saw with intense irony and grimness that no reading of life can possibly outdo the strangeness of life itself, no symbol of caprice and unreason be too extreme to represent the astonishing circumstances of our existence.

But as we consider the great structure of the Wessex novels it seems irrelevant to fasten on little points—this character, that scene, this phrase of deep and poetic beauty. It is something larger that Hardy has bequeathed to us. The Wessex novels are not one book, but many. They cover an immense stretch; inevitably they are full of imperfections—some are failures, and others exhibit only the wrong side of their maker's genius. But undoubtedly, when we have submitted ourselves fully to them, when we come to take stock of our impression of the whole, the effect is commanding and satisfactory. We have been freed from the cramp and pettiness imposed by life. Our imaginations have been stretched and heightened; our humour has been made to laugh out; we have drunk deep of the beauty of the earth. Also we have been made to enter the shade of a sorrowful and brooding spirit which, even in its saddest mood, bore itself with a grave uprightness and never, even when most moved to anger, lost its deep compassion for the sufferings of men and women. Thus it is no mere transcript of life at a certain time and place that Hardy has given us. It is a vision of the world and of man's lot as they revealed themselves to a powerful imagination, a profound and poetic genius, a gentle and humane soul.

❋

How Should One Read a Book?[1]

❋

In the first place, I want to emphasise the note of interrogation at the end of my title. Even if I could answer the question for myself, the answer would apply only to me and not to you. The only advice, indeed, that one person can give another about reading is to take no advice, to follow your own instincts, to use your own reason, to come to your own conclusions. If this is agreed between us, then I feel at liberty to put forward a few ideas and suggestions because you will not allow them to fetter that independence which is the most important quality that a reader can possess. After all, what laws can be laid down about books? The battle of Waterloo was certainly fought on a certain day; but is *Hamlet* a better play than *Lear*? Nobody can say. Each must decide that question for himself. To admit authorities, however heavily furred and gowned, into our libraries and let them tell us how to read, what to read, what value to place upon what we read, is to destroy the spirit of freedom which is the breath of those sanctuaries. Everywhere else we may be bound by laws and conventions—there we have none.

But to enjoy freedom, if the platitude is pardonable, we have of course to control ourselves. We must not squander our powers, helplessly and ignorantly, squirting half the house in order to water a single rose-bush; we must train them, exactly and powerfully, here on the very spot. This, it may be, is one of the first difficulties that faces us in a library. What is "the very spot"? There may well seem to

[1] A paper read at a School.

be nothing but a conglomeration and huddle of confusion. Poems and novels, histories and memoirs, dictionaries and blue-books; books written in all languages by men and women of all tempers, races, and ages jostle each other on the shelf. And outside the donkey brays, the women gossip at the pump, the colts gallop across the fields. Where are we to begin? How are we to bring order into this multitudinous chaos and so get the deepest and widest pleasure from what we read?

It is simple enough to say that since books have classes—fiction, biography, poetry—we should separate them and take from each what it is right that each should give us. Yet few people ask from books what books can give us. Most commonly we come to books with blurred and divided minds, asking of fiction that it shall be true, of poetry that it shall be false, of biography that it shall be flattering, of history that it shall enforce our own prejudices. If we could banish all such preconceptions when we read, that would be an admirable beginning. Do not dictate to your author; try to become him. Be his fellow-worker and accomplice. If you hang back, and reserve and criticise at first, you are preventing yourself from getting the fullest possible value from what you read. But if you open your mind as widely as possible, then signs and hints of almost imperceptible fineness, from the twist and turn of the first sentences, will bring you into the presence of a human being unlike any other. Steep yourself in this, acquaint yourself with this, and soon you will find that your author is giving you, or attempting to give you, something far more definite. The thirty-two chapters of a novel—if we consider how to read a novel first—are an attempt to make something as formed and controlled as a building: but words are more impalpable than bricks; reading is a longer and more complicated process than seeing. Perhaps the quickest way to understand the elements of what a novelist is doing is not to read, but to write; to make your own experiment with the dangers and difficulties of words. Recall, then, some event that has left a distinct impression on you—how at the corner of the street, perhaps, you passed two people talking. A tree shook; an electric light danced; the tone of the talk was comic, but also tragic; a whole vision, an entire conception, seemed contained in that moment.

But when you attempt to reconstruct it in words, you will find that it breaks into a thousand conflicting impressions. Some must be subdued; others emphasised; in the process you will lose, probably, all grasp upon the emotion itself. Then turn from your blurred and littered pages to the opening pages of some great novelist—Defoe, Jane Austen, Hardy. Now you will be better able to appreciate their mastery. It is not merely that we are in the presence of a different person—Defoe, Jane Austen, or Thomas Hardy—but that we are living in a different world. Here, in *Robinson Crusoe*, we are trudging a plain highroad; one thing happens after another; the fact and the order of the fact is enough. But if the open air and adventure mean everything to Defoe they mean nothing to Jane Austen. Hers is the drawing-room, and people talking, and by the many mirrors of their talk revealing their characters. And if, when we have accustomed ourselves to the drawing-room and its reflections, we turn to Hardy, we are once more spun round. The moors are round us and the stars are above our heads. The other side of the mind is now exposed—the dark side that comes uppermost in solitude, not the light side that shows in company. Our relations are not towards people, but towards Nature and destiny. Yet different as these worlds are, each is consistent with itself. The maker of each is careful to observe the laws of his own perspective, and however great a strain they may put upon us they will never confuse us, as lesser writers so frequently do, by introducing two different kinds of reality into the same book. Thus to go from one great novelist to another—from Jane Austen to Hardy, from Peacock to Trollope, from Scott to Meredith—is to be wrenched and uprooted; to be thrown this way and then that. To read a novel is a difficult and complex art. You must be capable not only of great fineness of perception, but of great boldness of imagination if you are going to make use of all that the novelist—the great artist—gives you.

But a glance at the heterogeneous company on the shelf will show you that writers are very seldom "great artists"; far more often a book makes no claim to be a work of art at all. These biographies and autobiographies, for example, lives of great men, of men long dead and forgotten, that stand cheek by jowl with the novels and poems, are we to refuse to read them because they are not "art"? Or shall we read them, but read them in a different way, with a different aim? Shall we read them in the first place to satisfy that curiosity which possesses us sometimes when in the evening we linger in front of a house where the lights are lit and the blinds not yet drawn, and each floor of the house shows us a different section of human life in being? Then we are consumed with curiosity about the lives of these people—the servants gossiping, the gentlemen dining, the girl dressing for a party, the old woman at the window with her knitting. Who are they, what are they, what are their names, their occupations, their thoughts, and adventures?

Biographies and memoirs answer such questions, light up innumerable such houses; they show us people going about their daily affairs, toiling, failing, succeeding, eating, hating, loving, until they die. And sometimes as we watch, the house fades and the iron railings vanish and we are out at sea; we are hunting, sailing, fighting; we are among savages and soldiers; we are taking part in great campaigns. Or if we like to stay here in England, in London, still the scene changes; the street narrows; the house becomes small, cramped, diamond-paned, and malodorous. We see a poet, Donne, driven from such a house because the walls were so thin that when the children cried their voices cut through them. We can follow him, through the paths that lie in the pages of books, to Twickenham; to Lady Bedford's Park, a famous meeting-ground for nobles and poets; and then turn our steps to Wilton, the great house under the downs, and hear Sidney read the *Arcadia* to his sister; and ramble among the very marshes and see the very herons that figure in that famous romance; and then again travel north with that other Lady Pembroke, Anne Clifford, to her wild moors, or plunge into the city and control our merriment at the sight of Gabriel Harvey in his black velvet suit arguing about poetry with Spenser. Nothing is more fascinating than to grope and stumble in the alternate darkness and splendour of Elizabethan London. But there is no staying there. The Temples and the Swifts, the Harleys and the St. Johns beckon us on; hour upon hour can be spent disentangling their quarrels and deciphering their characters; and when we tire of them we can stroll on, past a lady in black wearing diamonds, to Samuel Johnson and Goldsmith and Garrick; or cross the channel, if we like, and meet Voltaire and Diderot, Madame du Deffand; and so back to England and Twickenham—how certain places repeat themselves and certain names!—where Lady Bedford had her Park once and Pope lived later, to Walpole's home at Strawberry Hill. But Walpole introduces us to such a swarm of new acquaintances, there are so many houses to visit and bells to ring that we may well hesitate for a moment, on the Miss Berrys' doorstep, for example, when behold, up comes Thackeray; he is the friend of the woman whom Walpole loved; so that merely by going from friend to friend, from garden to garden, from house to house, we have passed from one end of English literature to another and wake to find ourselves here again in the present, if we can so differentiate this moment from all that have gone before. This, then, is one of the ways in which we can read these lives and letters; we can make them light up the many windows of the past; we can watch the famous dead in their familiar habits and fancy sometimes that we are very close and can surprise their secrets, and sometimes we may pull out a play or a poem that they have written and see whether it reads differently in the presence of the author. But this again rouses other questions. How far, we must ask ourselves, is a book influenced by its writer's life—how far is it safe to let the man interpret the writer? How far shall we resist or give way to the sympathies and antipathies that the man himself rouses in us—so sensitive are words, so receptive of the character of the author? These are questions that press upon us when we read lives and letters, and we must answer them for ourselves, for nothing can be more fatal than to be guided by the preferences of others in a matter so personal.

But also we can read such books with another aim, not to throw light on literature, not to become familiar with famous people, but to refresh and exercise our own creative powers. Is there not an open window on the right hand of the bookcase? How delightful to stop reading and look out! How stimulating the scene is, in its unconsciousness, its irrelevance, its perpetual movement—the colts galloping round the field, the woman filling her pail at the well, the donkey throwing back his head and emitting his long, acrid moan. The greater part of any library is nothing but the record of such fleeting moments in the lives of men, women, and donkeys. Every literature, as it grows old, has its rubbish-heap, its record of vanished moments and forgotten lives told in faltering and feeble accents that have perished. But if you give yourself up to the delight of rubbish-reading you will be surprised, indeed you will be overcome, by the relics of human life that have been cast out to moulder. It may be one letter —but what a vision it gives! It may be a few sentences— but what vistas they suggest! Sometimes a whole story will come together with such beautiful humour and pathos and completeness that it seems as if a great novelist had been at work, yet it is only an old actor, Tate Wilkinson, remembering the strange story of Captain Jones; it is only a young subaltern serving under Arthur Wellesley and falling in love with a pretty girl at Lisbon; it is only Maria Allen letting fall her sewing in the empty drawing-room and sighing how she wishes she had taken Dr. Burney's good advice and had never eloped with her Rishy. None of this has any value; it is negligible in the extreme; yet how absorbing it is now and again to go through the rubbish-heaps and find rings and scissors and broken noses buried in the huge past and try to piece them together while the colt gallops round the field, the woman fills her pail at the well, and the donkey brays.

But we tire of rubbish-reading in the long run. We tire of searching for what is needed to complete the half-truth which is all that the Wilkinsons, the Bunburys, and the

Maria Allens are able to offer us. They had not the artist's power of mastering and eliminating; they could not tell the whole truth even about their own lives; they have disfigured the story that might have been so shapely. Facts are all that they can offer us, and facts are a very inferior form of fiction. Thus the desire grows upon us to have done with half-statements and approximations; to cease from searching out the minute shades of human character, to enjoy the greater abstractness, the purer truth of fiction. Thus we create the mood, intense and generalised, unaware of detail, but stressed by some regular, recurrent beat, whose natural expression is poetry; and that is the time to read poetry when we are almost able to write it.

> Western wind, when wilt thou blow?
> The small rain down can rain.
> Christ, if my love were in my arms,
> And I in my bed again!

The impact of poetry is so hard and direct that for the moment there is no other sensation except that of the poem itself. What profound depths we visit then—how sudden and complete is our immersion! There is nothing here to catch hold of; nothing to stay us in our flight. The illusion of fiction is gradual; its effects are prepared; but who when they read these four lines stops to ask who wrote them, or conjures up the thought of Donne's house or Sidney's secretary; or enmeshes them in the intricacy of the past and the succession of generations? The poet is always our contemporary. Our being for the moment is centred and constricted, as in any violent shock of personal emotion. Afterwards, it is true, the sensation begins to spread in wider rings through our minds; remoter senses are reached; these begin to sound and to comment and we are aware of echoes and reflections. The intensity of poetry covers an immense range of emotion. We have only to compare the force and directness of

> I shall fall like a tree, and find my grave,
> Only remembering that I grieve,

with the wavering modulation of

Minutes are numbered by the fall of sands,
As by an hour glass; the span of time
Doth waste us to our graves, and we look on it;
An age of pleasure, revelled out, comes home
At last, and ends in sorrow; but the life,
Weary of riot, numbers every sand,
Wailing in sighs, until the last drop down,
So to conclude calamity in rest,

or place the meditative calm of

whether we be young or old,
Our destiny, our being's heart and home,
Is with infinitude, and only there;
With hope it is, hope that can never die,
Effort, and expectation, and desire,
And something evermore about to be,

beside the complete and inexhaustible loveliness of

The moving Moon went up the sky,
And no where did abide:
Softly she was going up,
And a star or two beside—

or the splendid fantasy of

And the woodland haunter
Shall not cease to saunter
When, far down some glade,
Of the great world's burning,
One soft flame upturning
Seems, to his discerning,
Crocus in the shade.

to bethink us of the varied art of the poet; his power to make us at once actors and spectators; his power to run his hand into character as if it were a glove, and be Falstaff or Lear; his power to condense, to widen, to state, once and for ever.

"We have only to compare"—with those words the cat is out of the bag, and the true complexity of reading is admitted. The first process, to receive impressions with the utmost understanding, is only half the process of reading; it must be completed, if we are to get the whole pleasure from a book, by another. We must pass judgment upon these multitudinous impressions; we must make of these fleeting shapes one that is hard and lasting. But not directly. Wait for the dust of reading to settle; for the conflict and the questioning to die down; walk, talk, pull the dead petals from a rose, or fall asleep. Then suddenly without our willing it, for it is thus that Nature undertakes these transitions, the book will return, but differently. It will float to the top of the mind as a whole. And the book as a whole is different from the book received currently in separate phrases. Details now fit themselves into their places. We see the shape from start to finish; it is a barn, a pig-sty, or a cathedral. Now then we can compare book with book as we compare building with building. But this act of comparison means that our attitude has changed; we are no longer the friends of the writer, but his judges; and just as we cannot be too sympathetic as friends, so as judges we cannot be too severe. Are they not criminals, books that have wasted our time and sympathy; are they not the most insidious enemies of society, corrupters, defilers, the writers of false books, faked books, books that fill the air with decay and disease? Let us then be severe in our judgments; let us compare each book with the greatest of its kind. There they hang in the mind the shapes of the books we have read solidified by the judgments we have passed on them—*Robinson Crusoe*, *Emma*, *The Return of the Native*. Compare the novels with these—even the latest and least of novels has a right to be judged with the best. And so with poetry—when the intoxication of rhythm has died down and the splendour of words has faded a visionary shape will return to us and this must be compared with *Lear*, with *Phèdre*, with *The Prelude;* or if not with these, with whatever is the best or seems to us to be the best in its own kind. And we may be sure that the newness of new poetry and fiction is its most superficial quality and that we have only to alter slightly, not to recast, the standards by which we have judged the old.

It would be foolish, then, to pretend that the second part of reading, to judge, to compare, is as simple as the first

—to open the mind wide to the fast flocking of innumerable impressions. To continue reading without the book before you, to hold one shadow-shape against another, to have read widely enough and with enough understanding to make such comparisons alive and illuminating—that is difficult; it is still more difficult to press further and to say, "Not only is the book of this sort, but it is of this value; here it fails; here it succeeds; this is bad; that is good." To carry out this part of a reader's duty needs such imagination, insight, and learning that it is hard to conceive any one mind sufficiently endowed; impossible for the most self-confident to find more than the seeds of such powers in himself. Would it not be wiser, then, to remit this part of reading and to allow the critics, the gowned and furred authorities of the library, to decide the question of the book's absolute value for us? Yet how impossible! We may stress the value of sympathy; we may try to sink our own identity as we read. But we know that we cannot sympathise wholly or immerse ourselves wholly; there is always a demon in us who whispers, "I hate, I love," and we cannot silence him. Indeed, it is precisely because we hate and we love that our relation with the poets and novelists is so intimate that we find the presence of another person intolerable. And even if the results are abhorrent and our judgments are wrong, still our taste, the nerve of sensation that sends shocks through us, is our chief illuminant; we learn through feeling; we cannot suppress our own idiosyncrasy without impoverishing it. But as time goes on perhaps we can train our taste; perhaps we can make it submit to some control. When it has fed greedily and lavishly upon books of all sorts—poetry, fiction, history, biography—and has stopped reading and looked for long spaces upon the variety, the incongruity of the living world, we shall find that it is changing a little; it is not so greedy, it is more reflective. It will begin to bring us not merely judgments on particular books, but it will tell us that there is a quality common to certain books. Listen, it will say, what shall we call *this?* And it will read us perhaps *Lear* and then perhaps the *Agamemnon* in order to bring out that common quality.

Thus, with our taste to guide us, we shall venture beyond the particular book in search of qualities that group books together; we shall give them names and thus frame a rule that brings order into our perceptions. We shall gain a further and a rarer pleasure from that discrimination. But as a rule only lives when it is perpetually broken by contact with the books themselves—nothing is easier and more stultifying than to make rules which exist out of touch with facts, in a vacuum—now at last, in order to steady ourselves in this difficult attempt, it may be well to turn to the very rare writers who are able to enlighten us upon literature as an art. Coleridge and Dryden and Johnson, in their considered criticism, the poets and novelists themselves in their unconsidered sayings, are often surprisingly relevant; they light up and solidify the vague ideas that have been tumbling in the misty depths of our minds. But they are only able to help us if we come to them laden with questions and suggestions won honestly in the course of our own reading. They can do nothing for us if we herd ourselves under their authority and lie down like sheep in the shade of a hedge. We can only understand their ruling when it comes in conflict with our own and vanquishes it.

If this is so, if to read a book as it should be read calls for the rarest qualities of imagination, insight, and judgment, you may perhaps conclude that literature is a very complex art and that it is unlikely that we shall be able, even after a lifetime of reading, to make any valuable contribution to its criticism. We must remain readers; we shall not put on the further glory that belongs to those rare beings who are also critics. But still we have our responsibilities as readers and even our importance. The standards we raise and the judgments we pass steal into the air and become part of the atmosphere which writers breathe as they work. An influence is created which tells upon them even if it never finds its way into print. And that influence, if it were well instructed, vigorous and individual and sincere, might be of great value now when criticism is necessarily in abeyance; when books pass in review like the procession of animals in a shooting-gallery, and the critic has only one second in which to load and aim and shoot and may well be pardoned if he mistakes rabbits for tigers, eagles for barndoor fowls, or misses altogether and wastes his shot upon some peaceful cow grazing in a further field. If behind the erratic gunfire of the press the author felt that there was another kind of criticism, the opinion of people reading for the love of reading, slowly and unprofessionally, and judging with great sympathy and yet with great severity, might this not improve the quality of his work? And if by our means books were to become stronger, richer, and more varied, that would be an end worth reaching.

Yet who reads to bring about an end however desirable? Are there not some pursuits that we practise because they are good in themselves, and some pleasures that are final? And is not this among them? I have sometimes dreamt, at least, that when the Day of Judgment dawns and the great conquerors and lawyers and statesmen come to receive their rewards—their crowns, their laurels, their names carved indelibly upon imperishable marble—the Almighty will turn to Peter and will say, not without a certain envy when He sees us coming with our books under our arms, "Look, these need no reward. We have nothing to give them here. They have loved reading."